THE CHILD'S CONCEPTION OF NUMBER

THE CHILD'S CONCEPTION
OF NUMBER

by

JEAN PIAGET

*Professor at the University of Geneva
and at the Institute of J. J. Rousseau Geneva*

Author of
*Language and Thought of the Child, Child's Conception of Causality,
Moral Judgement of the Child, Psychology of Intelligence*

ROUTLEDGE & KEGAN PAUL LTD
Broadway House, 68–74 Carter Lane
London

La Genèse du Nombre chez l'Enfant
First published in Switzerland from the French, 1941
Child's Conception of Number translated by
C. Gattegno and F. M. Hodgson
First published in Great Britain 1952
by Routledge & Kegan Paul Limited
Broadway House, 68-74 Carter Lane
London, E.C.4.
Second impression 1961
Third impression 1965
Fourth impression 1969
Printed in Great Britain by
Fletcher & Son Ltd, Norwich
No part of this book may be reproduced
in any form without permission from
the publisher, except for the quotation
of brief passages in criticism
SBN 7100 3142 4 (c)
SBN 7100 6194 3 (p)

CONTENTS

v

FOREWORD

IN our earlier books (*The Language and Thought of the Child, Judgment and Reasoning in the Child, The Child's Conception of the World*, and *The Child's Conception of Physical Causality*), we analysed various verbal and conceptual aspects of the child's thought. Later on, we examined the beginnings of thought on the practical and sensory-motor planes (*La Naissance de l'Intelligence* and *La Construction du Réel chez l'Enfant*). It now remains, in order to discover the mechanisms that determine thought, to investigate how the sensory-motor schemata of assimilating intelligence are organized in operational systems on the plane of thought. Beyond the child's verbal constructions, and in line with his practical activity, we now have to trace the development of the operations which give rise to number and continuous quantities, to space, time, speed, etc., operations which, in these essential fields, lead from intuitive and egocentric pre-logic to rational co-ordination that is both deductive and inductive.

In dealing with these new problems, appropriate methods must be used. We shall still keep our original procedure of free conversation with the child, conversation which is governed by the questions put, but which is compelled to follow the direction indicated by the child's spontaneous answers. Our investigation of sensory-motor intelligence has, however, shown us the necessity for actual manipulation of objects. In *The Child's Conception of Physical Causality*, we saw, though it was not possible to take full advantage of the fact, that conversation with the child is much more reliable and more fruitful when it is related to experiments made with adequate material, and when the child, instead of thinking in the void, is talking about actions he has just performed. As far as the study of number is concerned, this is an essential condition, and the gifts of Mlle Szeminska have made it possible to discover techniques adapted to the various problems which needed to be solved and analysed separately. In another volume, written with the collaboration of Mlle Inhelder, the same methods will be used in the description of continuous quantities as the product of quantification of physical qualities (weight, volume, etc.).

In the present volume, it has not been possible to include all that we should have wished to say on the subject of the evolution of number. In particular, there is an inexhaustible mine of

vii

information, on which we have deliberately not drawn, in the observations collected at the Maison des Petits by Mlles Audemars and Lafendel, who constructed original material which they have been using for more than twenty years. It is to be hoped that these gifted teachers will shortly publish their findings concerned with the beginnings of arithmetic in the school. We have, of course, greatly benefited from the spirit of their research, and we are also greatly indebted to many works on the arithmetic of the child, particularly to those of K. Bühler, Decroly, Mlle Descœudres, and others. We have not entered into a detailed discussion of existing works because we have here deliberately restricted ourselves to the problem of the construction of number in relation to logical operations.

Our hypothesis is that the construction of number goes hand-in-hand with the development of logic, and that a pre-numerical period corresponds to the pre-logical level. Our results do, in fact, show that number is organized, stage after stage, in close connection with the gradual elaboration of systems of inclusions (hierarchy of logical classes) and systems of asymmetrical relations (qualitative seriations), the sequence of numbers thus resulting from an operational synthesis of classification and seriation. In our view, logical and arithmetical operations therefore constitute a single system that is psychologically natural, the second resulting from generalization and fusion of the first, under the two complementary headings of inclusion of classes and seriation of relations, quality being disregarded. When the child applies this operational system to sets that are defined by the qualities of their elements, he is compelled to consider separately classes (which depend on the qualitative equivalence of the elements) and asymmetrical relations (which express the seriable differences). Hence the dualism of logic of classes and logic of asymmetrical relations. But when the same system is applied to sets irrespective of their qualities, the fusion of inclusion and seriation of the elements into a single operational totality takes place, and this totality constitutes the sequence of whole numbers, which are indissociably cardinal and ordinal.

Although the facts recorded in this volume lead to this conclusion almost without any attempt at interpretation, its very simplicity seemed to us a cause for doubt. Discussion as to the relationship between number and logic has, as we know, been endless. The logisticians, with Russell, have tried to reduce cardinal number to the notion of 'class of classes', and ordinal number, dissociated from cardinal number, to the notion of 'class of relationships', while their opponents maintained, with Poincaré and Brunschvicg, that the whole number is essentially synthetic and irreducible. Our hypothesis seems to obviate the necessity for this alternative, for if number is at the same time both class and asymmetrical relation, it does not derive from one or other of the logical operations, but from their union, continuity thus being reconciled with irreducibility, and the relationships between logic and arithmetic being regarded not as unilateral but as reciprocal. Nevertheless, the connections established in the field of experimental psychology needed to be verified in the field of logistics, and we proceeded to attempt this verification.

In studying the literature on the subject, we were surprised to find to what extent the usual point of view was 'realist' rather than 'operational', with the exception of the interesting work of A. Reymond. This fact accounts for the connections, many of them artificial, established by Russell, which forcibly separated logistic investigation from psychological analysis, whereas each should be a support for the other in the same way as mathematics and experimental physics.

If, on the contrary, we construct a logistics based on the reality of operations as such, in accordance with, and not in opposition to, the psychogenetic processes, we discover that the natural psychological systems of thought, such as simple and multiple classifications, simple and multiple seriations, nesting of symmetrical relations, etc., correspond from the logistic point of view to operational structures closely akin to mathematical 'groups', and which we have called 'groupings'. The laws of these groupings, once formulated, proved to be of constant help in our psychological analysis. [1]

TRANSLATOR'S NOTE

While keeping as closely as possible to the French text, we have, with the author's permission, used a certain freedom on occasion, but only when it seemed desirable in the interests of clarity and when no essential idea was involved. In particular, we have omitted the logistic algorism introduced by the author in Chapters III and X to which reference can be made in the original text.

[1] Since this book was published (Geneva, 1941), this problem has been considerably developed in two further volumes, *Classes, relations et nombres* (Vrin, Paris, 1942) and *Traité de Logique* (A. Colin, Paris, 1950). (Translator's note).

The first chapter of this volume appeared in 1939 in the *Journal de Psychologie*, and the first paragraphs of Chapter VII form part of an article published in 1937 in the *Recueil de travaux de l'Université de Lausanne, publié à l'occasion du IVme Centenaire de la fondation de l'Université*.

In the *Compte rendu des séances de la Société de Physique et d'Histoire naturelle de Genève* (vol. 58, 1941) the theory of groupings appeared for the first time, in condensed form.

PART ONE

CONSERVATION OF QUANTITIES
AND INVARIANCE OF WHOLES

CHAPTER I

CONSERVATION OF CONTINUOUS QUANTITIES

EVERY notion, whether it be scientific or merely a matter of common sense, presupposes a set of principles of conservation, either explicit or implicit. It is a matter of common knowledge that in the field of the empirical sciences the introduction of the principle of inertia (conservation of rectilinear and uniform motion) made possible the development of modern physics, and that the principle of conservation of matter made modern chemistry possible. It is unnecessary to stress the importance in every-day life of the principle of identity; any attempt by thought to build up a system of notions requires a certain permanence in their definitions. In the field of perception, the schema of the permanent object[1] presupposes the elaboration of what is no doubt the most primitive of all these principles of conservation. Obviously conservation, which is a necessary condition of all experience and all reasoning, by no means exhausts the representation of reality or the dynamism of the intellectual processes, but that is another matter. Our contention is merely that conservation is a necessary condition for all rational activity, and we are not concerned with whether it is sufficient to account for this activity or to explain the nature of reality.

This being so, arithmetical thought is no exception to the rule. A set or collection is only conceivable if it remains unchanged irrespective of the changes occurring in the relationship between the elements. For instance, the permutations of the elements in a given set do not change its value. A number is only intelligible if it remains identical with itself, whatever the distribution of the units of which it is composed. A continuous quantity such as a length or a volume can only be used in reasoning if it is a permanent whole, irrespective of the possible arrangements of its parts. In a word, whether it be a matter of continuous or discontinuous qualities, of quantitative relations perceived in the sensible universe, or of sets and numbers conceived by thought, whether it be a matter of the child's earliest contacts with number or of the most refined axiomatizations of any intuitive system, in

[1] *La Construction du Réel chez l'Enfant*, chapter i.

each and every case the conservation of something is postulated as a necessary condition for any mathematical understanding.

From the psychological point of view, the need for conservation appears then to be a kind of functional *a priori* of thought. But does this mean that arithmetical notions acquire their structure because of this conservation, or are we to conclude that conservation precedes any numerical or quantifying activities, and is not only a function, but also an *a priori* structure, a kind of innate idea present from the first awareness of the intellect and the first contact with experience? It is experiment that will provide the answer, and we shall try to show that the first alternative is the only one that is in agreement with the facts.

§1.   *Technique and general results*

This chapter and the one that follows will be devoted to experiments made simultaneously with continuous and discontinuous quantities. It seemed to us essential to deal with the two questions at the same time, although the former are not arithmetical and were to be treated separately in a special volume,[1] since it was desirable to ascertain that the results obtained in the case of discontinuous sets were general.

The child is first given two cylindrical containers of equal dimensions (A_1 and A_2) containing the same quantity of liquid (as is shown by the levels). The contents of A_2 are then poured into two smaller containers of equal dimensions (B_1 and B_2) and the child is asked whether the quantity of liquid poured from A_2 into ($B_1 + B_2$) is still equal to that in A_1. If necessary, the liquid in B_1 can then be poured into two smaller, equal containers (C_1 and C_2), and in case of need, the liquid in B_2 can be poured into two other containers C_3 and C_4 identical with C_1 and C_2. Questions as to the equality between ($C_1 + C_2$) and B_2, or between ($C_1 + C_2 + C_3 + C_4$) and A_1, etc., are then put. In this way, the liquids are subdivided in a variety of ways, and each time the problem of conservation is put in the form of a question as to equality or non-equality with one of the original containers. Conversely, as a check on his answers, the child can be asked to pour into a glass of a different shape a quantity of liquid approximately the same as that in a given glass, but the main problem is still that of conservation as such.

The results obtained seem to prove that continuous quantities are not at once considered to be constant, and that the notion of conservation is gradually constructed by means of an intellectual

[1] J. Piaget and B. Inhelder, *Le Développement des Quantités chez l'Enfant (Conservation et Atomisme)*, 1941.

mechanism which it is our purpose to explain. By grouping the answers to the various questions, it is possible to distinguish three stages. In the first, the child considers it natural for the quantity of liquid to vary according to the form and dimensions of the containers into which it is poured. Perception of the apparent changes is therefore not corrected by a system of relations that ensures invariance of quantity. In the second stage, which is a period of transition, conservation gradually emerges, but although it is recognized in some cases, of which we shall attempt to discover the characteristics, it is not so in all. When he reaches the third stage, the child at once postulates conservation of the quantities in each of the transformations to which they are subjected. Naturally this does not mean that this generalization of constancy extends at this stage beyond the limits of the field studied here.

In our interpretation of these facts, we can start from the following hypotheses, some of which directed the research of this chapter while others arose in the course of our experiments. The question to be considered is whether the development of the notion of conservation of quantity is not one and the same as the development of the notion of quantity. The child does not first acquire the notion of quantity and then attribute constancy to it; he discovers true quantification only when he is capable of constructing wholes that are preserved. At the level of the first stage, quantity is therefore no more than the asymmetrical relations between qualities, i.e., comparisons of the type 'more' or 'less' contained in judgements such as 'it's higher', 'not so wide', etc. These relations depend on perception, and are not as yet relations in the true sense, since they cannot be co-ordinated one with another in additive or multiplicative operations. This co-ordination begins at the second stage and results in the notion of 'intensive' quantity, i.e., without units, but susceptible of logical coherence. As soon as this intensive quantification exists, the child can grasp, before any other measurement, the proportionality of differences, and therefore the notion of extensive quantity. This discovery, which alone makes possible the development of number, thus results from the child's progress in logic during these stages.

§2. Stage I: Absence of conservation

For children at the first stage, the quantity of liquid increases or diminishes according to the size or number of the containers. The reasons given for this non-conservation vary from child to child, and from one moment to the next, but in every case the child thinks that the change he sees involves a change in the total value of the liquid. Here we have some examples:

Blas (4;0). 'Have you got a friend?—*Yes, Odette.*—Well look, we're giving you, Clairette, a glass of orangeade (A1, ¾ full), and we're giving Odette a glass of lemonade (A2, also ¾ full). Has one of you more to drink than the other?—*The same.*—This is what Clairette does: she pours her drink into two other glasses (B1 and B2, which are thus half filled). Has Clairette the same amount as Odette?—*Odette has more.*— Why?—*Because we've put less in* (She pointed to the levels in B1 and B2, without taking into account the fact that there were two glasses).— (Odette's drink was then poured into B3 and B4.) *It's the same.*—And now (pouring Clairette's drink from B1 + B2 into L, a long thin tube, which is then almost full)?—*I've got more.*—Why?—*We've poured it into that glass* (pointing to the level in L), *and here* (B3 and B4) *we haven't.*— But were they the same before?—*Yes.*—And now?—*I've got more.*' Clairette's orangeade was then poured back from L into B1 and B2: 'Look, Clairette has poured hers like Odette. So, is all the lemonade (B3 + B4) and all the orangeade (B1 + B2) the same?—*It's the same* (with conviction).—Now Clairette does this (pouring B1 into C1 which is then full, while B2 remains half full). Have you both the same amount to drink?—*I've got more.*—But where does the extra come from?—*From in there* (B1).—What must we do so that Odette has the same?—*We must take that little glass* (pouring part of B3 into C2).—And is it the same now, or has one of you got more?—*Odette has more.*—Why?—*Because we've poured it into that little glass* (C2).—But is there the same amount to drink, or has one got more than the other?—*Odette has more to drink.*— Why?—*Because she has three glasses* (B3 almost empty, B4 and C2, while Clairette has C1 full and B2).'

A moment later, a new experiment. Clairette was again shown glasses A1 and A2, ¾ full, one with orangeade for herself and the other with lemonade for Odette. 'Are they exactly the same?—*Yes* (verifying the levels).—Well, Odette is going to pour hers (A2) into all those (C1, C2, C3, C4, which were thus about half full). Have you both the same amount?—*I've got more. She has less. In the glasses there's less* (looking carefully at the levels).—But before, you both had the same?—*Yes.*—And now?—*Here* (pointing to the level in A1) *it's more, and here* (indicating the 4 glasses C) *it's less.*'

Finally she was given only the big glass A1 almost full of orangeade: 'Look, Clairette does this: she pours it like that (into B1 and B2, which are then ⅘ full). Is there more to drink now than before, or less, or the same?—*There's less* (very definitely).—Explain to me why.—*When you poured it out, it made less.*—But don't the little glasses together make the same?—*It makes less.*'

Sim (5;0). She was shown A1 and A2 half full. 'There's the same amount in the glasses, isn't there?—(She verified it) *Yes.*—Look, Renée, who has the lemonade, pours it out like this (pouring A1 into B1 and B2, which were thus about ⅔ full). Have you both still the same amount to drink?—*No. Renée has more because she has two glasses.*—What could you do to have the same amount?—*Pour mine into two glasses.* (She poured A2 into B3 and B4.)—Have you both got the same now?—(She looked for a long time at the 4 glasses *Yes.*—Now Madeleine (herself) is going to pour her two glasses into three (B_3 and B_4 into C_1, C_2 and C_3). Are they the same now?—*No.*—Who has more to drink?—*Madeleine, because she has three glasses. Renée must pour hers too into three glasses.* (Renée's B_1 and B_2 were poured into C_5, C_6 and C_7). There. —*It's the same.*—But now Madeleine pours hers into a fourth glass (C_4, which was filled with a little from C_1, C_2 and C_3). Have you both the same amount?—*I've got more.*—Is there more of the lemonade (C_5, C_6 and C_7) or of the orangeade (C_1, C_2, C_3 and C_4)?—*The orangeade.*— (The two big glasses A_1 and A_2 were then put before her.) Look, we're going to pour back all the lemonade into this one (A_1) as it was before, and all the orangeade into that one. Where will the lemonade come up to?—(She indicated a certain level)—And the orangeade?— (She indicated a higher level.)—Will the orangeade be higher than the lemonade?—*Yes, there's more orangeade* (pointing to the level she had indicated) *because there's more orangeade here* (pointing to C_1, C_2, C_3 and C_4).—You think it will come up to here?—*Yes.*—(This level was marked by an elastic band and she herself poured in the liquid and was delighted to find that it came up to the band. But when she poured the lemonade into A_1 she was very much surprised to find that it reached the same level.) *It's the same!*—How's that?—*I think we've put a little back, and now it's the same.*'

It is clear that so far the child had thought that there were changes in quantity when the number of glasses varied, but with the next question the level intervenes: 'Look, Madeleine pours the orangeade into that glass (A_2 was poured into L, which was longer and narrower. L was then $\frac{3}{4}$ full, whereas the lemonade in A_1 came only half way up.)— *There's more orangeade, because it's higher.*—Is there more to drink, or does it just look as if there is?—*There's more to drink.*—And now (pouring the lemonade into B_1 and B_2 and the orangeade into D_1 and D_2 which were wide, low glasses)?—*It's the orangeade that's, more, because there* (in D_1 and D_2) *there's a lot.*—So if we pour the lemonade and the orangeade back here (A_2 and A_1), will the orangeade come up higher or will they be the same?—*Higher.*' She poured D_1 and D_2 back into A_2, and B_1 and B_2 back into A_1, and was again much surprised to see that the levels were the same.

Lac (5;6). 'Here are two glasses (A_1 half full of orangeade and A_2 slightly less full of lemonade.) The orangeade is for you and the lemonade for Lucien. Lucien is cross because he has less. He pours his drink into these two glasses (pouring A_2 into B_1 and B_2). Who has more?— (Lac looked at the levels) *Me.*—Now you pour your drink into these two glasses (B_3 and B_4, the levels being thus slightly higher than in B_1 and B_2). Who has more?—*Me.*—And now Lucien takes this glass (B_1) and divides it between these two (C_1 and C_2, which are then full, whereas B_2 remains half-full). Who has more?—(Lac compared the levels and pointed to glasses C) *Lucien.*—Why?—*Because the glasses get smaller* (and therefore the levels rise).—But how did that happen? Before it was you who had more and now it's Lucien?—*Because there's a lot.*—But how did it happen?—*We took some.*—But where?—...—And how?—...—Has one of you got more?—*Yes, Lucien* (very definitely).

—And if I pour all the orangeade and all the lemonade into the two big glasses (A_1 and A_2) who will have more?—*I shall* (thus showing that he remembered the original position).—Then where has the extra you had gone to?— . . . —What could you do to have the same amount as Lucien? You can use any of the glasses.—Lac then took B_3 and poured some of it into C_3, an empty glass. He filled it, and put it opposite Lucien's C_1 and C_2. Then he compared B_3 to Lucien's B_2 and saw that there was less in B_3 than in B_2. He then took C_3 again, poured it back into B_3, and then, showing great disappointment, cried: '*But why was it quite full there* (C_3), *and now* (B_3) *it isn't full any longer?*'

Mus (5;0). This child, like those quoted earlier, relied on the number of glasses or the level, but in her case as in several others there was also a new factor, the size of the glasses. Nevertheless she followed three successive lines of thought:

I. *Size of the containers.*—She was given A_1 and A_2, ¾ full: 'Is there the same amount in both of them?—*Yes.*—Olga pours hers out like this (A_2 into B_1 and B_2, almost full). Has she still the same amount?—*No.* —Who has more to drink?—*Gertrude* (A_1).—Why?—*Because she has a bigger glass.*—How is it that Olga has less?— . . . —And if I pour these (B_1 and B_2) back into that one (A_2) how will it be?—*The same amount* (as in A_1).—(I did so.) And if Olga pours it back again like this (A_2 into B_1 and B_2, almost full) is it the same?—*No.*—Why?—*It makes less.*'

II. *Level.*—'Now Gertrude pours hers like this (A_1 into C_1 and C_2, almost filling C_1 and C_2 and leaving A_1 ⅓ full). Who has more, Gertrude with those ($A_1 + C_1 + C_2$), or Olga with those (B_1 and B_2)? —(She looked at the levels, which were about equal) *Both the same.*— Olga pours some of hers into another glass (B_3, thus lowering the general level in her glasses).—*Gertrude will have more. Olga will have less.* —Olga pours again into these glasses (B_1 and B_2 into C_3 and C_4, which were then full).—*She will have more* (level).—But before she had less; has she more now?—*Yes.*—Why?—*Because we put back here* (C_3 and C_4) *what was in the big glasses* (B_1 and B_2).' The reasoning here was thus just the opposite of what it was in I.

III. *Number of glasses and level.*—'If I give you some coffee in one cup, will it still be the same if you pour it into two glasses?—*I'll have a little more.*—Where?—*In the two glasses of course.*—Mummy gives you two glasses of coffee (B_1 and B_2). Then you pour that one (B_2) into those (C_1 and C_2).—*There's more there* (C_1 and C_2): *there are two glasses quite full. There, there's only one.*—And of those (B_1 and the 4 C) which would you rather have, that one (B_1) or all those (4 C)?—*The big one* (B_1).— Why?—*Because there's more: the glass is big.*'

Such then are the earliest reactions of the child confronted with the problem of conservation of quantities. He is not prepared to believe that a given quantity of liquid remains the same irrespective of changes in shape when it is poured from one container to another.

It might of course be argued that the child may not really have grasped the question. Does he always understand that it refers to the total quantity, or does he think he is merely being asked about changes in the number, level or size of the glasses? But the problem is precisely to discover whether the child is capable of grasping a quantity as being a whole, as a result of the co-ordination of the various relationships he perceives. The fact that these children isolated one of these relationships may therefore be due as much to lack of understanding of the notions in question as to failure to grasp the verbal question.

On the other hand, it might be suggested that when the liquid is poured from one container to another before the eyes of the child there are certain illusions of perception that counteract his judgement as to conservation.[1] We are well aware that perception of the quantifiable qualities such as length, weight, etc., leads to systematic distortions, and that the child finds it extremely difficult to perceive the constancy of these qualities. Hence, when the constancy is directly perceived, there is no problem as far as we are concerned. Our only problem is to discover by what means the mind succeeds in constructing the notion of constant quantity in spite of the indications to the contrary provided by immediate perception. Judgement comes into play precisely when perception proves inadequate, and only then. For instance, the discovery that a given quantity of liquid does not vary when poured from a container A into one or two containers B of a different shape, requires on the part of the child an effort of intellectual understanding which will be the greater and the more easily analysable the more deceptive the immediate perception. We are therefore not concerned to discover why this perception is deceptive, but why children at a certain level accept it without question, whereas others correct it by the use of intelligence. Moreover, either perception must be studied 'from the angle of the object', in which case intelligence will in the final resort be the origin of the constancy, or else perception presupposes an organization which elaborates the constancy on its own plane, in which case the functioning and the successive structures of perception imply a sensory-motor activity that is intelligent from the start. If the latter is the case, the development of the notion of invariant quantities (like that of 'object') would be a continuation, on a new, abstract plane, of the work already undertaken by sensory-motor intelligence in the field of conservation of the object.

We shall attempt to interpret the examples given above from this second point of view. What is most striking at this first stage is the inadequate quantification of the perceived qualities, and the lack of co-ordination between the quantitative relations involved

[1] E. Brunswik, *Wahrnehmung und Gegenstandwelt*. Leipzig u. Wien, 1939.

in the perception. For example, Blas (4;0) begins by thinking that
the quantity of liquid diminishes when the contents of a large
glass three-quarters full are poured into two smaller glasses, but
that it increases when poured from these small glasses into a long,
narrow tube. It is therefore only the level and not the number or
the cross section of the glasses which seems to be Blas's criterion.
But a moment later he thinks there is more liquid in three small
glasses than in two medium-sized ones filled with the same quantity. There are two noteworthy features in this reaction. In the first
place, the child continually contradicts himself. At one moment he
thinks there is more orangeade than lemonade, at another he
thinks the opposite, and yet it does not occur to him to question his
previous assumption. Obviously, if it is accepted that a liquid is
capable of expansion or contraction and has no constancy, there is
no contradiction. The real contradiction lies in the fact that the
child attempts to justify his opposing statements by resorting to
explanations that he cannot co-ordinate one with another, and
that lead to incompatible statements. Thus Blas sometimes finds
his evidence in the level of the liquid and thinks that the quantity
diminishes when it is poured from a large glass into several small
ones: sometimes he bases his statement on the number of glasses
involved, in which case the same operation is thought to imply an
increase in quantity. Alternatively, the child will use the cross
section of the containers in his estimate of the change, disregarding
the number of glasses and the level, and will then take one of these
factors into account and arrive at the opposite conclusion. This
brings us to the second feature of the reaction: the child behaves as
though he had no notion of a multi-dimensional quantity and
could only reason with respect to one dimension at a time without
co-ordinating it with the others. What has been said is true not
only of Blas, but of all the children quoted above.

The reactions of this stage can therefore be interpreted in the
following way. We must first look for the principle of differentiation between quantity and quality, and this from the first perceptual contact with the object. In every case, perception and
concrete judgement attribute qualities to objects, but they cannot
grasp these qualities without thereby relating them one to
another. These relations can only be of two kinds: symmetrical
relations expressing resemblances, and asymmetrical relations
expressing differences. Now resemblances between qualities can
only result in their classification (e.g., glasses C_1, C_2, C_3 . . . are
'equally small'), whereas asymmetrical differences imply 'more'
and 'less' and thus indicate the beginnings of quantification (e.g.,
'A_1 is larger than B_1' or 'A_1 is narrower than D'). In its primitive
form, therefore, quantity is given at the same time as quality,

since it is constituted by the asymmetrical relations that necessarily link any qualities one to another. Qualities *per se* do not in
fact exist; they are always compared and differentiated, and this
differentiation, since it includes asymmetrical relations of differences, is the germ of quantity. From this point of view, the judgements characteristic of the first stage are obviously already
quantitative in this sense. For instance, when Sim says: 'There's
more orangeade because it's higher', she is merely expressing in
terms of quantity a perceptual relation of difference between two
qualities (the heights of the liquids).

At this first level, however, which we shall call that of 'gross
quantity', quantification is restricted to the immediate perceptual
relationships, just as 'gross quality' (i.e., directly perceived
quality) is incapable of giving rise to a complete classification. The
relationship of similarity between qualities will of course eventually result in a system of classes, but this only becomes possible
with the elaboration of sequences of hierarchical inclusions involving the whole logic of classes and asymmetrical relations. As for
the relations of difference, with which alone we are for the
moment concerned, they will lead to a systematic quantification
whose stages we shall study in subsequent chapters. But before
this is achieved they must be able to satisfy two conditions that are
lacking at this level, which accounts for the absence of measurable
quantity and conservation.

The first of these conditions is that, from being mere perceptual
relationships, they shall become true relations, thus giving rise to
systems of graduations or 'intensive quantities'. (See Glossary.)
Obviously a perceptual relationship does not as such constitute a
relation. The criterion for the psychological existence of relations
is the possibility of their composition, or in other words, the
construction of their logical transitivity (or, if they cannot become
transitive, the justification for their non-transitivity). The main
characteristic of the perceptual relationships of gross quantity
used by the child at this first level is that they cannot be composed one with another either additively or multiplicatively.
When the child thinks that the quantity increases because the
level rises, he is disregarding the cross section, and when he takes
the cross section into account he disregards the level, and so on.[1]

The following experiment makes this plain. The child is given

[1] By addition of asymmetrical relations we mean their actual or virtual
seriation and the resulting graduation of the seriated terms. By multiplication
of these relations we mean their seriation from two or more points of view
simultaneously. In the examples quoted above, the simple series do not appear,
but the children had to compare two quantities from several points of view,
height, cross-section, number of glasses, etc., which constitutes multiplication
of relations.

two containers A and L of equal height, A being wide and L narrow. A is filled to a certain height (one-quarter or one-fifth) and the child is asked to pour the same quantity of liquid into L. The dimensions are such that the level will be four times as high in L as in A for the same amount of liquid. In spite of this striking difference in the proportions, the child at this stage proves incapable of grasping that the smaller diameter of L will require a higher level of liquid. Those children who are clearly still at this stage are satisfied that there is 'the same amount to drink' in L when they have filled it to the same level as A.

Blas (4;0): 'Look, your mummy has poured out a glass of lemonade for herself (A) and she gives you this glass (L). We want you to pour into your glass as much lemonade as your mummy has in hers.—(She poured rather quickly and exceeded the level equal to that in A that she was trying to achieve.)—Will you both have the same like that?— *No*.—Who will have more?—*Me*.—Show me where you must pour to so that you both have the same.—(She poured up to the same level.)— Will you and mummy have the same amount to drink like that?—*Yes*. —Are you sure?—*Yes*.—Now watch what I'm doing (putting L' next to L). I'm going to pour that one (A) into this one (L'). Will that make the same here (L') as there (L)?.—*Yes*.—(When I did so, the child laughed): *Mummy has more*.—Why?—...'

Mus (5;0): 'Look (same story as for Blas). Show me with your finger how far I must pour.—*There* (indicating the same level in L as in A).— (I filled it slightly higher). Will there be the same amount to drink?— *You've put too much. There's a little more there* (in L). *I've a little more to drink* —What could you do to see if it's the same? (putting L' next to L).— ... —Where will it come up to if we pour that one (A) into this one (L')?—*To there* (pointing to the same level as in A).—(I did so.).— *Mummy has more* (with great surprise).—How did that happen?— *Because the glass* (L') *is smaller*. (Mus thus appeared to have grasped the relation height × cross-section, but it was only a momentary glimpse, as we shall see.)—And if I pour this (L') back into that (A), which will have the most?—*Both a little, both the same*.—(I poured it back). Who has more to drink?—*Both less*.'

These reactions show that the child at the first stage is unable to reckon simultaneously with the height and cross section of the liquids he has to compare. It is not that he fails to notice the width of glass A when circumstances oblige him to make the comparison (e.g. Mus, when A is poured into L'), but when he merely has to estimate the quantities in A and L' he takes into account only the height.

The child at this stage has therefore not yet acquired the notion of multi-dimensional quantity, owing to lack of composition between the relationships of differences. For him the quantity of liquid does not depend on the combination of the various relations of height, cross section, number of glasses, etc., since each of these relations is considered separately, as though independent of the others. Each relation therefore constitutes merely a 'gross quantity' that is essentially uni-dimensional. Even when the child uses terms such as 'big' or 'large' this quality is still, as the case of Mus shows, merely perceptual data not susceptible of composition with others, and therefore again constituting a uni-dimensional 'gross quantity'.

The second condition to be satisfied before these perceptual relations can lead to true quantification, namely that there shall be partition into equal units, is even more impossible of fulfilment at this first stage than is intensive graduation. Before there can be acceptance of the notion of conservation of the liquid, and therefore construction of the notion of extensive quantity (see Glossary), there must be understanding that every increase in height is compensated by a diminution in width, these two qualities being inversely proportional. Yet even in the very simple problem of the increase in the number of glasses, children at this stage show clearly that they are unable to grasp the fact that a quantity of liquid poured from one glass into two or three smaller glasses remains the same. Composition by partition is therefore as impossible as by relations.

§3. Stage II. Intermediary reactions

Between the children who fail to grasp the notion of conservation of quantity and those who assume it as a physical and logical necessity, we find a group showing an intermediary behaviour (not necessarily found in all children) which will characterize our second stage. Two at least of these transitional reactions are worthy of note. The first of these shows that the child is capable of assuming that the quantity of liquid will not change when it is poured from glass A into two glasses B1 and B2, but when three or more glasses are used he falls back on to his earlier belief in non-conservation. The second reaction is that of the child who accepts the notion of conservation when the differences in level, cross section, etc., are slight, but is doubtful when they are greater. Here we have some examples of the first type:

Edi (6;4): 'Is there the same in these two glasses (A1 and A2)?— *Yes.*—Your mummy says to you: Instead of giving you your milk in this glass (A1), I give it to you in these two (B1 and B2), one in the morning and one at night. (It is poured out.) Where will you have most to drink, here (A2) or there (B1 + B2)?—*It's the same.*—That's right. Now, instead of giving it to you in these two (B1 and B2), she gives it to you in three (pouring A2 into C1, C2 and C3), one in the morning, one at lunch-time and one at night. Is it the same in the two as in the three, or not?—*It's the same in 3 as in 2 . . . No, in 3 there's more.*—Why?— . . . —(B1 and B2 were poured back into A1.) And if you pour the three ($C_1 + C_2 + C_3$) back into that one (A2) how far up will it come?—(He pointed to a level higher than that in A1.)—And if we pour these 3 into 4 glasses (doing so into $C_1 + C_2 + C_3 + C_4$, with a consequent lowering of the level) and then pour it all back into the big one (A2), how far up will it come?—(He pointed to a still higher level.)—And with 5?— (He showed a still higher level.)—And with 6?—*There wouldn't be enough room in the glass.'*

Pie (5;0): 'Is there the same amount here (A1) and there (A2)?— (He tested the levels.) *Yes.*—(A1 was poured into B1 + B2). Is there the same amount to drink in these two together as in the other?—(He examined the levels in B1 and B2, which were higher than in A1.) *There's more here.*—Why?—*Oh yes, it's the same.*—And if I pour the two glasses (B1 and B2) into these three ($C_1 + C_2 + C_3$), is it the same?— *There's more in the 3.*—And if I pour it back into the 2?—*Then there'll be the same* (B1 + B2) *as there* (A2).'

Here is an example of the second type:

Fried (6;5) agreed that A1 = A2. A1 was poured into B1 + B2. 'Is there as much lemonade as orangeade?—*Yes.*—Why?—*Because those* (B1 + B2) *are smaller than that* (A2).—And if we pour the orangeade (A2) as well into two glasses (doing so into B3 + B4, but putting more in B3 than in B4), is it the same?—*There's more orangeade than lemonade.'*— (B3 + B4 thus seemed to him more than B1 + B2).

A minute later he was given A1 half full, and A2 only a third full. 'Are they the same?—*No, three's more here* (A1).—(A1 was then poured into several glasses C.) *It's the same now as there* (A2).' He finally decided, however: '*No, it doesn't change, because it's the same drink* (i.e. A1 = $C_1 + C_2 + C_3 + C_4$ and A1 < A2).'

These two types of intermediary reactions are important and enable us to dismiss an objection that doubtless occurred to the reader in §2. Instead of concluding that the notion of conservation has its origin in quantification properly so called (itself the result of progressive co-ordination of the relations involved), could we not explain the absence of the notion as being due merely to failure to understand the question as referring to the quantity as a whole? The child might simply be comparing one level with another or one width with another, without considering the total quantity of liquid, but that would not necessarily prove that he was incapable of so doing. If this were so, as soon as the idea of the whole quantity made its appearance, the child would suddenly discover conservation; he would at once understand that the liquid remains the same since nothing is added to or subtracted from it. And indeed, when Edi and other children state, when first questioned, that (A2) and (B1 + B2) are 'the same', they give the impression that the difference between them and the children in §2 is due merely to the fact that they interpret the question differently. The correct solution would then be the result of a kind of immediate identification and there would be no need for a complex process of quantification. But the intermediary reactions of this second stage make it clear that this too simple interpretation is not valid. If the child hesitates, if he gives a correct answer when the variations are slight but does not assume conservation when the variation in shape is greater, it is obvious that he understands the question but is not convinced *a priori* of the constancy of the whole quantity.

This being so, how are we to interpret the progress shown by children at the second stage? The two conditions laid down in §2 as defining the transition from 'gross quantity' to true quantification are beginning to be fulfilled.

At this stage the child is attempting to co-ordinate the perceptual relations involved and thus to transform them into true, operational relations. Whereas the child at the first stage is satisfied that two quantities of liquid are equal if the two levels are the same, irrespective of the width of the containers, the child at the second stage tries to take the two relations into account simultaneously, but without success, hesitating continually between this attempt at co-ordination and the influence of the perceptual illusions. This reaction is already apparent in the most advanced children of the first stage, but generally speaking it is typical of the second period. Here we have some examples, of which the first belongs to the earlier stage:

Lac (5;6): 'Your brother Lucien has this orangeade (A, $\frac{1}{4}$ full). Pour the same amount for yourself into this glass (L).—(He filled L. to a higher level than that in A.) *No, I've got too much* (he poured some back so that L was $\frac{1}{5}$ full, i.e. the same level as in A).—Are they the same?— *No* (bringing L nearer to A and saying to himself): *Who has the most?*— Yes, who has the most?—(He pointed to A): *It's that one, because it's bigger.*—But you must have as much as Lucien.—(He added a little to L and compared the two levels.) *It's too much.* (He poured back the contents of L and began again. He gave himself the same level as in A, then added a little more so that L was about $\frac{2}{5}$ full.) *Oh! it's too much! It's not the same.* (In order to arrive at an equal quantity in L and A he then made the levels the same.)—You think you have the same amount to drink like that?—*Yes.*—(A was then poured into L'.)—*Oh! it's more!* (greatly astonished.)' Lac thus showed that he was still at the first stage, although his first reactions suggested the second stage.

Edi (6;4). Glass A was $\frac{1}{5}$ filled. 'Pour as much orangeade into this one (L) as there is there (A).—(He filled L to the same level as that in A.)—Is there the same amount to drink?—*Yes.*—Exactly the same?— *No.*—Why not?—*That one* (A) *is bigger.*—What must you do to have the same amount?—*Put some more in* (filling L).—Is that right?—*No.*— Who has more?—*Me* (pouring some back).—*No, the other one has more* (A).—(He continued to add more and then pour some back, without reaching a satisfactory conclusion).'

Wir (7;0): 'Can you pour as much into this one (L) as there is in that (A)?.—*As much?*—(He filled it to the same level.)—Are they the same?—*No.* (He added some to L till it was ½ full and then compared the levels.) *No, it's too much.* (He made the levels equal again.)—Who will have most to drink?—*Mummy* (A), *because the glass is bigger* (adding some to L).—Now are they the same?—*No, I've got more* (pouring some back).—Are they the same now, or has one of you got more?—*Mummy* (A), *because she has a bigger glass.* (He added some to L.) *No, now I've got more.* (He poured some back and again equalized the levels.) *No, mummy has more now* (no satisfactory solution).'

In each of these cases, the child begins, as at the first stage, by filling the narrow glass L to the same level as the wide glass A. But unlike the earlier children, he then discovers, by comparing the two columns of equal height, that one is wider than the other and decides that the first glass contains more because it is bigger. Thus a second relation, that of the width, is explicitly brought into the picture and 'logically multiplied' (see Glossary) with that of the levels. In order to arrive at equality, the child pours a little more liquid into glass L, thus proving the reality of this multiplication of relations. But as soon as the level of the liquid in the narrow glass is higher than that in the wide one, the child forgets the cross sections and thinks that L contains more than A, thus showing clearly the difficulties of this multiplicative operation. When he is concerned with the unequal levels, he forgets the width, and when he notices the difference in width he forgets what he has just said about the relation between the levels. Hence it is only when the levels are equal that he attempts a logical multiplication of the relations of height and width, and when the attempt has been made, one or other of the relations becomes all-important and he is left hesitating between them.

It is obvious, however, that even if the operation of logical multiplication of relations were carried through by the child of this stage it would not suffice for the construction of conservation of the whole quantity unless the height and width were simply permutated. A column of liquid whose height increases and whose width diminishes with respect to another column may be greater, equal, or less in volume than the other. In order to be certain that there is equality, the intensive graduation must be completed by an extensive quantification, i.e., it must be possible to establish a true proportion, and not merely a qualitative correlation, between the gain in height and the loss in width. In other words, there must be partition of some kind to supplement the co-ordination.

Now it is during the second stage, and in close connection with the logical co-ordination just described, that the child begins to understand that a whole remains identical with itself when it is divided into two halves. Edi and Pie, examples of the first stage, stated this fact when A1 was poured into B1 + B2, but this understanding of partition is short-lived and discontinuous, like the multiplication of relations. As soon as B1 and B2 are poured into C1 + C2 + C3, Edi and Pie no longer think there is conservation. 'In three there's more', they say, and Edi even goes so far as to think that the more a given quantity is sub-divided the more there will be of it.

In conclusion, then, multiplication of relations and partition go hand in hand. Both of them make their appearance and begin to develop during this second stage, both are halted as a result of the same limitations. What then is the link that unites these two types of operation? The analysis of the third stage will provide the answer.

§4. Stage III: Necessary conservation

In the replies characteristic of the third stage children state immediately, or almost immediately, that the quantities of liquid are conserved, and this irrespective of the number and nature of the changes made. When the child discovers this invariance, he states it as something so simple and natural that it seems to be independent of any multiplication of relations and partition. Our problem is therefore to discover whether this independence is real or only apparent, and if the latter is the case, to determine how the various intervening factors are linked.

Here are some examples:

Aes (6;6). A_1 and A_2 were $\frac{3}{4}$ filled, and then A_1 was poured into P_1, which was wide and low. 'Is there still as much orangeade as there was in the other glass?—*There's less.*—(A_2, which was supposed to be his glass, was poured into P_2.) Will you still have the same amount to drink now?—*Oh yes! It's the same, It seems as if there's less, because it's bigger* (=wider), *but it's the same.*—(P_1 and P_2 were poured back into A_1 and A_2, and A_1 was then poured into $B_1 + B_2$.) Has Roger got more than you now?—*He's got the same* (definitely).—And if I pour yours into 4 glasses (A_2 into $C_1 + C_2 + C_3 + C_4$)?—*It'll still be the same.*'

Geo (6;6). Her glass was A_1, $\frac{1}{2}$ full, and A_2, only $\frac{1}{3}$ full was supposed to be Madeleine's. 'Who has more?—*I've got more.*—That's right. But Madeleine wants to have the same amount. She divides hers by pouring it into two glasses ($C_1 + C_2$) and says: "Now I've got more, or at any rate the same amount as you."—Who has more now?—(After some thought) *It's still me.*—She then pours it into 3 glasses ($C_1 + C_2 + C_3$). Who has more now?—*Still me.*—Then she pours it into a lot of glasses (C_1, C_2 and C_3 were poured back into A_2, the contents of which

were then divided between 6 little glasses C). Who has more now?—
Madeleine has more, because it's been poured into the other glasses.—And if we
put it all back into here (A_2) where will it come up to?—(She reflected.)
No, Madeleine has less. I thought she had more, but she hasn't.—Can't it be
more?—*No.*—(Glasses C were poured back into A_2, then A_2 was poured
into 8 little glasses.) And now?—*No, it's still the same. It's the same all the
time.*' Finally she was given two new glasses A_3 and A_4, both half-full,
and A_3 was poured into $B_1 + B_2$: '*She has the same.*—Are you sure it's the
same?—*Yes, it's only been poured out.*'

Bert (7;2): 'The orangeade (A_1, $\frac{2}{3}$ full) is for Jacqueline, the lemonade (A_2, $\frac{1}{2}$ full) is for you. Who has more?—*Jacqueline.*—You pour yours
(A_2) into these two ($B_1 + B_2$, which were then full). Who has more?—
It's still Jacqueline.—Why?—*Because she has more.*—And if you pour this
(B_1) into those ($C_1 + C_2$)?—*It's still Jacqueline, because she has a lot.*—
Every change produced the same result: '*It's Jacqueline, because I saw
before that she had more.*' Then A_3, equal to A_4, was poured into $C_1 + C_2$:
'*It's still the same, because I saw before in the other glass that it was the same.*
—But how can it still be the same?—*You empty it and put it back in the
others!*'

Eus (7;2). A_1 was $\frac{2}{3}$ full and A_2 was $\frac{1}{2}$ full. A_2 was poured into $C_1 +
C_2 + C_3$: 'Are they the same now?—*No, You've poured it out of the same
glass* (A_2). *Like that you can never make them the same.*' Then with A_1
equal to A_2, A_2 was poured into $B_1 + B_2$, etc.: '*It's still the same, because
it still comes from the same glass.*'

These few examples are sufficient to show clearly which of the
hypotheses in §3 corresponds to what actually occurs. If we merely
consider the answers of Bert and Eus, who are 7, it seems that the
global comparison between the initial and final state of the liquid
is sufficient to enable the child to see that there is conservation,
independently of any multiplication of relations or partition. 'It's
still the same', Eus says, 'because it always comes from the same
glass'. At a certain level of development, therefore, the notion of
conservation seems to be the result of an *a priori* analytic deduction
(see Glossary) which makes it possible to dispense with observation
of the relations and even with the experiment itself. If, however,
we examine the replies of Aes and Geo, who still hesitate for a
moment before being quite certain, the mechanism of their construction becomes apparent, and we are compelled to recognize
that the reasoning that leads to the affirmation of conservation
essentially consists in co-ordination of the relations, with its twofold aspect of logical multiplication of relations and mathematical
composition of parts and proportions. Aes, for instance, begins by
thinking that the liquid in glass A becomes less when poured into
glass P, but immediately afterwards says: 'It seems as if there's
less, because it's bigger (=wider), but it's the same.' In other
words, he corrects his mistake by co-ordinating the relations of

height and width. In general, when children of this stage are confronted with the problem of glasses A and L, their answers show, unlike those of the earlier stages, correct co-ordination of the relations involved.

Aes (6;6). Although he began by pouring into L (long and narrow) a column of liquid the same height as in A in order to obtain the same quantity, he very soon corrected himself: 'Is it the same?—*Yes, it's the same height. . . . Oh no! that one* (L) *is narrower and this one* (A) *is wider* (and he added more to L).'

Geo (6;6) at once filled glass L ⅔ full to equal ⅕ in glass A: 'Is that right?—*It's about right.*—Is there the same amount to drink?—*Yes, it's the same.*—Why?—*Because it's narrower here* (L) *and wider there* (A).— What can you do to be sure it's the same (giving her the glasses)?— (She took glass A₂ and poured into it the liquid in L: it was approximately the same quantity as in A₁.)'

Bert (7;2) began by filling L to the same level as in A, then added some more '*because the glass is smaller: you think it's the same, but it's not true.*'

Eus (7;2) at once poured into L a column of liquid higher (¾) than in A (⅕) and explained his action by saying: '*Here* (A), *it's lower, but it's the same as there* (L).'

Ela (7;0): '*In this one* (L) *we must put more, because it's narrower,*' and '*in the other there's more room because it's wider.*'

These children, all of whom show in other experiments that they recognize conservation of quantity, succeed without difficulty in the present experiment in multiplying the relations of height and width in glasses A and L. It should be stressed that this question of the relation between A and L was put to all our children before the questions relating to conservation of quantities. It is not, therefore, the discovery of conservation which makes possible the multiplication of relations, but the contrary. Moreover, this question appears to be on the whole rather easier than that of conservation in general, since correct answers are given slightly earlier than those assuming invariance. This fact constitutes a further reason for assuming that conservation of quantities, even when it is affirmed categorically, as though it was an *a priori* judgement, presupposes a much more complex construction than would at first appear.

It is obvious that logical multiplication of relations is not sufficient to ensure the discovery of the invariance of whole quantities, and we shall now see why. When the child, after estimating the quantities from one point of view only, begins to co-ordinate the relations one with another, he does indeed construct a multidimensional whole, but it is a whole that remains 'intensive' and is not susceptible of 'extensive' measurement so long as the logical multiplication is not supplemented by truly mathematical considerations.

What, in fact, is logical multiplication of the relationships of height and width? If we have a series of containers of the type A $(A_1, A_2, A_3,$ etc.) containing liquid at increasing levels, we shall say that the child can add relations if from $A_1 < A_2$, and $A_2 < A_3$ he can deduce that $A_1 < A_3$, the operation obviously taking place only on the practical plane, the levels being clearly perceptible. If we take another series of containers of increasing width (L, B, A, P, etc.) we shall again say that there is addition if there is unidimensional co-ordination of the relationships. But we shall say that there is logical multiplication of relationships when the child compares the containers from the point of view of the two relationships *simultaneously*, e.g., when the column of liquid in L is both higher and narrower than that in A.

These logical multiplications of relationships are essential to the child's solutions, since he cannot assign any numerical value to the two dimensions and is therefore unable to multiply them arithmetically. Moreover, this logical operation makes possible the conception of a further relationship, that of total quantity, which is the logical product of height and width. For instance, if A is one-fifth full and P is quite full, the liquid in P being at the same time higher and wider than that in A, no child will have any hesitation is saying that P contains more than A. When Geo compares A_1, which is half full with A_2, one-third full, he at once deduces that since the cross-sections are equal there is more liquid in the container in which the level is higher. In a word, logical multiplication of relationships is the necessary intermediary between gross, uni-dimensional quantity and extensive quantification, which we shall consider presently.

But obviously these elementary operations can only lead to simple seriations or 'intensive' graduations, since the only possible conclusions are the following: (1) if the two relationships vary in the same direction, or (2) if one remains constant and the other varies, or (3) if both remain constant, then it is possible to discover whether the total quantity increases, decreases, or remains the same. If, on the other hand, the height increases and the width decreases, or conversely, it is impossible to know whether the total quantity increases, decreases, or remains constant. In general, the child will therefore be able to grasp increasing or decreasing series in certain conditions, but he will not be able to tell by how much one quantity is greater or less than another, or whether the total quantity increases or decreases when the relationships that intervene vary in opposite directions.

Now the notion of conservation of wholes, which is acquired by children at this stage, presupposes a quantification wide enough to cover the case in which elementary relationships vary in opposite directions, and it therefore presupposes the discovery of 'extensive' quantities. Indeed, if the child is to assume conservation, he must not only be aware that when the width and height of the columns are the same the total quantity remains constant, but also that it remains constant in spite of the fact that the height increases and the width decreases. But this conclusion is impossible within the limits of logical multiplication of relationships. How then does the child succeed in going beyond these limits if he has no numerical data or measurements in the true sense? This is the problem that we must consider, and it is bound up with the whole question of the transition from intensive to extensive quantity.

We might, of course, at this point, confine ourselves to saying, like Geo, that there is conservation because 'it's only been poured out', or like Eus, because 'it still comes from the same glass'. Conservation would then be identified with mere logical permanence, without the intervention of mathematics. But in our view, it then becomes legitimate to ask why the child does not make this discovery before he reaches the third stage. Children of 4 or 5 know as well as older children that 'it's only been poured out' or that 'it still comes from the same glass', and yet for them the quantity varies. How is it that they do not see the final and initial states as being identical, whereas at 6 or 7 they will find no difficulty in doing so?

The reason is that here a second process intervenes, one which is synchronic but distinct from the earlier one, its relations with which need careful examination, since they dominate the whole development of mathematical notions. It is the intervention of the notion of the 'unit', i.e., extensive quantification in the form either of arithmetical partition, or, which comes to the same thing, of proportions.

To take a concrete example, when Aes tried to put into L a quantity of liquid equal to that in A (one-fifth full), he poured in a higher column and said 'it's the same . . . because this one (L) is narrower and that one (A) is wider'. What does this mean? If he was merely using logical multiplication, he could only conclude that the liquids in A and L were equal if the height of the one and the width of the other were interchangeable. Something more is therefore implied in his reasoning, the feeling of a definite proportion such that L lost in width what it gained in height, or that the height of A was to its width as the height of L was to its width, or, to put it more simply, that the increase in height when A was poured into L was equivalent to the decrease in width.

At the first stage, the child confines himself to establishing simple, qualitative differences. During the following stages, when he is using only logical multiplication of relationships, he progressively grades these differences, in one or more dimensions, into 'intensive' seriations of two or more terms. But these series, except when there is complete equality, involve only asymmetrical relationships of difference. Since these differences can be seriated, they result in intensive quantification, but when two given quantities show two relationships of difference, there is no means of equating them. In other words, multiplication of relationships is a multi-dimensional seriation leading only to further seriations, and in no way allowing of the division of a given quantity into units that are recognized as equal and yet distinct. On the other hand, both proportion and numerical partition imply the fusion of asymmetrical relationships of difference with those of equality, and it is this combination of equalities and differences, or, to put it more briefly, this equating of differences, which constitutes the transition from intensive to extensive quantity, and explains the arithmetization of logical multiplication.

We shall now attempt to express what occurs in terms of actual operations that are psychologically real. First of all, it is clear that the child would have no means of gauging the equality or non-equality of the various quantities in A_1 and $(B_1 + B_2)$ or in P, L, etc., if he were merely asked to compare them. The fact that the liquid is poured from one container into another does, of course, suggest equality, but as we have seen, this action is not sufficient to explain conservation, since the younger children think that the change in shape involves a change in quantity. The action of pouring does, however, lead to the notion of invariance of the quantity when it is supported by the following operations. The empty glass A is filled to one-fifth. When A is poured into L, the liquid in L will be higher but narrower. While the child is still on the plane of qualitative seriation, he is capable of co-ordinating two relationships of level, or width, or both together. This means that, on comparing the liquids in A and L he can at once see that the level in L is higher than that in A, i.e. that it is equal to that in A plus a difference. Similarly, he can compare the liquids and see that L is narrower than A, the width of L thus being equal to that of A, less a difference. But there is no means, in these simple comparisons, of quantifying these relationships otherwise than as 'more' or 'less'. Our contention is that at a given moment the child grasps that the differences compensate one another, and this is the beginning of extensive quantification, because then two heterogeneous qualitative relationships (increase in level and decrease in width) are seen to be equal, though still preserving their value of asymmetrical difference. It is thus that proportion comes into being, through the combination of equality and asymmetrical relationship.

In a sense, this proportion is already a partition, for the equating of the increase in level with the decrease in width means that the quantity as a whole is no longer viewed as a qualitative totality whose value changes with each change of shape, but is structurized as a sum susceptible of division into units. The criterion is the following. There is arithmetical partition as soon as the elements of a whole can be equated with one another and yet remain distinct.

Moreover, the equating of differences, which we have just stated to be the principle of extensive quantification, gives rise during the third stage to truly numerical partition, which is not only synchronic but complementary to the discovery of proportions. Thus for Aes, it is obvious that when A_1 is poured into 2B or 4C it still remains A_1, and although Geo is at first reluctant to accept 6C as being equal to A, when he finally does so he generalizes and assumes that the same is true of 8C; etc. During the first stage, and during the second except in very simple cases of partition, this was not so.

In order to explain this evolution we must understand that, for instance, half a quantity is not only a quantity which is equal to another quantity and which when added to it constitutes the original quantity, but also that it is equal to the difference between the whole and the other half. Without this second condition, the relationship between the half and the whole could not be understood and the notion of the whole would cease to exist after the division. Numerical partition is therefore essentially an equating of differences, like proportion itself, but in the case of $A = B_1 + B_2$, the two halves B_1 and B_2 are seen as equal, whereas in the case of $A = L$, it is only the differences that are equated.

In conclusion, we have shown the extreme simplicity, at bottom, of the process of quantification as revealed in the child's discovery of the conservation of quantities. He begins—and makes no further progress during the first stage—by considering only unco-ordinated perceptual relationships of qualitative equality or difference, thus acquiring the notions of gross quantities and qualities not susceptible of composition. During the second stage, there begins a process of logical co-ordination, which is completed at the third stage and leads to classification when there is equality and to seriation when there is difference, this seriation resulting in intensive quantities. Finally, the third stage is characterized by the construction of extensive quantities through the

c

equating of intensive differences and therefore through the arithmetization of logical groupings (see Glossary).[1]

[1] For the sake of simplicity, we have here restricted ourselves to explaining the discovery of conservation of quantities of liquid in terms of the proportion established by the child between differences in height and width of columns of water, this being the method used by our subjects. It would obviously be possible also to envisage a purely logical (non-arithmetical) conservation in cases in which the displaced parts could be abstracted individually, or in which the differences in height and width could be compensated merely by substitution, height becoming width and vice versa.

CHAPTER II

CONSERVATION OF DISCONTINUOUS QUANTITIES AND ITS RELATION TO ONE–ONE CORRESPONDENCE[1]

THE experiments described in the previous chapter can all be repeated with discontinuous quantities that can be evaluated globally when the elements are massed and counted when they are separated. Sets of beads, for instance, can be used. If they are put into the containers used in Chapter I, they can serve for the same evaluations as the liquids (level, cross-section, etc.), and in addition they are material for a further global quantification with which children are familiar: that of the length of necklaces made from the beads. The evaluation of this length can thus be used in each case to check the quantification of the contents of the various containers used. On the other hand, when the beads are considered as separate units they can be used in operations of correspondence. If the child is told, for instance, to put beads into a container, one by one, at the same time as the experimenter is putting beads one by one into another container, he can then be asked whether the total quantities are the same, with or without identity in the shape of the two containers.

In going on from the analysis of continuous quantities to that of discontinuous quantities we are therefore not merely checking our earlier findings. We are also making a preliminary study of the relationship between conservation of quantities and the development of one–one correspondence, which is, as is well known, one of the origins of number. We shall then be in a better position to approach the question of cardinal and ordinal correspondence as such.

It should be noted that the stages we shall find here correspond exactly to those of the previous chapter.

§1. Stage I: Absence of conservation

During the first stage there is no conservation of the sets of beads, just as there was no conservation of the quantity of liquid. The child not only thinks that the total quantity changes when a

---

[1] With the collaboration of M. Juan Jaen.

set of beads is poured from one container into another of a different shape, but he also thinks that a necklace made of the beads will not be of the same length in the two cases.

Port (5;0): 'What are these?—*Little green* (A₂) *and red* (A₁) *beads.*—Is there the same amount in the two glasses?—*Yes.*—If we made a necklace with the red ones and another with the green ones, would they be the same length?—*Yes.*—Why?—*Because there's the same height of green and red.*—If we put the beads in there (L), what would happen?—*They would be higher.*—Would there be the same amount?—*No.*—Where would there be more?—*There* (L).—Why?—*Because it's narrow* (A₁ was poured into L).—Do you really think there are more beads there (L) than here (A₂)?—*Yes.*—Why?—*Because it's narrow and they go higher.*—If I poured them all out (making as though to pour the red beads on one side and the green on the other), would they be the same or not?—*More red ones.*—Why?—*Because that one* (L) *is narrow.*—And if I make a necklace with the red beads and one with the green beads, will they be the same, or not?—*The red one will be longer.*—Why?—*Because there'll be more in there* (L).—(The red beads were put back into A₁.) And now? —*They're the same height again.*—Why?—*Because you've poured them into that one* (A₁).—Are there more red ones or green ones?—*The same.*— (The red ones were poured from A₁ into M.)—*It's higher.*—But does it make the same amount?—*No. There* (M), *there are more.*—Where did the extra beads come from?—*From there* (A₁).—And if I pour the red beads back into that glass (A₁), what will happen?—*They'll be the same* (red and green).—If I make a necklace with those (M) and those (A₂)?—*There'll be more red beads.*—And if I pour this glass (M) into that one (G)?—*It'll be the same as there* (A₁) *because you'll have poured it into a thing that's too big.*—Where will there be more?—*There'll be less there* (G) *then there* (M) *because you'll have poured that one* (M) *into this one* (G) *and it's bigger.*—(The beads in M were poured into G.) If I made two necklaces, one with those (the red ones in G), and the other with those (the green ones in A₂), would they be the same?—*It would be bigger green* (A₂) *than red* (G).—Which would be longer?—*The red would be longer because before we had them here* (M) *and there were more. If you pour the green ones into this one* (M) *and then into that one* (G), *we'll see if there are more green or red ones.*—And if I pour that one (A,₂ green) into this one (E), what will happen?—*It'll be a smaller necklace because you've poured them into a smaller glass.*—And if I take these green beads (A₂) to make a necklace, and measure it, and then pour the beads into this one (E) and then make the necklace again? *It'll be shorter because you've poured them into a very small glass* (E).—But will there be more beads, or less, or the same?—*Less beads.*—(The green beads were then poured into E, without comment.) *Oh! there are more!*—And what did you think?— *That there'd be less.*—Why?—*Because this one* (E) *is smaller than that one* (M) *and it's higher than that one. No, it's narrower.*—Are there more or less beads than before, or the same?—*More, because you've poured them out.*— And if we made a necklace with these beads, would it be the same as the other?—*Longer!*'

Port was then told to put a red bead into A_1 with her right hand every time she put a green one into A_2 with her left hand. After a moment she was stopped: 'Have you got the same amount in the two glasses?—*Yes.*—(A_1 was poured into B.) Are they the same?—*No, less there* (B) *and more there* (A_2).—Why?—*Because you poured them into a little glass.*' Etc.

Gfe (5;0). There were as many red beads in A_1 as green ones in A_2: '*They're the same.*—Now listen, if I thread the red beads on one string and the green on another, will the necklaces be the same length?—*Yes, both will be the same.*—(He was told that the green beads were going to be poured into P.) Will there be the same amount?—*No. More green.*—Why?—*Because they'll all be flat; they won't be one on top of the other.* (A_2 was poured into P, and Gfe declared that there were then more green ones in P than red ones in A_1.)—And if we do this with the red ones (pouring A_1 into L)?—*More red ones.*—And if we make a red necklace and a green one, will they be the same?—*No, this one* (red) *will be longer, because there are more here* (L).'

Gfe was then told to put a large bean into V_1 every time the experimenter put one into V_2. 'When we've finished, will we have the same amount, or not?—*Yes.*—(V_1 was poured into L.) And now?—*Three are more there* (L) *than here* (V_2). *Because it's higher. They're long there* (L) *and here* (V_2) *they're lying down.*—But what difference does that make?—*It makes more beans.*—Why?—*Because they're in another glass.*—And if we eat them, will there be the same amount?—*More in that one* (L). Etc.

Roc (5;0). The red beads were in A_1 and the green in A_2: 'Are they they same?—*Yes.*—If we make two necklaces . . . etc.?—*The same length.*—Why?—*Because there's the same amount of beads.*—(The green ones in A_2 were poured into L.)—*There are more green ones.*—If we make two necklaces?—*The green one will be longer because there are more.*'

There is no need to quote further examples. Those we have given confirm our findings in the case of the conservation of liquids. As soon as the beads are poured from one container to another of different shape and dimensions, the child thinks that the quantity increases or diminishes, basing his estimate now on the level of the beads, now on the width of the glass, now on the number of glasses. In other words, as in the case of the liquids, the quantities are estimated merely from perceptual relationships unco-ordinated one with another. This initial lack of coherence explains both the continual contradictions in the various judgements of the child, and the absence of any criterion for conservation.

On the other hand, however, these same examples make it possible to be more explicit with regard to certain points. As long as we were considering continuous quantities such as the liquids used in the experiments in Chapter I, we might perhaps have thought that the child's failure to see that there was conservation was due rather to physical than to mathematical reasons, since liquids might be imagined to contract or expand according to the shape of the containers. But when we come to discontinuous quantities, a new feature intervenes. In spite of the fact that the elements of the sets are discrete, the child thinks that they increase or diminish in number with the change in the shape of the set in passing from one container to another. Thus a set of beads poured from A to L is thought to produce a longer necklace if the beads are taken from L than if they are taken from A. The child does not, of course, count the beads one by one, but as his estimate of the quantity is in terms of length of necklace, his attention is certainly drawn to the fact that the set is composed of discontinuous units. When therefore he assumes that the same set can be made now into a longer, now into a shorter necklace, there is definitely non-conservation in the mathematical sense.

Moreover, as we have seen, in order that the child may be well aware that the elements in the two sets to be compared are equal, he himself is made to put one bead into a given container each time the experimenter puts one into the other container. Even this one-one correspondence, which amounts to a practical enumeration, is not sufficient for conservation to be assumed. The child grasps that the two corresponding sets are equal only so long as the containers are equal. When one set is put into a container of a different shape, the two sets are no longer considered as equal.

As a confirmation of this, let us see what happens to the one-one correspondence when the containers are of different shape:

Bab (4;6) put one bean on the table every time the experimenter did so. 'Have we both got the same?—*Yes*.' He then put one bean into L each time the experimenter put one into P, and with each bean the child said spontaneously: '*It's the same.*' But when there were ten in each glass, and L was ½ full, Bab cried: '*I've got a lot.*—And what about me?—*Mine's nearly quite full.*—Are they the same?—*I've got a lot.*—And what about me?—*Look! you've only got a few.*—Why?—*Look there* (pointing to the levels).'

Bab then put a bead into E each time the experimenter put one in P: 'Make sure that we've both got the same.—(Bab then said the number aloud each time.) *Me one and you one; me two and you two; me three and you three*; . . . (up to 6, when glass E was quite full).—Are they the same?— . . . (conflict between the appearance and the correspondence).—If we made one necklace with your beads and one with mine, would they be the same?—*No, mine would be longer.*—But if we took all your beads and all mine?—*No, yours won't be as long; we must fill your glass to have a necklace as long as mine.*—Count them.—(He counted 1 . . . 6 in E and 1 . . .6 in P.)—Well?—*You'll have a little necklace.*—But why have you got a lot? —*Look, they're low in your glass. It's me that got a lot, mine's quite full.*'

Coc (5;0) put one bean into A_1 each time the experimenter put one into A_2, and then said spontaneously: '*They're both the same.*—How do

you know?—*Because we put both* (=the two corresponding beans) . . .
No, because the two glasses are the same.' He was then told to put one bean
in P each time the experimenter put one in L: 'Does that make the
same amount?—*No, here* (L) *there are more.*—Why?—*Because it's quite
small* (=narrow) *and there* (P) *it's big.*'

These interesting reactions are very characteristic of the first
stage. Obviously, if there is no conflicting factor, the one-one
correspondence between two sets ought to lead to equivalence of
the corresponding sets. This is what we find at the second stage,
during which the conflict is between the correspondence and the
perceptual appearances. But at the first stage, quantification is so
little developed that there is no conflict; perception completely
over-rules the correspondence. Goc, for instance, thinks that A_1
and A_2 are equal 'because the two glasses are the same' rather
than because the two corresponding beans are put in at the same
time, as if the first criterion were more reliable than the second. As
for Bab, although he says 'it's the same' each time the two corresponding beans are put in, he disregards this estimate once L is
half full, and judges only by the levels. Moreover, in spite of having
counted six beads in both E and P, he still concludes that the
necklace made from the beads in E will be longer, because in E
there are 'a lot, quite full'. Thus not only the one-one correspondence, but also the actual enumeration, seem to the child at
the first stage to be less sure means of quantification than direct
evaluation through global perceptual relationships (gross quantities). When he is required by his social environment to count up
to a certain number, his counting is still only verbal and has no
operational value. As for the one-one correspondence, it would be
a great mistake, as we shall see in the following chapters, to consider it as being already a quantifying operation: it is as yet only
a qualitative comparison.

§2. *Stage II: Beginnings of construction of permanent sets*

As in the case of continuous quantities, we can distinguish here
also a second stage characterized by intermediary solutions. In
general, the situation is as follows. On the one hand, the child
tends to think that there is conservation, either because the two
sets are put into two identical containers (A_1 and A_2) or because
the two sets have been built up by a one-one correspondence. But
on the other hand, this tendency comes into conflict with the
appearance of the sets, i.e. with the difference in level, cross-
section, etc. Two new features are then observable, as distinct
from the reactions of the first stage. In the first place, there is a
real conflict; the factors of conservation do not immediately give

way before the factors of change, and the struggle between the two is most instructive. Secondly, as a result of this conflict, the perceptual relationships are co-ordinated as relations, and are integrated in a system susceptible of justifying conservation while taking into account the concomitant variations.

Here we have two examples in which the one-one correspondence does not intervene:

Marg (5;6): 'Is there the same number of beads (in A_1 and A_2)?—*Yes, the same.*—And if we made necklaces, etc.?—*The same length.*—Why?— ... —And if I pour this into that (A_1 into L)?—*There are more there* (A_2).—Why?—*Because it gets bigger here* (pointing to the narrower column in L).—Where is there more?—*In the big one* (=the wide one, A_2).—And if we make two necklaces (with L and A_2)?—*They'll be the same length.*—And if we pour these (L) into those ($M_1 + M_2$)?—*There'll be more in the two little ones.*—Why?— ... —And if we make a necklace? —*It will be longer with the two little ones* (than with A_2).—And before, when the beads were here (A_1 and A_2)?—*The necklaces were the same length.*—And if I put those (A_2) here ($E_1 + E_2 + E_3 + E_4$), will the two necklaces be the same (i.e. 2 M and 4 E)?—*No, it'll be longer from the little ones* (4 E).'

Ari (5;6): '*They're the same* (A_1 and A_2).—And if we make two necklaces, etc.?—*The same length.*—And if we pour these (A_2) into that (L)? —*There'll be more there* (L).—Why?—*Because it's higher.*—And if we make two necklaces?—*They'll be the same length.*—And if we pour them like this (A_1 into 4 E)?—*There'll be more there* (4 E).—And if we make a necklace?—*It'll be longer.*'

The first point to notice here is that, as in the case of continuous quantities, the child at this level is capable of postulating conservation when there is only a slight change in pattern, but not when the change is more significant. Thus Marg and Ari think that the two necklaces will still be the same length if the beads in A are poured into L, but not if they are poured into 2M or 4E. But this is not all. By the very fact that he hesitates to assume conservation because of the change in shape, the child comes to distinguish between evaluations based on mere perception of the relationships of height and width and those which result from representation of the length of the necklaces. For instance, although Marg and Ari think that the quantity changes in passing from A to L because the level rises, they still think that the necklace made from the beads in L will be the same length as the one made from those in A. Hence there is conservation when the child is thinking of the row of discontinuous elements, and non-conservation when he is thinking of one or other of the dimensions of the set as a whole. Such distinctions between the various evaluations are extremely instructive. On the one hand they indicate how many and varied are the operations that the child has to co-ordinate in quantification. On the other hand, the fact that the evaluations based on representation of the necklace are more correct than the others suggests that the notion of conservation involves decomposition into elements. We shall now see whether this is borne out by the facts:

Tis (5;1) put one bead into V_1 each time the experimenter put one into V_2: 'Are they the same?—*Yes, because I put the same as you every time.* —If we make two necklaces, etc.?—*They'll be the same length, because there are a lot of beads, and you've got a lot as well.*—(V_1 was poured into L + M.) Are they still the same?—*In yours* (L + M) *there are a lot.*—And in yours?—*Not many.*—And if we make two necklaces, etc.?—*Yours will be longer; mine won't be so long.*—Why?—*Because there are more beads in yours.*—But how did we put the beads in?—*Two each time.*—Then why have I got more?—*There are two big lots in yours, look.*' So far then, Tis's reaction is characteristic of the first stage, but we shall now see the transition from this reaction to the conflicts typical of the second stage.

Tis put one bead into L every time the experimenter put one into P. He counted each bead as he put it in and reached the correct total of 12. L was then full, and Tis cried spontaneously: '*I've got more.*—Why? *There are more in mine.*—And if we make two necklaces?—*This one* (L) *will be longer.*—Why?—*The glass is bigger, and that one* (P) *is smaller* (pointing to the height).—But are there more beads?—*In that one* (L).— Why?—*It's bigger.*—How did we put the beads in?—*We put two every time.*—Have we got the same, or have you more or less?—*Both the same.*—Why?—*Because we put two every time.*—What will the necklaces be like?—*Yours will be long and mine will be the same length.*—Why?— *Because this one* (L) *is big, and mine* (P) *is little. You've got a lot of beads in yours.*—And what about you?—*Not as many, but a lot all the same.*' It is clear that as soon as the child is reminded of the one-one correspondence there is a conflict between it and his perception of the dimensions, the former tending towards equality and the latter towards difference, with the result that no real synthesis is achieved.

Von (5;10) also failed to reconcile the correspondence with the perceptual relationships. When 11 pink beads were put into E and 11 blue ones into P, one at a time, he said that they were the same, although E was full. 'Why?—*Because I counted, and I know it's right.*— And if we make a pink necklace and a blue one?—*There'll be the same difference for both, the same size necklace.*—How do you know?—*I counted. There's the same number of beads.*—Then why are they like that here (pointing to the level in E)?—*Yours* (E) *is round and thinner, mine* (P) *is round and bigger* (with a gesture indicating the width).—Well?—*They're the same, because I counted. We put in the same number; I put the same as you every time.*'

Von then put one bead into G each time I put one into L. '*It's the same in both.*—Why?—*We put them in together.*—And if we make two necklaces?—*Both the same.*—Well why is L full and not the other?— *Because here* (L) *it's round and long, and there* (P) *it's round and bigger*

(=wider) *and we put in the same amount.*—(The beads in G were then poured into another glass Gp, the same shape but smaller, which was then full.) Now what about this (L) and that (Gp)?—*They're the same.* —Why?—*Because that one* (Gp) *is smaller* (=lower) *and flatter, and this one* (L) *is longer; it's bigger and so there's more.*—More what (Gp and L were full to the brim and Von was therefore not distinguishing between the volume of the glasses and the quantity of beads)?—*More beads. There are more beads there* (L).—And if we made two necklaces?—*You* (L) *have more, the blue necklace will be longer.*—And what about the pink one (Gp)?—*Shorter, because there are less beads.*'

These intermediary reactions are very interesting both from the point of view of quantification in general and of the significance of correspondence itself.

There is obviously a systematic conflict in the case of Tis and Von, and all the other cases typical of this stage, between a factor of equalization and conservation and a factor of difference. Every one of these children concludes that there is equality if the same number of elements is dropped, one at a time, into two containers, irrespective of the shape of the containers, But when the child afterwards considers the result obtained when the shapes are different, his belief in the equivalence is shaken by an evaluation based on the perceptual relationships. Although he himself has just made the one-one correspondence, he reacts like the child at the first stage and thinks that any variation in height or width entails a change in the quantity as a whole. But whereas at the first stage his belief in the equivalence was destroyed, now there is merely a conflict between the two tendencies, neither of which definitely triumphs. When the child considers the sets of beads he thinks that there is non-equivalence, and when he remembers the correspondence he again thinks that the sets are equivalent. Even when, as in the case of Tis, a final decision appears to have been reached, the words the child uses express his doubt ('You have got a lot. . . . I've not got so many, but a lot all the same').

How is the child going to reconcile these two opposing tendencies? It is interesting to find that he solves the problem of the beads in exactly the same way as that of continuous quantities. The synthesis of the real equivalence and the apparent variations is achieved through co-ordination of the relations in question, and here again this co-ordination first takes the form of mere logical multiplication, which rapidly develops into true proportionality. This is begun at the second stage and completed during the third. Von, for example, who begins by accepting the equivalence because of the correspondence, explains the apparent variations in quantity by saying that the width of P compensates for the height of L. But his attempt at the operation of multiplication of relations

('They're the same . . . because here (L) it's round and long, and there (P) it's round and bigger'), is as yet so ill-founded that the second time he does it he forgets to correlate the height of L with the width of the other container and suddenly decides that L 'is longer and bigger and so there's more'!

§3. Stage III: Conservation and quantifying co-ordination

Let us now examine how the intensive and extensive quantification begun during the second stage reaches completion. Our first examples are of reactions to questions involving conservation only, independently of correspondence:

Lin (6;0) recognized the equality of A_1 and A_2. 'Suppose I pour this one (A_1) into that one (L)?—*It'll still be the same.*—And if I pour that one (L) into this one (G)?—*Still the same.*—Will it really?—*Of course, because there, in the little one* (i.e. L, the narrow one), *there's more* (pointing to the height, and thus indicating that the increase in height compensated for the narrowing of the column).'

Jup (5;6). 'Suppose I pour this (A_2) into those ($M_1 + M_2$)?—*It's the same.*—Why?—*There's the same amount of beads.*—How many glasses?— *Two and one.*—Aren't there more beads in the two?—*No, because the two are smaller.*—And if I pour them ($M_1 + M_2$) into these ($E_1 + E_2 + E_3 + E_4$)?—*The same.*—And if we make a necklace with these (A_1) and another neckalce with those (4 E)?—*They'll be the same.*—And if we pour these (A_1) into that one (G)?—*It's just the same.*'

Pel (6;0). Same replies. '*It's the same in the little glasses as in a big one* '

It is at once obvious that the difference between these answers and all those given earlier lies in the fact that the child no longer needs to reflect in order to be certain that there is conservation of the total quantities: he knows it *a priori*. At first sight, therefore, is might seem that the notion of the invariance of the whole results merely from a global judgement, counteracted hitherto by perceptual factors, but standing out plainly once the perceptual factors are overcome. Yet the arguments used by these children show that the co-ordinations of relations achieved during the preceding stage are still the essential factors, but are now a single act instead of being constructed step by step. Lin, for example, simply says 'in the little one (L) there is more' to justify the total invariance of which he is convinced. Similarly Jup at once sees that the whole remains constant when divided into two parts, 'because the two are smaller'.

In order to see the real significance of the discovery of the invariance of wholes—which is a decisive stage in quantification— it is therefore essential to make a further analysis of the operations of co-ordination involved in the earlier reactions. It is, however, no longer sufficient to oppose the one-one correspondence to the changes in shape, since at this stage the factor of equivalence over-rides that of change. Our technique will therefore be to some extent modified. We shall give the child two sets of different shapes whose equivalence he cannot check, and we shall ask him whether he thinks they are or are not equivalent, afterwards checking by one-one correspondence, with retrospective explana-tion, the hypothesis he makes. Here are some examples:

Sum (6;10) compared glasses L and P (each containing 18 beads) without having counted or made the correspondence between the beads. 'Are they the same or not?— . . . —How can we find out?— *There are more in that one* (P).—Why?—*Because it's bigger. You can't put as many in this one* (L).'

L and P were emptied, and Sum put one bead into L each time the experimenter put one into P. '*They're the same.—Why?—That one* (P) *is bigger, but it's not full, and this one's narrower but it's quite full.*—How do you know they're the same?—*Because we put them in together.*'

Sum was then given glass G containing a single layer of beads and was asked to put the same number in L. He filled L $\frac{2}{3}$ full and said: '*I don't know how to do it, I think there are more there* (G).—(We then filled up L.)—*I think they're the same.—Why?—That one* (G) *is bigger, but if we made it long* (making as though to elongate G and so to make the beads vertical), *it would be the same as there* (L).'

Lea (7;7) compared L and P (16 beads in each): '*Here* (L) *there are more, they're higher.*—Well?—*It's not so wide, but it's higher. That one* (P) *is wider, but it's smaller. But if we filled it, it would make more beads.*—Why? —*Because it's wider.*—Explain how.—*If we cut it* (L) *in the middle and put the two bits there* (in P), *it would still be not so wide.*—Why?—*Because it's very narrow.*'

L and P were emptied, and the beads put in one by one. '*They're the same.—Why?—Because we put them in together each time.*—But there (L) it's higher. How's that?—*If I emptied this one* (P) *into that one* (L), *or that one* (L) *into this one* (P) *they'd be the same.*—Why?—*If I put those* (the beads in P) *in a pile they'd be the same.*—Well?—*That one* (P) *is wider, it holds a lot* (with a gesture indicating width), *but here* (L) *the glass is narrow, so it doesn't hold many* (in width), *but they go up.*'

Dur (7;8), after thinking that L 'had more' than P, put in one bead each time the experimenter put one into P. '*They're both the same.—* How do you know?—*Because we finished together; we began at the same time and we finished at the same time.*—But is that one (L) narrower?—*It's narrow, but it's higher, and this one* (P) *is low but it's bigger.*'

Dur was then asked to put into G (=4 E) a quantity equal to that in E (full). He pointed to a level that was about $\frac{1}{4}$G. 'How do you know? —*I fill it in my mind and I can see where it comes up to.*—What do you mean by "where"?—*I lay the glass* (E) *on its side, and then I can see that there's more here* (G), *because there's still some room left.*'

Ler (7;8). Same beginning, then, after making the correspondence: '*There's the same amount, because we put them in together, so there can't be more in one than in the other.—Why?—Because there* (P) *it's wide. and here* (L) *it's high.*' Similarly, he compared E and G, and discovered the exact relationship. 'How did you find out?—*By looking! I lay that one* (E) *on its side, and when I do that I can see that there's some room left.*'

Chai (7;8): '*There* (L) *you have to put them one after the other* (=put the beads one on top of the other), *because it's narrow, but here* (P) *you can put a lot at once in a row* (horizontally.' In the case of glasses E and G, Chai estimated that the contents of E would reach half-way up G. 'Why?—*That one* (G) *is twice as wide* (as E), *so if I put them in once, they make just one row; that's half, and then we can put another one.*'

Gar (8;2): '*There* (P), *they're close together, in a heap.*—Well, what difference does that make?—*Here* (P), *they're spread out. If I put them close together, they'd be the same as there* (L).'

Kor (8;6): '*That glass* (P) *is wider, it goes out more at the sides, so they don't go up so fast* (as in L).' In comparing G and E, Kor said at once that G contained more than E. 'Why?—*If we wanted to make it* (G) *narrow and high, it would be as narrow as the other* (E) *but higher.*' These remarks were accompanied by gestures indicating that by compressing the broad column in G we could make a narrow column like that in E, but taller.

Gui (9;0): '*In the little glass* (L), *there's only one bead on another* (cf. Chai), *and there* (P), *there are more at a time: there are only two layers, but it's the same* (as in L).' In the case of E and G, '*It goes 4 times.*—How do you know?—*I cut it in the middle, and then again. I make quarters, I fill up each quarter and then I see that it goes 4 times.*' On the other hand, Gui thought G was bigger than L, as a result of the following reasoning: '*I cut it* (G) *into lines* (the last gesture he made to illustrate what he meant showed the circumference of G divided into 4 sections each corresponding to the width of L), *and then afterwards I compared with that one* (L). *I put it like that* (L on its side) *and then measured with one portion of it* (L divided into two unequal parts, one of which corresponded to the width of G). He was therefore comparing the width of G with the height of L. As for the width of L and the thickness of G, he finally made the following comparison: '*I cut this one* (G) *like that* (into two layers), *and I saw that that layer is just right if we cut that one* (L) *in two* (lengthwise).' Hence half a column in L was equal to one layer in G!

These various methods of comparison—all of them discovered spontaneously by the child—enable us both to verify the interpretations of the previous chapter and to see the problem of correspondence more clearly.

With regard to the first point, it will be remembered that as soon as the child is capable of co-ordinating differences in height and cross-section, in a 'multiplication of relations' that leads to intensive quantification, he is also capable of equating the differences and therefore of achieving extensive quantification. But in the case of continuous quantities, all that we could observe was that the child grasped the inverse proportion between the height and cross-section of two columns of liquid, or the partition of a given quantity into two or more unit-glasses. In the case of discontinuous quantities, however, the reactions at this stage provide evidence which is both more significant and more precise as to the origins of extensive quantification.

In the first place, it should be observed that each of these reactions, like those quoted at the beginning of this section, has as its starting point logical multiplication of the relations of height and cross-section. In order to remove the contradiction between the one-one correspondence of the elements of the two sets and the apparent variations, the child at once assumes that the latter constitute a whole. Thus for Sum, P is 'bigger but not full', while L is 'narrower but quite full', and for Lea, L is 'not so wide but higher', etc., each relation being multiplied by another, usually its inverse.

But as was clearly apparent when the comparison between L and P was made without the equivalence of their contents being previously verified, such an operation is quite inadequate for the constitution of the notion of a permanent quantity or the equality of two quantities. It merely enables the child to deduce, provided that he already knows that the two quantities are equal, that an increase in height necessarily corresponds to a decrease in width, and conversely. This explains the fact that it is when the child is already conscious of the invariance owing to the one-one correspondence, and only has to explain the apparent variations, that he resorts to multiplication of the relations, thereby co-ordinating all the relationships in question in an intensive quantification. This co-ordination does not of itself result in that case in the construction of the notion of invariance, since it could only do so if the relations of height and width were merely permuted. But as soon as the child has mastered the operation of co-ordinating the differences, i.e. when he multiplies the relations, he assumes that the differences can be equated. As we have just seen, he even formulates this hypothesis very clearly. For Sum, for instance, the set in G is equal to that in L because 'if we made it long it would be the same', or in other words, because the difference in cross-section between G and L is exactly equivalent to the difference in height. In the same way Lea says that P is 'wider' than L and consequently 'holds a lot', with the result that the height is less, but that 'if we put them in a pile they'd be the same'. Again, Gar says: 'If I put them (P) closer together they'd be the same (as L)' and Kor: 'If we wanted to make it narrow and high, it would be as narrow as the other but higher', etc. In a word, as soon as the perceived differences are co-ordinated operationally, they are measured one against the other, each increase in cross-section being equated or compared to the concomitant decrease in height, and conversely.

Most of the children at this stage show clearly that this proportion, which constitutes the beginning of extensive quantification, goes hand in hand with arithmetical partition, as we assumed in the previous chapter. For instance, for Lea, L contains more than P (when P is full), because 'if we cut it (L) in the middle and put the two bits in there (P), it would still be not so wide', and Chai divided the height of G into two, and equated each section to E. The case of Kor, who was older, shows how far such decomposition can lead in the absence of any enumeration of the elements.

Generally speaking, it can be seen that these proportions, this equating of differences and these numerical partitions come into being as a result of the inverse operations which the child can now perform, precisely because the transformations hitherto considered to be mere perceptual relationships have become 'operational'. When, for instance, Lea says 'if I emptied this one (P) into that one (L), or that one (L) into this one (P), they'd be the same', he is expressing the reversibility characteristic of any logical, mathematical operation, and it is this reversibility that makes possible the notion of equalization and decomposition. This is clearly illustrated in the case of Dur, who says: 'I fill it in my mind and I can see where it comes up to' and 'I lay the glass (E) on its side, and then I can see that there's more here (G), because there's still some room left' (cf. also the cases of Ler, Gar, and more particularly Gui).

The conflict between the one-one correspondence and the perceptual relationships thus comes to an end only during the third stage, with the triumph of correspondence over perception. But what is the connection between one-one correspondence and co-ordination of the perceptual relationships?

So far, we have approached the problem from one point of view only. We have considered the progressive co-ordination of relations merely as the means by which the child explains the changes in shape of the sets from the two angles of intensive and extensive quantification, and thus reconciles these changes with the invariance of the corresponding sets, the correspondence thus being viewed as the initial reason for the invariance. But one considerable difficulty still remains: how is it that it is not until the third stage that the one-one correspondence implies lasting equivalence in the sets, and that during the first two stages it is inadequate to override perceptual appearances? As far as the first stage is concerned, it might be argued that since co-ordination is lacking, the perceptual relationships make so firm an impression on the mind that the equivalence is conceived of as not lasting. But during the second stage, co-ordination of the relationships does take place, and yet the equivalence still does not triumph over perceptual appearances.

The truth of the matter may be that co-ordination of the relationships occurs as soon as correspondence itself has been constructed, and that the mechanisms involved in this evolution form a much more integrated whole than has hitherto appeared. It may in fact be that the correspondence that leads to lasting equivalence is not the same operation as the one-one correspondence without lasting equivalence between corresponding sets. If by further experiments it were found possible to distinguish between these two forms of correspondence, it would then be natural that the perceptual correspondence of the first stage should be subordinated to the apparent changes, and that only the correspondence of the third stage should develop into co-ordination of the relationships, because the latter are already implied in it. The intermediary stage would then be merely the period during which the correspondence itself is being organized. The two chapters that follow will provide the answers to these questions.

PART TWO

CARDINAL AND ORDINAL
ONE–ONE CORRESPONDENCE

CHAPTER III

PROVOKED CORRESPONDENCE AND
EQUIVALENCE OF CORRESPONDING SETS

IN analysing the beginnings of quantification, we find ourselves
confronted with the problem of correspondence. To compare
two quantities is indeed either to compare their dimensions, or
to make a one-one correspondence between the elements. As a
result of the work of Cantor, the second of these processes has been
seen to be fundamental to the construction of the integer, since it
provides the simplest and most direct measurement of the equivalence of two sets. The fact that the discovery of this operation
came so late is due, as Brunschvicg clearly proved, to its very
primitive character. Both counting on the fingers and the exchange
of one object for another are indications of the considerable part
played by correspondence in the synthesis of number.

Yet although one-one correspondence is obviously the tool used
by the mind in comparing two sets, it is not adequate, in its
original form or forms, to give true equivalence to the corresponding sets, i.e. to give each set the same cardinal value, which
is seen as constant as a result of the correspondence. As we saw in
the previous chapter, either the correspondence is held in check
by perceptual factors, or the correspondence itself develops from
mere global correspondence between configurations into truly
quantifying correspondence, which issues in necessary equivalence and thus in cardinal invariance. We shall now proceed to
examine the question of the possibility of such development of
correspondence.

We must first make a distinction between two kinds of situations in which the child is led to discover or to make the one-one
correspondence. On the one hand, there are those cases in which
he is required to assess the value of a given set of objects by comparing them with objects of the same kind. For instance, if two
children are playing marbles, and one puts four or six on the
ground, his partner will want to put one opposite each of them
and thus obtain an equivalent set, without needing to be able to
count. This correspondence between like objects raises the whole
problem of cardination, and we shall therefore leave the analysis

of it for the next chapter, in which we shall deal with the construction of spontaneous correspondence in general. On the other
hand, there is an even simpler situation, which we shall first
study, namely, correspondence between objects that are heterogeneous, but qualitatively complementary, a correspondence which
is thus, as it were, provoked by external circumstances. During a
meal, for instance, the child might be asked to put an egg in each
egg-cup, to put a glass opposite each bottle, or a flower in each of
the little vases, etc. We must also include in this category the
exchange of one object for another, for example one flower or one
sweet for each penny, etc. In this chapter, our investigation will be
restricted to situations in which the correspondence is provoked,
with a view to establishing whether the one-one correspondence
made by the child, or with his help, necessarily entails in his mind
the idea of lasting equivalence between the corresponding sets.
We shall in fact find that this is not so, but we cannot be too careful in our choice of examples, and shall therefore confine ourselves
first to the analysis of these elementary behaviours, leaving the
study of correspondence in general to the next chapter.

The procedure will be as follows. We shall first examine the
correspondence between six to ten glasses and bottles. Since this
experiment does not give rise to the notion of lasting equivalence,
we shall go on in §2 to the analysis of the correspondence between
flowers and vases, which would seem to be even simpler, since the
flowers are actually put into the vases and not merely near to them.
The result being the same as before, we shall check the position by
an even simpler correlation: that of eggs and egg-cups. It is
simpler because each egg-cup can contain only one egg, whereas
the relation between the number of glasses and bottles, or flowers
and vases, is arbitrary. As the reactions remain the same, in §3 we
shall study one-for-one exchange without counting aloud, and in
§4 with counting aloud. We shall find that when counting is introduced the results are in no way different from those of the experiments in §1 to §3.

§1. One-one correspondence between glasses and bottles

Six little bottles (about one inch high, of the kind used in dolls'
games) are put on the table, and the child is shown a set of glasses
on a tray: 'Look at these little bottles. What shall we need if we
want to drink?—Glasses.—Well, there they are. Take off the tray
just enough glasses, the same number as there are bottles, one for
each bottle.' The child himself makes the correspondence, putting
one glass in front of each bottle. If he takes too many or too few,
he is asked: 'Do you think they're the same?' until it is clear that

he can do no more. Mistakes occur in fact only with children of the first stage (4–5 years). The correspondence can be made easier by getting the child to empty the bottles into the glasses, each bottle just filling one glass. Once the correspondence is established, the six glasses are grouped together and the child is again asked: 'Are there are many glasses as bottles?' If he says 'no', he is then asked: 'Where are there more?' and 'Why are there more there?' The glasses are then rearranged in a row and the bottles grouped together, the questions being repeated each time.

I. Stage I: No exact correspondence and no equivalence

Bon (4;0): 'Look at all these little bottles. What shall we need if we want to drink?—*Some glasses.*—Well, there are a lot here (putting them on the table). Now put out enough glasses for the bottles, just one for each.—(He took the 12 glasses, but put them close together, so that the 6 bottles made a rather longer row.)—Where are there more?—*There* (the bottles).—Well then, put one glass for each bottle.—(He made the 12 glasses into a row the same length as that of the 6 bottles.)—Are they the same?—*Yes.*—(The bottles were then put further apart.) Is there the same number of glasses and bottles?—*Yes* (but he spread out the glasses a little more.)—(The bottles were then put still further apart.) —*There are only a few here* (the 12 glasses), *and there* (the 6 bottles) *there are a lot.*'

Gol (4;0) began by pouring the contents of each bottle into a glass. When he came to the 4th bottle he suddenly saw that he could not make the 6 bottles correspond to the 12 glasses, and cried: '*There aren't many bottles.*—Then you can take some glasses away.—(He left 7 glasses for 6 bottles, putting the glasses rather closer together.)—Is there the same number of glasses and bottles?—*Yes.*—(One glass was then put in front of each bottle, so that one could be seen to have no corresponding bottle.)—*We'll have to have another bottle.*—(He was given one.) Is it right now?—(He so arranged them that the first bottle corresponded to the second glass, and so on up to the 7th bottle, for which there was thus no glass.) *No, here there's a glass missing, and there there's a glass that hasn't a bottle.*—What do we need then?—*One bottle and one glass.*—(He was given them, but he put them opposite one another and never made the correct correspondence.)'

Car (5;2): 'Arrange them so that each bottle has its glass.—(He had taken all the glasses, so he removed some and left 5. He tried to make these correspond to the 6 bottles by spacing them out so as to make a row the same length.) Is there the same number of glasses and bottles? *Yes.*—Exactly?—*Yes.*—(The 6 bottles were then moved closer together so that the two rows were no longer the same length.) Are they the same?—*No.*—Why?—*There aren't many bottles.*—Are there more glasses or more bottles?—*More glasses* (pushing them a little closer together.) —Is there the same number of glasses and bottles now?—*Yes.*—Why did you do that?—*Because that makes them less.*'

These reactions are those of an earlier stage than that of correspondence in the true sense, a stage at which evaluation takes place through global comparison of the length of the sets in question. The case of Car shows this very clearly. He thinks that a row of five glasses contains more elements than a row of six bottles that are closer together, but he also thinks that by closing up the first row 'it makes them less' and that it then becomes equivalent to the row of six bottles! It follows that the notion of lasting equivalence between two sets is impossible, since equivalence depends on variable factors such as the length of the rows.

II. Stage II: One-one correspondence, but without lasting equivalence of corresponding sets

The following examples are those of children who are perfectly capable of making without hesitation the one-one correspondence between bottles and glasses. But although they are certain that there are as many glasses as bottles when they can see the corresponding elements opposite one another, they cease to believe in the equivalence when the rows are no longer of equal length.

Hoc (4;3): 'Look, imagine that these are bottles in a café. You are the waiter, and you have to take some glasses out of the cupboard. Each bottle must have a glass.' He put one glass opposite each bottle and ignored the other glasses. 'Is there the same number?—*Yes.*— (The bottles were then grouped together.) Is there the same number of glasses and bottles?—*No.*—Where are there more?—*There are more glasses.*' The bottles were put back, one opposite each glass, and the glasses were then grouped together. 'Is there the same number of glasses and bottles?—*No.*—Where are there more?—*More bottles.*— Why are there more bottles?—*Just because.*'

Mog (4;4) estimated that he needed 9 glasses for the 6 bottles, then made the one-one correspondence and removed the 3 that were left over, and said spontaneously: '*No, it wasn't the right number.*—And are they the same now?—*Yes.*—(The glasses were put closer together and the bottles spread out a little.) Is there the same number of glasses and bottles?—*No.*—Where are there more?—*There are more bottles.*'

Gin (4;11): 'Take just enough glasses off this tray for the bottles, one for each.—(He took all the glasses.) Do you think it's the same number?—*No.*—Take away the extra ones then.—(He made the one-one correspondence merely by looking at them, and left 6 glasses on the tray without counting.) Are they the same?—*Yes.*—Well, now put them so that we can see if it's right.—(He placed them correctly opposite the bottles.) *There.*—Is there the same number?—*Yes.*—(The glasses were then grouped together.) Is there the same number of glasses and bottles?—*No.*—Where are there more?—*There are more bottles.*—Why?—*Because there are more here* (pointing to the row of 6 bottles).—(The glasses were spread out and the bottles grouped together.) Are they the same?—*No.*—Where are there more?—*Here* (the glasses).'

Gal (5;1) made 6 glasses correspond to 6 bottles. The glasses were then grouped together: 'Is there the same number of glasses and bottles?—*No, it's bigger there* (the bottles) *and smaller here* (the glasses).— (The bottles were then grouped together and the glasses spread out.)— *Now there are more glasses.*—Why?—*Because the bottles are close together and the glasses are all spread out.*—Count the glasses.—*1, 2 . . . 6.*—Count the bottles.—*1, 2 . . . 6.*—They're the same then?—*Yes.*—What made you say they weren't the same?—*It was because the bottles are very small.*'

Mül (5;3) made the correct correspondence between bottles and glasses, but only after estimating at a glance that he would need 2 extra glasses. 'Were they the same?—*No, there were too many glasses.*— And are they the same now?—*Yes, they're the same.*—(The glasses were then grouped together and the bottles spread out.)—Are they the same? —*No, because that's bigger.*—Can you count?—*Yes.*—How many glasses are there?—*Six.*—And how many bottles?—*Six.*—So there's the same number of glasses and bottles?—*There are more where it's bigger.*'

Os (5;10) at once made the correspondence: 'Is there the same number of glasses and bottles?—*Yes, I've counted them.*—(The glasses were then grouped together.)—Is there the same number of glasses and bottles?—*No.*—Why?—*Because there are a lot here* (bottles) *and only a few there.*—(The bottles were grouped together and the glasses spread out.) Are they the same now?—*No.*—Why?—*Because here* (glasses) *it's a lot and there it's only a few.*'

Fu (5;9) poured the contents of the 6 bottles into 6 glasses and put the glasses in front of the empty bottles. 'Is there the same number of bottles and glasses?—*Yes.*—(The bottles were grouped together in front of the glasses.) Are they the same?—*No.*—Where are there more? —*There are more glasses.*—(The reverse process then took place.) And now?—*There are more bottles.*—What must we do to have the same number?—*We must spread out the glasses like this, no, we'll need some more glasses.*'

Fra (6;3). Same reaction: when the glasses were grouped together, there were more bottles, and vice versa: '*There are more because they're not spread out.*' When finally he was told: 'Make it so that they're the same', he reconstructed the one-one correspondence.

Such are the reactions of the second stage. The first point to notice is that all these children are capable of making the one-one correspondence, but that as soon as the visual correspondence is destroyed, the quantitative equivalence and even the qualitative correspondence no longer exists for the child. It is as though, for the child, quantity depended less on number (a notion which, if our hypothesis is correct, is still only verbal, although the child can count correctly) or on the one-one correspondence between the objects, than on the global appearance of the set, and in particular on the space occupied by it. Even Mül, for instance, who could count, thought that 'there are more where it's bigger', although he had counted that there were six glasses in the group and six bottles in the row.

It might be argued that the mistakes are due to lack of understanding of the words used. May it not be that the child does recognize that the number of bottles and glasses remains the same when one set is grouped together, and that when he says 'there are more' he is merely expressing the idea that the shape of the set has changed and the space it occupies is greater? It is precisely because of this possibility, and because of the difficulty of ensuring that there shall be no verbal misunderstanding that we shall give a wide variety of examples and situations in the course of these two chapters. By continuing our analysis in the light of further facts we shall be able to choose between these two interpretations.

Even at this point, however, it seems desirable to make the following observations. In the first place, while it is difficult to find terms for the expression of quantitative equivalence that can be easily understood by children of between 4 and 6, we have on the other hand no proof that a child of 5 like Mül is using the words 'six glasses' or even 'six' in general, in the same sense as we ourselves do. All that we can see is that Mül can apply the first six numerals to six objects, that is to say he can make words correspond to glasses as well as glasses to bottles. But does that prove that this verbal enumeration expresses a better quantification, from the child's point of view, than the space occupied, or that the fact of attributing numbers to objects answers the question 'how many?' in a truly numerical sense? We are obviously in no position to assert that this is so, since it is possible that at this level the correspondence between numerals and objects is still purely verbal, and that the child has not yet acquired the notions necessary for the construction of number itself, i.e. permanence and equivalence of sets irrespective of the distribution of the elements of which they are composed. The argument concerning the language used thus has another side, and all that can safely be said is that there is a discrepancy between the labelling with numbers and the visual intuition.

In the second place, when the child expresses a quantitative change, he does not always merely say 'there's more' or 'there's less', which would suggest that he was making a purely spatial evaluation without taking into account the discontinuous quantities, but frequently he is quite explicit, 'there are more glasses', or 'there are more bottles' (cf. Hoc, Mog, Gin, Du, Fu, etc.). Os says 'there are a lot here and only a few there'. Gal, who, unlike Mül, is finally convinced of the equivalence of the two sets on discovering that they contain the same number of elements, makes the position quite clear. He begins by saying 'it's bigger here', which he then translates into 'there are more glasses', and goes on to say that when the bottles are grouped together they 'are very small'. This last statement can only mean that the child had expected that the actual quantity would decrease, and on finding that the number of elements remained the same, reconciled this permanence of the number 6 with the contraction of the space occupied, by reducing the size of the elements.

In the third place—and this seems to us the decisive argument— when the correct answer is arrived at, it is clear what the child was thinking earlier. We shall see that, at the third stage, the child discovers, and states explicitly, that the fact of grouping together or spacing out the elements in no way affects their number. This achievement is characteristic of the higher level, whereas before this level is reached, spatial alterations appear to the child to affect the quantification of the element.

III. Stage III: One-one correspondence and lasting equivalence of corresponding sets

Here are two examples of correct answers, which will serve for comparison with the answers given earlier:

Pel (5;6) began by putting 5 glasses opposite 6 bottles, then added one glass: 'Are they the same?—*Yes.*—And now (grouping the glasses together)?—*Yes, it's the same number of glasses.*—Why?—*That hasn't changed anything.*—And if they're like that (grouping the bottles together and spacing out the glasses)?—*Yes, it's the same.*'

Lau (6;2) made 6 glasses correspond to 6 bottles. The glasses were then grouped together: 'Are they still the same?—*Yes, it's the same number of glasses. You've only put them close together, but it's still the same number.*—And now, are there more bottles (grouped) or more glasses (spaced out)?—*They're still the same. You've only put the bottles close together.*'

It is clear that for these children, once the sets have become equivalent through the one-one correspondence, they remain so, irrespective of the arrangement of their elements. The difference between this and the earlier stage is brought out most obviously by Lau, for whom the number of glasses remained the same because 'you've only put them close together'. These answers indicate that the quantities remain equivalent although the space occupied changes, which suggests that earlier on, the problem for the child was to know whether the number varied with the configuration. The operation of one-one correspondence is thus constituted, and triumphs over mere intuitive or optical comparison.

We can now proceed to examine the significance of the three stages we have just described, or at least to state our hypotheses, which will be tested in the experiments of the following section.

As far as the first stage is concerned, the situation is clear. The child confines himself to a kind of global comparison, without one-one correspondence, merely making a spatial evaluation (length of rows, etc.). The third stage also is perfectly clear: one-one correspondence and lasting equivalence between sets. The explanation of the second stage, therefore, seems to lie in the fact that it is the transition between the two others, and the reactions of the children at this level must be taken at their face-value, without attempting to translate their thoughts in terms of higher concepts. For them, there is quantitative equivalence between two sets when there is one-one correspondence, but this correspondence is perceptual, or intuitive, thus involving a perceived contact between the corresponding elements. In the examples we gave this perceived contact was visual, but it might equally well be auditory or tactual. Precisely because of this limitation, once the contact is no longer perceived, the correspondence ceases to exist for the child, and the only criterion for evaluation remaining to him is the global, spatial criterion of the previous stage. Mül, for instance, although he can count up to six, says 'there are more where it's bigger'.

What does the child who knows that there are six glasses and six bottles mean, then, by the expression 'there are more'? And more generally speaking, what does the child mean by expressions such as 'there are more glasses' and 'here there are a lot and there there are only a few'? It would be absurd to suggest that they imagine that the actual number of objects varies, since the basis of our whole interpretation is our belief that these children do not yet possess the notion of number. On the other hand, and for the same reason, the child cannot simply mean that the space has increased while the number remains the same. The only possible interpretation, therefore, is to assume a kind of lack of differentiation between the number and the space occupied. The child's evaluation is, as we have already said, global, and not as yet analytic, the only evaluation at his disposal being perceptual correspondence. Fu illustrates this very clearly when he says that in order to restore the correspondence between six glasses in a group and six bottles in a row, either the glasses must be spaced out, or more glasses must be added, as though the two solutions were equivalent.

We are thus confronted with two problems. The first is that of the transition from global quantification by means of perceptual relationships of length or space occupied, to intuitive one-one correspondence; the second is that of the change from this intuitive correspondence to operational correspondence with lasting equivalence. Further examples will, however, be necessary before these problems can profitably be discussed.

§2. Correspondence between flowers and vases, and between eggs and egg-cups

It seems obvious that the closer the one-one correspondence between the elements, the more lasting the equivalence of the corresponding sets will be. If therefore, a flower is put into a vase, or an egg into an egg-cup, the link between the corresponding elements will be closer for the child than when a glass is merely put opposite a bottle. He will therefore have less difficulty in understanding that the quantity of flowers or eggs remains equal to that of vases or egg-cups when the flowers or eggs have been taken out and piled together.

This is an important situation from two points of view. In the first place, it provides further evidence of the correctness of our interpretations, for if the same children answer the same questions better when the correspondence is intuitively closer, they show that it is not a matter of verbal misunderstanding, but that the quantifying value of the correspondence is greater or less according to the content of the particular problem. In the second place, the difference in the degree of ease with which the questions are answered will enable us to analyse the answers better than if there were a general lack of understanding on the part of the child.

The technique used was as follows. In the case of flowers and vases, the child's interest was first aroused by a little game: 'What shall we put into these vases?—*Some flowers*.—Then we must go and get some from the garden, one flower for each vase, as many flowers as vases.' A number of flowers were then put before the child, more than there were vases, and we observed how he made the correspondence. He either put one flower opposite each vase, or made a more or less compact row the same length as the row of vases. He was then asked to check his result by putting one flower into each vase, thus obtaining a one-one correspondence. The flowers were then taken out and bunched together (or the vases grouped) and as before the child was asked whether there was still the same number of both. In the case of eggs and egg-cups, the technique was the same, but in addition the eggs were clustered first close to the egg-cups, and then some distance away, in order to test whether optical contact does in fact affect the estimate of equivalence.

I. Stage I: Global comparison without one-one correspondence or lasting equivalence

Here we have some examples of children who merely made a row of flowers the same length as the row of vases:

Fum (4;4) began by taking the flowers one at a time, looking at each vase in turn, but he was only able to keep this up for a few units and then made a global estimate. 'Are they the same?—*Yes.*—Try them and see.—(He put the flowers into the vases and found that he was 3 short.) *I need some more flowers there* (adding them).—And now are they the same?—*Yes.*—Now we'll take the flowers out for a minute and change the water (closing up the cases and spacing out the flowers). Is there the same number of vases and flowers?—*There are more flowers.*—Try them.—(He spaced out the vases.) *No, they're the same.*—(The vases were again closed up.)—*There are more flowers.*—Why?—*Because there's a flower here* (pointing to a flower which wasn't opposite a vase).—Do you think all the flowers will go in?—*I think we'll have to take those away* (the two flowers that were beyond the end of the row of vases). *I'll put the flowers in quickly.* (He did so, and finding that he needed the two he had taken away he added them).—Now we'll change the water again, shall we? (The flowers were again taken out and bunched together.) If we put the flowers back in the vases, will there be the same number or not?—*I think they're the same. No, there are too many vases.*—Well then, you do it yourself so that they're the same.—(He closed up the vases!) Do you think that's right?—*Yes, I think that's all right.*'

Gui (4;4) put 13 flowers close together in a row opposite 10 vases rather more spaced out, although he had counted the vases from 1 to 10. Since the rows were the same length, he thought that the flowers and vases were '*the same*'. 'Then you can put the flowers into the vases?—*Yes.*' He did so, and found he had 3 flowers over. The flowers were taken out and bunched together in front of the vases. 'Is there the same number of vases and flowers?—*No.*—Where are there more?—*There are more vases.*—If we put the flowers back into the vases, will there be one flower in each vase?—*Yes.*—Why?—*Because there are enough.*—(The vases were closed up and the flowers spaced out.)—And now?—*There are more flowers.*'

Here are three examples of reactions at this stage to eggs and egg-cups, the most primitive of them showing (like Fum in the case of the flowers) that the child could not yet grasp even the idea that the original situation could be restored:

Fra (4;3): 'Take just enough eggs for the egg-cups, not more and not less, one egg for each cup.—(The child made a row the same length but containing far too many eggs.) Is there the same number of eggs and egg-cups?—*Yes.*—Well then, put the eggs in, to see whether they're right.—(He did so.)—Were they the same?—*No.*—Are they the same now?—*Yes* (removing the extra eggs).—Now we'll take all the eggs out (making them into a heap in front of the egg-cups). Are they the same now?—*No.*—Why?—*There are more egg-cups.*—Are there enough eggs for the egg-cups?—*I don't know.*—(The egg-cups were put closer together and the eggs spread out.) Look, now is there the same number of eggs and egg-cups?—*No, there are more eggs.*—Are there enough egg-cups for the eggs?—*No, I don't know.*'

Zu (4;9) also began by putting opposite the egg-cups a row of the same length but containing too many eggs. He put the eggs in and removed the extra ones. He himself then took out the eggs and made a pile of them in front of the egg-cups. 'Is there the same number of eggs and egg-cups?—*No, there are a lot of egg-cups and less eggs.*—Are there enough eggs for the egg-cups?—*No.*' All the eggs were then removed and (for 7 egg-cups) only 4 were put back, well spaced out. 'Are there enough eggs for these egg-cups?—*Yes* (the length of the rows was the same).—Put them in yourself, to see.—(He put them in and seemed very much surprised that there were not enough.)—And now, are they the same (having removed the 4 eggs and put opposite the 7 egg-cups a row of equal length, but composed of 12 eggs).—*Yes.*—Exactly?—*Yes.*—If we put them into the egg-cups, will there be any over?—*No, they'll all go in.*—Try it.—(He was again very much surprised.) *There are some left over!*' With only 3 eggs, widely spread, for 7 egg-cups, Zu replied correctly that '*There'll be some empty egg-cups,*' but with 5 eggs spaced out he again thought that they would exactly correspond!

It is clear that these children were not capable, by themselves, of making the one-one correspondence, and that they would not have discovered it if they had not been forced to do so by the relations between container and content as exemplified by vases and flowers or egg-cups and eggs. As for the equivalence of the two sets, it is obviously entirely based on a perceptual comparison of the length of the rows, and as soon as the elements in one set are put closer together or further apart than those of the other, the equivalence is no longer recognized. Thus Fum, in spite of having put one flower into each vase, thinks that the one-one correspondence breaks down when the flowers are taken out of the vases and put further apart, and he even goes so far as to remove some flowers in order to restore the correspondence! Similarly Zu's estimates are so completely dependent on the space occupied that he attempts to put first four, then twelve and then five eggs into seven egg-cups, and yet estimates that the seven eggs that he himself had put in, then taken out and placed in a more compact row, could not be made to correspond to the seven egg-cups! These amazing reactions indicate how little the child differentiates during the first stage between the discontinuous quantity and the space occupied. At this level, even when the one-one correspondence has been established through force of circumstances, the child doubts, if the perceptual aspect of one set is changed, whether a return to the original position will restore the correspondence. When, like Gui, the child thinks it will do so, the reason may well be that he merely remembers the correspondence perceived earlier, and there is no proof that in the meantime he considered the equivalence to be lasting. He says, in fact, that 'there are more flowers' when the vases are put closer together, and conversely.

II. Stage II: Intuitive one-one correspondence without lasting equivalence
Children at this stage are more advanced than those at the first stage in that they can spontaneously make the one-one correspondence, but they are as incapable as the others of deducing that the correspondence involves lasting equivalence of the sets irrespective of the arrangement of the elements. Here we have some examples:

Dal (4;6), after examining the 10 vases, took 9 flowers, thinking he had seen the exact number he needed. When he came to the seventh vase he saw that he wouldn't have enough, and took another. When all the flowers had been put into the vases, they were taken out and bunched together: 'Is there the same number of flowers and vases?— *No.*—Why?—*There are more vases.*—And now (reversing the process)?— *There are more flowers.*'
Sim (5;7) put one flower into each vase. They were taken out and bunched together: 'Is there the same number of flowers and vases?— *No.*—Why?—*There are more vases.*—Are there enough flowers for the vases?—*Yes.*—They're both the same amount then?—*No, here* (vases) *there are more, because they're spread out.*'
Sim (5;7) took six eggs to correspond to six egg-cups and put the eggs in. They were taken out and spaced further apart: 'Is there the same number of eggs and egg-cups?—*No.*—Where are there more?—*Here* (eggs).—If we wanted to put one egg back in each egg-cup would there still be the right number?—*Yes . . . I don't know.*'
Dum (5;8) also took 6 eggs to correspond to 6 egg-cups and put them in himself. When they were taken out and put in a pile in front of the egg-cups, Dum thought they weren't the same. 'Why?—*Because you did that* (making a gesture to indicate closing up).—Are there enough eggs for the egg-cups?—*No.*—(The egg-cups were put closer together and the eggs further apart.)—Are they all right now?—*No, because there are more eggs.*'

These few examples are sufficient to confirm that there is a second stage, which occurs between the stage of spontaneous non-correspondence and the stage of lasting equivalence. The child can by himself produce a one-one correspondence, but it is still intuitive, since there is no longer equivalence once the configuration of the set is changed. Moreover, although some children at this stage think that a return to the original position is possible they do not see it as necessary. Sim, for instance, who assumes it in the case of the flowers and vases, is less certain for the eggs and egg-cups. In addition to this, even when the child accepts the possibility of a return to the original position, he does not draw the conclusion that the equivalence persists during the interval. It is again Sim who says that 'there are more flowers' than vases when the vases are close together, although he thinks that one flower could be put back in each vase, and says explicitly, when asked 'Are they both the same, then?', 'No, here there are more, because they're spread out'. There could be no better indication that, for the child of this level, quantification is reducible neither to number (most of these children can count up to ten), nor to one-one correspondence, but to an intuitive correspondence depending on the perceptual configuration of the sets.

III. Stage III: Operational correspondence and lasting equivalence

The interest of these experiments lies in the fact that, being slightly simpler than those involving glasses and bottles, they provide us with examples of an intermediary nature, which facilitate the analysis of the method by which the child finds the correct solution. Here are some examples:

Du (5;8) was still at the second stage as far as the experiment with glasses and bottles was concerned. He made the correct correspondence between flowers and vases, and when the flowers were taken out and bunched together, he began by saying '*there are more vases*'. When the opposite was done, he said '*there are more flowers*'. He was then given another bunch of flowers of a different colour: 'Put one in each vase.— (When he had done so, they were taken out and bunched together in front of the vases.) And now, is there still the same number of flowers and vases?—*Yes.*—Why?—*Because we'd put them all there* (in the vases).' When, however, the vases were put closer together and the flowers spaced out some distance away, he again fell into his original mistake.

Mou (5;8) also said that there were still as many vases as flowers when the flowers were bunched together. But when the vases were together, he thought they were more numerous: '*There are more.*'

Os (5;10) was also at the second stage as far as glasses and bottles were concerned. In the case of the flowers, he wavered between the solutions of the second stage and those of the third. He began by counting 10 vases, and then 10 flowers, putting them one by one into the vases as he counted. They were then taken out and bunched together near the vases: 'Is there the same number?—*Yes, because there are ten* (vases) *and here* (flowers) *there are ten.*—(The vases were closed up and the flowers spaced out some distance away.) And now?—*No, here* (vases) *there are only a few.*—Well look, here are some pink flowers. Take the right number for the vases (which were again in a row).—(He counted quietly as he put them into the vases.)—(They were then removed and spread out on the other side of the vases, the blue flowers remaining near the child.)—Is there the same number of pink flowers and blue flowers?—*Yes, there are 10 here and 10 there.*—And is there the same number of pink flowers and vases?—*No.*'

Here are a few reactions of the same type with respect to eggs and egg-cups. (It is to be noted that the child sometimes assumes equivalence when one set is grouped in close proximity to the other, but that this assumption diminishes with distance!)

Gal (5;1), whose reactions at the second stage we have already seen in §1, at once took 7 eggs to correspond to 7 egg-cups. When the eggs were removed and grouped in front of the egg-cups, he still thought they were equivalent. 'Why do you say they're the same?—*Because.*—(The eggs were spread out some distance away.) Are they still the same?—*No.*—Why?—*Because there they're spread out and here they're close together.*—But if we put them back, would there be the same number of eggs and egg-cups?—*Yes.*'

Os (5;10) counted the same number of eggs and egg-cups. The eggs were taken out and grouped together in front of the egg-cups: 'Is there the same number?—*Yes.*—(The eggs were put some distance away.) Are they still the same?—*No.*—Where are there more?—*There are more eggs.*—Would all the eggs go into the egg-cups?—*Yes.*'

The significance of these intermediary reactions is obvious. Generally speaking, they mark the beginnings of the construction of operational correspondence as distinct from optical or intuitive correspondence. Du, for instance, after saying that the sets were not equivalent when the one-one correspondence was no longer visible, was able to grasp that the number of flowers bunched near the vases was the same as the number of vases, for the very good reason that 'we'd put them all there', i.e. that the flowers had earlier been contained in the vases. But he was not capable of applying the same reasoning when the same flowers were spaced out, and thought they were more numerous because they were further away. Mou thought that the quantity of flowers remained constant, but that there were more vases when they were grouped together, thus using the criterion of density rather than of space occupied. The reaction of Os is extraordinary, in that he assumed that there was an equal number of vases and flowers when the flowers were bunched together but not when they were spaced out, and that there was an equal number of pink and blue flowers when both were spaced out but not as many pink flowers as vases when the vases were grouped and the flowers spaced out. Obviously the explanation is that when the flowers were bunched together near the vases they reminded him that they had all been in the vases, whereas when they were spaced out, and there was no optical contact, he forgot this. This is confirmed in the experiment with eggs and egg-cups. Os thinks that they are equivalent when the eggs are clustered near the egg-cups, but not when they are some distance away, and Gal shows clearly that when he is thinking of the possibility of putting back the eggs into the egg-cups he still believes in the equivalence, but ceases to do so when the eggs are further away. In a word, the child is beginning to free himself from perception and to construct a correspondence with equivalence that is truly intellectual. When the eggs are grouped together, but remain close to the egg-cups, the child assumes equivalence because the optical contact is a sufficient reminder of the correspondence, although the configuration has been changed. But when the eggs are widely spaced, thus being some distance from the egg-cups, the equivalence is no longer recognized, because the operation of correspondence is not yet completely freed from perception.

In the case of children who definitely reached the third stage, however, the operation is no longer affected by intuition and these children therefore grasp both reversibility and equivalence.

Fet (5;5) arranged 10 flowers in a row in front of the vases and then put them in. They were taken out and bunched together: 'Is there still the same number of both?—*Yes.*—And if we put them like that (widely spaced some distance away)?—*Yes.*—Why?—*Because they were inside the vases.*'

Bet (5;8). After he had made the correspondence without counting, the flowers were bunched together some distance away from the vases. 'Is there the same number?—*Yes.*—Why?—*Because they go in* (i.e. into the vases).
And with the eggs grouped together in front of the egg-cups: 'Is there the same number?—*Yes.*—Why?—*Because they're like that* (making the gesture of grouping together).—And now (with eggs spaced out and egg-cups close together)?—*Yes.*—Why?—*If you spread the eggs out, it's the same number.*'

Pit (6;11). Same reactions. When the eggs were spread out, they were still the same '*because they all go into the egg-cups.*'

On reading these very simple answers, one wonders how it can have taken the child so long to grasp the lasting equivalence of corresponding sets. Yet the difference between these children and those quoted earlier is an essential one, indicating the triumph of the operation properly so called over perception.

Hitherto, the only quantification of which the child was capable was based on modifications of a perceptual and spatial character, and the one-one correspondence itself was not quantifying. In other words, in the first stages, the qualities perceived by the child give rise only to simple quantitative relationships (more or less 'big', 'long', 'small', 'narrow', etc.) without operations in the true sense. These qualities are, indeed, not co-ordinated or multiplied one with another: the child does not see, for instance, that if the elements of a row are spaced out the number per unit of length diminishes, and that if they are closed

E

up, this relative number increases. Thus during the first stage, the child judges the quantity only by the length of the row, without constructing even intuitive correspondences. During the second stage, the child has become capable of co-ordination of relationships, but only on the intuitive plane, i.e. he can make the correspondence when the elements of the two sets are opposite one another, but he no longer assumes equivalence when there is a change in the distribution of the elements of one set. The reason for this is that quantifying correspondence presupposes, in addition to merely perceptual correspondence, even if it is qualitatively exact, a more advanced operation, namely the equalization of differences, i.e. a co-ordination of the displacements such that they can offset one another when they become reversible. As long as the child is incapable of this multiplication, which is mathematical, and no longer merely qualitative, the correspondences he makes do not lead to lasting equivalence. That is why, even when the children who think that the bunched flowers are less numerous than the vases to which they correspond, assume that they could be put back one into each vase, it is not a case of a logically reversible operation, but only of foreseeing an empirical return to the original position. During the third stage, it is precisely this multiplication that takes place, because the child discovers that any spatial modification in the distribution of the elements can be corrected by an inverse operation. This is expressed by Fet and Bet when they give as reasons for their belief that the two sets remain the same, 'because they were inside the vases', 'because they go in', 'if you spread the eggs out, it's the same number', and 'because they all go into the egg-cups'. These reasons, which have no value for the children of the earlier stages, only become valid when reversibility is understood, and understood as a source of equivalence. It is therefore clear that the triumph of the operation over perceptual intuition is the outcome of the progressive reversibility of thought. Perception is essentially irreversible, but as it progressively resolves itself into judgements of relations, the reversible operations which result are able to dominate it, and thus to replace the intuitive correspondence by a quantifying operational correspondence which guarantees, in spite of appearances, the necessary and lasting equivalence of corresponding sets.

§3. One for one exchange of pennies and objects

In this section, we shall study the dynamic correspondence which one for one exchange provides, and we shall begin with a technique which is merely an extension of those used in the earlier

experiments. The child is told that we are going to have a shop-
ping game, and he is given some pennies to buy flowers, sweets,
etc., the price of each object being one penny. He can first be
asked to estimate how many things he will be able to buy (which
will show whether he is using global comparison, one-one correspondence, or numeration). The actual exchange then takes
place, after which we try to discover whether or not there is
equivalence, for the child, between the number of pennies and the
things he has bought. As however these methods of correspondence
are essentially the same as those we shall be examining in the next
chapter, it is more particularly the question of the equivalence of
corresponding sets with which we shall be concerned here.

I. Stage I: Global comparison and lack of equivalence
Naturally, all children at the first stage can make the correct
one for one exchange of pennies for objects. But on the one hand
they are incapable of estimating, through correspondence, how
many elements they will have to exchange, and on the other they
do not conclude that the two sets exchanged are equivalent.

Gui (4;4) put 5 flowers opposite 6 pennies, then made a one for one
exchange of 6 pennies for 6 flowers (taking the extra flower from the
reserve supply). The pennies were in a row and the flowers bunched
together: 'What have we done?—*We've exchanged them.*—Then is there
the same number of flowers and pennies?—*No.*—Are there more on one
side?—*Yes.*—Where?—*There* (pennies). (The exchange was again
made, but this time the pennies were put in a pile and the flowers in a
row.)—Is there the same number of flowers and pennies?—*No.*—
Where are there more?—*Here* (flowers).—And here (pennies)?—
Less.'
Mic (4;4) was also unable to make a correct estimate of the number
of flowers required for the pennies.—A one for one exchange of 6
flowers for 6 pennies was made, the flowers being put in a row and the
pennies close together: 'Is there the same number of both?—*No, there
are more flowers.*—Why?—*Because the flowers are more spread out.*'
Duc (4;6) also succeeded only in making a global estimate of the
number of flowers required. Then 6 flowers were exchanged for 6
pennies, the pennies being spread out: 'Have we got the same number
of flowers and pennies?—*No, there are more pennies.*—(The money was
returned and the exchange again made, the pennies being put in a
pile.) And now?—*No, there are more flowers.*'

It is unnecessary to comment on these examples before examining those of the second stage.

II. Stage II: Correct correspondence but not lasting equivalence
The only progress shown at this stage is that the child is capable
of making a correct estimate, through visual correspondence, of

the number of elements to be exchanged. In spite of this, and of the fact that the estimate is empirically confirmed by the exchange, he still does not believe that the two sets are equivalent:

Nic (4;1) counted 10 flowers and 10 pennies, but did not total them into a single cardinal number: 'How many pennies are there, then?—*One, two, three, four . . . ten* (counting from memory).—Well then, buy.— (He gave one penny for each flower, up to 10, but the pennies were put in a row while he kept the flowers in his hand.)—Is there the same number of flowers and pennies?—*There are more pennies* (but he then spontaneously made the correspondence by putting one flower opposite each penny). *Oh, yes! They're the same.*—(The flowers were then bunched together.) And now?—*There are more pennies.*—(The pennies were put in a pile and the flowers in a row.) And now?—*No, because there are a lot of flowers.*'

Lid (4;5) put 4 pennies opposite 4 flowers: 'Is there the same number of pennies and flowers?—*Yes, they're the same.*—All right, now you're going to buy some flowers. Here are your pennies (six).—You must give one penny for each flower.—(We exchanged 6 flowers for 6 pennies the pennies being arranged in a row while the flowers were in his hand.) Is there the same number of flowers and pennies?—*Yes, they're the same . . . No, they're not. Here there are more* (pointing to the flowers).—Could we put one flower opposite each penny?—*No, there are too many flowers* (he tried it and found that they corresponded exactly.) *Yes, they're the same.*—Let's begin again, shall we? (The exchange was again made, with the pennies spaced out and the flowers bunched together.)—Will that be all right?—*There'll be too many flowers. You'll see.* (He made the correspondence and was very much surprised at the result!).'

Par (5;2): 'You must pay a penny for each flower. How many flowers can you buy with that (1)?—*One.*—And with those (3)?—*Three flowers for three, because there are three pennies.*—All right, now you're going to buy all those (he exchanged 6 pennies for 6 flowers, and the flowers were put in a row and the pennies in a pile). Is there the same number of both?—*No.*—Why?—*Because there are more flowers.*—If I wanted to buy those flowers with these pennies (i.e. the 6 pennies that the child himself had paid out one by one), could I do it?—*No, yes.*— They're the same then?—*No, there are more flowers.*—And if I put a penny opposite each flower (doing so opposite the first two flowers to make sure he understood)?—*No, there'll be some flowers left over.*'

Fur (5;9) exchanged 7 pennies for 7 flowers after correctly making the correspondence 5 to 5. The flowers were still in his hand and the pennies were in a row: 'Is there the same number of both?—*No, there are a lot of pennies and not many flowers.*—(The flowers were then arranged in a row but rather closer together than the pennies.) Is there the same number?—*No, there are more pennies. There's one past the end.*—Count the flowers.—*Seven.*—And count the pennies.—*One . . . seven.*—So they're the same?—*No, there are some past the end.*—Let's see (the one for one exchange was again made.)—So there's the same number?—(He remained silent, and was obviously shaken.)—If we counted the

pennies and the flowers (the latter were now further apart) would we
have to count longer, or would it be the same?—*We'd have to count
longer for the flowers.*'
Aud (6;7): 'We're going to play at selling flowers. Here are your
pennies.—(He counted them correctly.) *Eight pennies.*—Each flower
costs a penny. How many will you be able to buy?—*Eight.*—(The one
for one exchange was made, and the pennies were put in a row while
the child kept the flowers in his hand.) Is there the same number of
flowers and pennies?—*No. There* (pennies) *there are more.*—Why?—
They're spread out.—Could we put one flower on each penny?—*Yes.*—
Then is there the same number of both?—*No. There are more there*
(pennies), *because they're spread out.*'

These reactions show quite clearly that one for one exchange is
no guarantee that the child sees two equivalent sets as being
bound by the same cardinal number.

Children of the second stage do not differ from those of the
first stage as far as equivalence is concerned.

It is in no way surprising that Gui, Mic and Duc (stage I), who,
before the exchange takes place, cannot make the correspondence
between two sets of objects, and estimate quantities by the space
they occupy, are also unable to see after the exchange that the sets
are necessarily equivalent. What is extraordinary, however, is that
Nic, who makes the correspondence spontaneously in order to see
if the two sets are equivalent, Lid, who before the exchange makes
the correct correspondence between four pennies and four sweets,
and Par, who uses numbers in estimating that he will get three
flowers for three pennies, are incapable of assuming the equivalence of the sets they themselves have exchanged.

The most curious cases are those of Par, Fur and Aud, who use
numeration. Par states, before he makes the experiment, that he
can buy three flowers with three pennies, but as soon as the
flowers are spread out, he no longer sees the equivalence. Fur,
when the seven pennies are piled together and the seven flowers
spread out, counts both sets, discovers that they have the same
cardinal number, but refuses to accept that they are equivalent:
'No, there are more pennies. There's one past the end.' Similarly
Aud counts eight pennies, says that he will be able to buy eight
flowers, makes the exchange, and then cannot see that the sets are
equivalent: 'There are more, because they're spread out.' These
cases clearly show that perception of spatial properties carries
more weight than even verbal numeration.

As to the question of the possibility of restoring the original
situation, the children were asked, when they thought that the
flowers and pennies exchanged were not equivalent, whether one
flower could be put on each penny. Most children at this stage

think that this could not be done. Lid says, 'There'll be too many flowers, you'll see', and Par, 'No, there'll be some flowers left over'. Only Aud thinks it could be done, but does not deduce from this fact that there is equivalence, although he is very near it.

III. Stage III: Lasting equivalence

To begin with, we have here two reactions that are intermediary between stages II and III:

Pit (6;11). Ten flowers were exchanged for 10 pennies. Pit kept the flowers in his hand and the pennies were put in a row: 'Is there the same number of flowers and pennies?—(He made the flowers into a row, putting one opposite each penny, in order to check the number, and then said): *Yes, there are as many flowers as pennies.*—(The pennies were spaced out and the flowers bunched together.) Is there the same number of both?—*No, there are more here* (pennies).—And now (flowers spaced out, pennies in a pile)?—*They're not the same. There are more flowers* (he re-made the correspondence of his own accord). *Oh yes! They're the same.*—But before, you said there were more flowers, didn't you?—*Yes, but they were like that* (with a gesture to indicate that the pennies were close together).'

Fran; (6 3) at once counted the 10 pennies he was given. 'How many flowers can you buy if each one costs a penny?—*Ten* (the exchange was made, the flowers remaining in his hand and the pennies spaced out on the table.)—Is there the same number of flowers and pennies?—*Yes.*—Why?—*Because they're the same.*—(The exchange was again made, and the pennies were spread out.) Are they the same?—*Yes.*—(The pennies were put together and the flowers spaced out.) And now?—*No.*—Why? *There are more there* (pointing to the pennies).—Could we cover each penny with a flower?—*Yes.*—Well then?—*They're the same.*'

These two cases, in which the correct answer is arrived at, are extremely interesting, particularly the spontaneous verification of Pit, who was obviously using abstract operations that were as yet barely mastered, in order to combat perceptual appearances. Fran finally succeeded in arriving at this abstraction, i.e. at the operation proper.

Here, finally, are some examples of correct reactions:

Gin (4;11) counted his 10 pennies and estimated that he would have 10 flowers. After the exchange, he said '*they're the same*' whatever the configuration, but without giving any reasons.

Du (5;8) exchanged 10 for 10, the flowers remaining in his hand and the pennies spread out on the table. 'Is there the same number of pennies and flowers?—*Yes.*—Why?—*Because we've used them all.*—(The flowers were spaced out and the pennies put together.) Are they the same now?—*Yes.*—Why?—*Because we've used them all.*'

Ler (5;8) kept the flowers in his hand after the exchange: 'Is there the same number of both?—*Yes.*—Why?—*Because they go like that* (spontaneously putting one flower opposite each penny).'

Clav (5;8). Same situation: 'Are they the same?—*Yes.*—Exactly?—*Yes.*—Why?—*Because I gave you my pennies.*'

For these children, it is clear that the equivalence has become obvious and logically necessary. The reasons they give to justify their assumption are interesting because of their operational character. For Ler, it is the fact that there is one-one correspondence, and hence the possibility of returning to the visible correspondence after the exchange; for Du and Clav, it is the exchange itself, because by it, the two sets were exhausted simultaneously: 'I gave you my pennies' and 'we've used them all'.

In conclusion, the results of the test using one for one exchange are exactly the same as those found in the case of static, visible correspondence between objects. This constitutes a valuable aid to the understanding of the notion of correspondence. It indicates that the importance given to the procedure of one for one exchange, in which so many authors have attempted to see the beginnings of cardination, is unjustified, since this procedure does not in itself result in the notion of necessary equivalence of exchanged sets. Before this result can be achieved, one for one exchange, like intuitive correspondence, must become operational, i.e. it must be grasped as a reversible system of displacements and relations.

§4. One for one exchange in conjunction with counting aloud

We have just seen, from the reactions of Par, Fur and Aud, that counting aloud appears to have little influence on the belief in the equivalence of two sets as a result of one-one correspondence. We have already frequently had occasion, in earlier sections, to point out that there is no connection between the acquired ability to count and the actual operations of which the child is capable.

We have now reached the point at which this needs to be examined systematically. We first of all find out how far the child can count without difficulty. We then repeat the above experiment with one for one exchange, choosing a number of pairs of objects smaller than the highest number to which the child can count. We then ask him to count the objects he has been given, and we cover with our hand the pennies he has given us in exchange (so that he cannot count them). We then ask him merely to guess how many pennies are hidden.

The results show that counting aloud makes no difference, and we find the same stages as those we found with the earlier techniques.

I. Stage I: Global comparison and lack of equivalence

Ras (3;6) could only count up to 4 or 5. He was given 2 pennies and asked to give in exchange 'the same number of sweets'. He gave 5 and then 2. For 3 pennies, he gave 4 sweets, etc. I then exchanged 4 pennies for 4 sweets, one at a time. When I hid the sweets with my hand, he thought that there were none left when 3 had been taken out, and then thought that there was still one left after I had taken out the fourth.

Ber (3;11) could count correctly up to 5, but had difficulty in making the correspondence between two sets containing more than 2 or 3 elements. I made the one for one exchange of 3 sweets for 3 pennies and covered up the 3 pennies. I then brought one out and said: 'Are there any left?—*Yes.*—How many?— . . . —And now (there was 1 left)?—*No.*—And now (when the last had been brought out)?—*Yes.*—How many?—*There's one penny left.*' When 2 pennies were exchanged for 2 sweets, Ber answered correctly, but as soon as there were 3 or 4 his answers were again given quite at random. Finally I made a one for one exchange of 4 pennies for 4 sweets and asked: 'How many sweets have I given you?—*One, two, three, four.*—And how many pennies have I in my hand?— . . . —How many do you think?—*I don't know.*'

II. Stage II: Correct correspondence, without lasting equivalence

The only difference between this and the preceding stage is that the child can make the correspondence before the actual exchange is made.

Mard (5;6): 'Look, I'm going to buy some sweets from you. Here are my pennies (7, in a row). Give me as many sweets as there are pennies.—(He counted) *1, 2, 3 . . . 7.*—And how many pennies?—*1, 2, 3 . . . 7.*—Good. And how many sweets have you given me (having covered them with my hand)?— . . . —How many did you give me for one penny?—*One.*—Yes. And for two pennies?—*Two.*—That's right. And for three pennies?—*Three.*—That's right. And how many pennies have you there?—*1, 2, 3 . . . 7.*—Good. And how many sweets did you give me? How many sweets are there here (uncovering them for a moment and then hiding them again with my hand)?—*1, 2, 3, 4, 5.*' I tried it again: 'Look. Here are some pennies (5, in a row). How many are there?—*1, 2, 3, 4, 5.*—That's right. (I picked them up.) Now, when I give you a penny, you'll give me a sweet (we made a one for one exchange up to 3). How many pennies have you?—*1, 2, 3.*—(Two more were exchanged.) And now how many pennies have you?—*1 . . . 5.*—Good. And how many sweets have I got (covering them)?— . . . —*9.*'

Cauch (5;6) was also able to make the one-one correspondence between sweets and pennies, when the pennies were in a row, even up to 15 or 17. He could count the pennies he was given up to and beyond 10. But after a one for one exchange of 8 pennies for 8 sweets he did not conclude that there was necessary equivalence: 'How many sweets have I given you?—(He counted.) *8.*—That's right. How many pennies have you given me (they were hidden under my hand)?—*10.*'

Per (6;0) made 7 sweets correspond to 7 pennies, and then made the exchange: 'How many pennies have you?—(Counting) 7.—And how many sweets have you given me (hidden under my hand)?— . . .' I began again with 5: 'How many pennies have you?—5.—And how many sweets have you given me?— . . . 7.' At a third attempt, he counted 10 pennies and thought he had had 9 sweets; etc.

It is not difficult to interpret these facts. When the child makes the one for one exchange, he knows very well that there is equivalence. Mard, for instance, knows that he has to give one sweet for one penny, two for two pennies, three for three, and so on. But once the exchange has been made, and one of the sets is no longer visible, the child no longer considers it to be equivalent to the one he can see. These reactions, therefore, are exactly the same as those of the corresponding stages studied earlier. If the child has not yet reached a certain level of understanding which characterizes the beginning of the third stage, counting aloud has no effect on the mechanism of numerical thought.

III. Stage III: Lasting equivalence

When, as here, one for one exchange is accompanied by counting aloud, interesting cases sometimes occur in which the child who has reached the stage of being able to give the correct answer, checks the equivalence by counting the number of exchanges, but does not as a result assign a definite number to the equivalent sets.

Mad (5;6) made a one for one exchange of 7 pennies for 7 sweets, counting them as he did so: 'How many sweets have you?—1, 2 . . . 7.— And how many pennies have you given me?—1, 2 . . . 7.' When, however, she did not count the elements as they were being exchanged, she showed that she was still at the earlier level. When 5 sweets were exchanged for 5 pennies, she said: ' There are 5 sweets.—And how many pennies under my hand?—4,' Etc.

Ferd (6;0) also exchanged 5 sweets for 5 pennies and evaluated the two sets correctly by repeating the series of numbers: '1 . . . 5.' But afterwards, when he was asked how many pennies were hidden, it did not occur to him to count the 5 sweets in a row in front of him.

Such reactions clearly indicate progress over the earlier stages in the direction of the construction of true equivalence between the sets in question. But the equivalence recognized by Mad and Ferd is in reality only the equivalence of the operations they have just performed, i.e. the action of moving a sweet and the action of moving a penny. As long as the child confines himself to the enumeration of these exchanges, he can accept the notion that the correspondence is lasting, but when he tries to abstract the cardinal number from the operations by means of which he arrived at it, he does not yet see that there is necessary equivalence.[1]

Finally, we have two examples of genuine cases of stage III, children for whom the one for one exchange involves the notion of lasting equivalence:

Sim (6;6). We made a one for one exchange of 6 pennies for 6 sweets. 'How many pennies have you?—*6.*—And how many sweets have I?—*6.*—Are you sure?—*Quite sure.*—Why?—...'

Far (6;6) exchanged 8 pennies for 8 sweets: 'How many sweets are there?—*8.*—And how many pennies here (raising my hand and showing the pile of pennies)?—*8.*—Are you sure?—*Yes.*' Same result with 11, etc.

This, then, is the evolution of estimates of equivalence.

It is in this way, then, that the child's capacity to estimate equivalence develops in cases where he makes use of numeration. It is therefore no exaggeration to say that the verbal factor plays little part in the development of correspondence and equivalence. We find here the same stages, corresponding to approximately the same ages, as we found in the experiments of §§1–3. At the point at which correspondence becomes quantifying, thereby giving rise to the beginnings of equivalence, counting aloud may, no doubt, hasten the process of evolution. Our only contention is that the process is not begun by numerals as such.

It remains to explain the relationship between correspondence and equivalence. Before we can do so, we must first examine the evolution of correspondence itself, i.e., of its mechanism in its spontaneous form, not when it is provoked. We shall attempt to do this in the following chapter, in which we shall investigate how the child estimates quantities, how he thereby discovers one-one correspondence, and how he makes use of it in the case of correspondence between similar objects that are not qualitatively complementary.

[1] A. Rey also observed children who counted the actions they were doing, and found that they did not all, as a result, acquire the notion of equivalence. (*L'Educateur*, May 1931, p. 151.)

CHAPTER IV

SPONTANEOUS CORRESPONDENCE
CARDINAL VALUE OF SETS[1]

IN the previous chapter, we tried to show that there are various types of correspondence, which can be distinguished by their relationship to the idea of equivalence they entail. While the highest level can be termed 'quantifying correspondence' because it results in the notion of necessary, lasting equivalence, the lower levels are intuitive, because the equivalence of the sets is recognized only when the correspondence is actually perceived, and ceases to exist when it is no longer in the field of perception.

Before going any further, we must now analyse the mechanism of correspondence, no longer considering its results, but examining its spontaneous development, i.e. in situations in which the child is compelled to find the correspondence of his own accord and to make what use of it he can. The type of situation required, therefore, is one in which the child spontaneously attempts to estimate the cardinal value of a set in such a way that we can discover what types of correspondence he uses, and what methods he adopts before, and immediately after, one-one correspondence.

For this purpose, what is most suitable is correspondence between like objects, the child being required to find a quantity equal to that contained in a given model. A problem of this kind is, of course, similar to those we examined in the previous chapter, when the child was told, before being asked about the equivalence, to pick out the required number of corresponding elements. But in the first place, here our material will not be of such a kind that the correspondence is suggested by the fact that the objects are qualitatively complementary; the objects will be similar, and this may make some difference. In the second place, and more important, the child will not be told to 'put one A opposite (or into) each B,' or to 'exchange one A for each B'. We shall say to him: 'There is a number of objects: pick out the same number', without suggesting any method. In other words, whereas the earlier problems imposed the correspondence so that we could examine its results, the problem to be studied here is merely one of evalu-

[1]With the collaboration of Mlle. Zoé Trampidis and Mme. Rafia Mehmed-şemin.

65

ation, requiring no suggestion of the method to be used, but enabling us to see what the child's procedure actually is.

These were the techniques used. In the first place, we presented the child with a succession of figures made with counters, and asked him to take the same number of counters as each figure contained. If, as we were led to suspect in the previous chapter, correspondence is based on qualitative comparison, our first task must be to analyse how the child compares quantitatively two sets with different configurations. There were five types of figures: I, 'badly-structured' figures, e.g., a collection of counters distributed at random, but neither touching nor overlapping; II, open series, e.g., two parallel rows of counters; III, closed figures, the shape of which did not depend on the number of elements used, e.g. a circle, a house, a right angle; IV, closed figures of which the shape depended on the number of counters, e.g. a square, a cross, etc. V, more complex closed figures, less familiar to the child, e.g. a rhombus, etc.[1]

With one of these figures in front of him, the child was told to look at it, and to pick out of a box the same number of counters.

In the second place, the child was shown a row of six beans, representing sweets or pennies, one to two centimetres apart, and he was asked to pick out the same number. Obviously this second technique, which is similar to those of the previous chapter, is only a special case of the first.

The results obtained with these two kinds of test can be classified into three types, corresponding to the three stages found in the earlier chapters. During the first stage, the child uses only global comparison, imitating the configuration of the model without attempting exact quantification. When he is dealing with rows, he makes a row of the same length as the model, but of different density. During the second stage, there is one-one correspondence, but it ceases to exist when the figure is distorted. Finally, in the third stage, there is exact correspondence and lasting equivalence.

§1. Reproduction of figures

W. A. Lay[2] made a detailed study of the way in which various figures made with three, four, five, etc., objects arranged as triangles, squares, etc., are distinguished by the child, from the point of view of perception of number. The number four, for

---

[1] When the counters are presented to the child in this way, care must be taken to avoid stressing the figure. Otherwise the test would become the reproduction of the figure rather than the estimate of the number of elements.

[2] *Führer durch Rechnen Unterricht gegründet auf didaktische Experimente.* Leipzig (Nemnich), 1907 (2nd edition.)

instance, is more easily recognized when the objects are placed at the four corners of a square than when they are placed at random. A. Descœudres[1] and O. Decroly[2] made use of these investigations in their interesting research into the development of number. Our point of view here will be different, for while these authors examined what has come to be called perception of number, i.e. the application of already existing numerical schemata to discrete objects perceived in the same field, we shall examine what might be called quantifying operations, i.e. the elementary operations of correspondence, equating, etc. which constitute the logic of number. In a word, we shall ignore the problems of perception and shall concentrate on the problem of the genesis of operations as such. This being so, our analysis of the reproduction of figures will serve merely as an introduction to the study of the mechanism of correspondence. We shall therefore not consider each of the figures separately, but shall describe simultaneously the whole set of reactions obtained by the first technique.

Stage I: Global comparison

The characteristic feature of children at the first stage is that they do not as yet feel the need for a quantitative evaluation, since they have no precise notions of the cardinal number. They therefore confine themselves, in evaluating the given sets, to global qualitative comparisons, without co-ordination of the qualities that are compared. Our first examples are cases of non-structured figures:

Pa (4;6). To find the required number of counters to correspond to a collection of 15 elements, he took small handfuls of them and tried to arrange them so that they looked the same: 'Are they the same?—*No.* —Why?—*There are more here* (the collection he had just made did in fact contain 2 extra elements).—Well then?—(He did not remove any of the counters, but moved the ones that were too close together, so as to produce a configuration more like that of the model.)—Is there the same number of counters?—*No, yes, I've put the same amount.'*

Hug (5;0), for a collection of 15 counters, said: '*I don't know how many there are. I don't know how to do it* (to find the same number).—Try.— (He collected a few counters and then spaced them out so that they resembled the model.)—Are they the same?—*Yes.*—How many are there there (model)?—*I don't know.*—Then how do you know they're the same?—*I looked twice* (model and copy). *It's right.'*

In the case of the series, children at this stage attempt to reproduce both the configuration and the dimensions of the model, but are not concerned with details:

[1] *Le Développement de l'Enfant de 2 à 7 ans* (Delachaux & Niestlé, S.A., 1920.)
[2] *Etudes de Psychogenèse* (Lamertin, 1932).

Mül (4;1) reproduced the model by a series of the same shape and approximately the same length, but with the elements closer together and thought '*there's the same number of counters.*'

Li (4;9), in order to reproduce the model first put 5 counters in a row, then made 4 of them into pairs by adding 4 more: 'Are they the same?—*Yes.*—Why?—(She made a movement of the hand to indicate the direction of the row.)—Are there as many?—*Yes.* (She looked at the model and saw that her copy was a little shorter. She added 2 counters: her series was then composed of 11 counters instead of 8 as in the model, but it was the same length.)—Where are there more?—*There* (pointing to her copy).—I want them to be the same.—(She removed the 2 counters, leaving 9 as against 8, but the model series was longer, so she spaced out her counters to make hers longer.)—Is there the same number?—*Yes.*'

In the case of closed figures, children at this stage can reproduce correctly those which require a definite number of elements, provided that the form is familiar (category IV), but if the shape is unfamiliar (V), or does not involve a definite number of elements (III), the copy is no longer numerically correct:

Mül (4;1), in attempting to find the same number of elements as there were in a circle of 10 counters, made a circle of 14. Similarly, for a circle made by 6 matches arranged as radii, he made one with 12 matches: 'Is there exactly the same number of match-sticks?—*Yes.*— Where are those (indicating on the copy some that were particularly close together)?—*There* (pointing at random to those of the model).'

For a right angle with 6 counters (sides of 4 and 3 elements), Mül made, three times in succession, angles with 4 counters (sides of 3 and 2): 'Is there the same number of counters?—*No. I don't know.*—Try again.—(He then made an angle with 8 counters.)—Is there exactly the same number?—*Yes.*—Who has more?—*Me.*—Well then, take away the extra ones.—(He removed two and altered the spacing of the counters to make them like the model.—Are they the same?—*Yes.*— Who has more?—*Me* (which was incorrect since there were 6 in both. He then put back the 2 he had removed.)' Similarly, for a house of 6 counters, Mül made one of 13, then removed 1 'so that it should be just right', etc.

In the case of figures whose shape depended on the number of elements, Mül successfully reproduced a square of 4 counters and a triangle of 6, but made a cross with 6 instead of 5. He also failed with a square of 9 counters, being careful to make the elements at the 4 corners correspond, but putting 1 counter too many in between. The rhombus of 13 counters was copied as a vague quadrilateral containing 15 elements.

Mar (4;6), in the case of figures whose shape depended on the number of elements, successfully copied a cross of 5 counters, a square of 4 and even a triangle of 6, but failed with a square of 9, his square containing 15 elements. The figures in category III, circle, right angle, etc., were copied, but with more elements.

The reactions of this first stage are of great importance to the psychology of number. It might at first seem that these children feel no need for a quantitative evaluation, and that they merely make a more or less correct copy of the model. Such an assumption would be too sweeping. Even if the child sometimes forgets, in making his copy, that he was told to 'put the same number of counters', he shows by his answers to the questions put to him that he understood perfectly what he had to do. Par, for instance, says 'there are more here', and Li recognizes the differences and attempts to correct them. But the expressions 'more counters' and 'less counters' have a quite different meaning for the child of this stage than for us, and do not as yet represent a cardinal evaluation.

For the adult, cardinal evaluation always presupposes that units have been added or merged in order to form the whole obtained by correspondence with the set to be evaluated. For the child of this stage, on the contrary, the evaluation is based merely on the global qualities of the sets in question, these qualities being quantified by comparison as 'more' or 'less', without co-ordination of the comparisons. In other words, this experiment, like those in Chapters I and II, shows that the only quantification of which the child at this stage is capable takes place through the relationships 'more' and 'less'. The child does not, however, co-ordinate the global qualities he perceives, but focuses on one at a time in comparing his copy with the model. Thus Mül thinks that his series of pairs is equal to the model because it is the same length, and he disregards the distribution of the elements, while Par thinks there are more counters in his copy because they are closer together, and merely puts them further apart instead of removing some. In the case of the figure with matches, Mül thinks that a circle of twelve has the same number as one of six, because the diameter is the same.

This experiment, unlike the earlier ones, provides us with evidence that this failure to co-ordinate the quantitative relationships only makes its appearance when there are explicit judgements of comparison. The child's initial procedure is to co-ordinate the perceived qualities, but this co-ordination has not yet become operational or logical. It is still purely intuitive, and consists only in the attempt to produce a general resemblance between the model and the copy. This is why, when the child tries to find the same number of counters as he has been shown, he contents himself with a rough reproduction of the configuration of the model. The copy is only approximate precisely because the child cannot analyse the figure, i.e. he cannot find the relationships which, when logically composed, constitute its qualities. In a word, it is the general shape, i.e. the total surface covered, accompanied by a vaguely similar structure, that the child of this level takes as the criterion for cardinal evaluation. When this general shape involves number, and is fairly familiar to the child, there is in addition one-one correspondence, but as a result of the qualitative similarity, not as its cause. When the general shape does not depend on number (types I–III) or is unfamiliar (type V), the child fails to make the correspondence.

To sum up, the most general characteristic of this stage is the irreversibility of the reactions. The evaluations of children at this level are purely perceptual, with the result that qualities that are not comparable are related and the synthesis can only be global. This means, in other words, that the child's intuitive judgement is not yet combined with operations through which the elements isolated by his analysis can be put together again. It is precisely because the judgements of the child at this stage lack mobility, that his thought is essentially irreversible.

Stage II: Intuitive correspondence

We shall apply the term *qualitative* to correspondence that is based only on the qualities of the corresponding elements, as for example, when the child puts angles in his copy when there are angles in the model, irrespective of whether he knows how many there are, or whether there is the same number as in the model. *Numerical* correspondence, on the other hand, will be that in which each element is considered as a unit, irrespective of the qualities, e.g. *n* blue counters corresponding to *n* red counters, whatever their distribution. We shall call *intuitive* any correspondence that is entirely based on perception (or possibly on representative images) and is consequently not preserved outside the actual field of perception (or of clear recollection). We shall say, on the other hand, that correspondence is *operational* when it is based on relationships of an intellectual nature, its distinctive characteristics therefore being the fact that it is preserved independently of actual perception, and its 'reversibility'. Qualitative correspondence may therefore be either intuitive or operational, whereas numerical correspondence is essentially operational (except perhaps in the case of the first three or four numbers).

Having clearly defined our terms, we shall find that the second stage, that of intuitive qualitative correspondence, is merely a continuation of the first. As the copying of the models becomes more exact, it leads to one-one correspondence susceptible of greater precision. But by the very fact that this correspondence is based on perceptual comparison, it is not numerical from the start, in spite of appearances, but remains qualitative and intuitive. This can easily be proved by altering the configuration of the corresponding sets. As soon as this is done, the child no longer accepts the equivalence. This intuitive correspondence without lasting equivalence justifies our assertion that there is a second stage, which differs from the first in that there is systematic use of correspondence, and from the third in that the correspondence does not yet involve necessary equivalence. We must point out also that, while children at the first stage usually begin by putting a pile of counters on the table and then arrange them to imitate the model (adding or removing elements where they think necessary), children at the second stage usually begin by making the correspondence, taking the counters one by one to reproduce the various parts of the model.

First we have some examples related to category I:

Ha (4;5) first looked carefully at the pile of 15 counters, then put down 16 elements one at a time, copying the configuration of the model bit by bit, looking to see that he was making the correspondence (his one error being due to the fact that he counted one element twice): 'Are they the same?—*That one* (copy) *is bigger. I'll take some away* (removing the extra counter).—Are they the same?—*Yes.*—Are you sure?—(The elements of the model were then spaced rather further apart.) Is there the same number of counters?—*Yes . . . no* (he added some counters to the model in order to imitate the new configuration of the copy).'

We then distributed 13 counters in front of Ha, some in groups of 3 or 2, but making the configuration a recognizable whole. He was then asked to find as many matches as there were counters. He arranged 11 matches in groups of 3 and 2 so as to reproduce certain details of the model.—'Are there as many?—*There* (counters), *there aren't many, here* (matches), *there are a lot.*—Make it so that there's the same number in both. (Ha then spaced out the counters.)'

Finally, 8 matches were distributed in front of him: 'Find the same number of counters.—*I don't know how to make the pattern.*—Never mind, try.' He spaced out the matches a little, then took 14 counters one by one and tried to reproduce the pattern of the model. The correspondence thus broke down when the difference in shape of the objects prevented an exact copy of the model, whereas the copy was an exact reproduction of the model when counters only were used.

Ba (4;9) put down his counters one by one, looking at each of the 15 in the model in turn: 'Are they the same?—*Yes.*—Are you sure?—*Yes.*—Show me how you know.—*This one and that one*, etc. (pointing to the corresponding elements). He also succeeded in making the correspondence between counters and matches, by imitating the configuration. But when the configuration was changed, he was no longer certain of the equivalence, even without the matches.

The next examples are of category II:

Min (5;0) succeeded at once in reproducing series of four or more

F

pairs, but ceased to assume the equivalence when the counters were spaced out. When he had to make the correspondence between matches and counters, he could only make an approximation, e.g. 10 matches for 8 counters: 'Are they the same?—*Yes.*—Count them.—(He counted correctly 8 and 10.)—Are they the same then?—*Yes.*' There was thus no precise relationship between his counting and the quantitative evaluation. (When the terms to be compared are qualitatively equivalent, the evaluation is made by correspondence; when they are different, e.g. counters and matches, it is made by a combination of correspondence and the global relationships of the space occupied.)

Gis (5;5) provides another example of the distinction between verbal numeration and actual operations. She counted correctly up to 27, pointing to each counter in the row in turn. After 27, there ceased to be any co-ordination between the counters to which she pointed and the number she said, but she continued from memory up to 54. This verbal enumeration did not however correspond to any systematic colligation except in the case of the first few numbers, because although she said that $12>8$ and $10>7$, she also said that $9>13$ and $19>21$: 'Where are there more (with the counters she had just counted in front of her)?—*19.*—Why?—*Because there are a lot.*—And there?—*21.*—Well then?—*That's less because there aren't many.*'

It is interesting to note that, on the plane of actual operations Gis was at the second stage: correct correspondence, but without lasting equivalence. For example, she made the correspondence between four or more pairs correctly, but no longer thought they were equivalent when one set was spaced out.

We find the same reactions for categories III–V:

Nil (5;0) began by putting 2 extra elements in copying a cross of 9 counters, but corrected himself by pointing to the corresponding terms. He at once correctly reproduced the square of 9 counters, a house of 11 and a circle of 10. In copying the circle, he kept the same diameter. When he was asked if it was exactly the same, he pointed with his finger to the one-one correspondence. One counter was then put opposite each element of the model so that the one-one correspondence would produce a concentric circle larger in diameter: 'Will there be enough counters to put opposite each one?—*Yes.*—Why?—*They're the same.*' But once the bigger circle was completed, he no longer thought they were equivalent: 'Is there the same number of counters?—*No.*—Why?—*Because it's bigger.*'

Ba (4;9) succeeded in reproducing, after one or two slight temporary errors, figures such as the circle of 9 counters, a right angle of 11, the square of 9, etc., and was also able to make the correspondence between matches and counters, in various combinations, by always copying the perceived figure. For the rhombus of 13 counters, he pu in the centre a row of 5 (correct) and below a triangle of 4 (correct). But above, he put only 2 elements instead of 4: 'Are there as many?—*Yes.*—How do you know?—(He pointed to each element in the model and each corresponding counter in the copy, and when he got to the top exclaimed): *I made a mistake, I did it wrong.*(He at once corrected himself.)'

In spite of this, however, Ba did not assume necessary equivalence when the distribution of one of the sets was changed, although he himself had just made the correspondence. For example, when a rectangle of twelve counters was turned so that the long side became the base, he no longer thought it was equivalent to the model.

These then are the reactions of the second stage. There is one-one correspondence, but it is always based on the particular properties of the figure, for without the figure, the child no longer thinks the two sets are equivalent.

Stage III: Operational correspondence

During the third stage, the correspondence no longer depends on the intuitive figure, and the child begins to use spontaneous operations as a check, breaking up the figures himself and arranging them in series. The correspondence thus becomes either qualitatively or numerically operational. Here we have some examples of categories I and II:

Hen (5;0) was shown a collection of 11 counters: 'Take the same number.—(He took 14, one at a time or in twos.) Are they the same?—(He made the correspondence in order to find out.) *No.* (He removed 3.)—And now (his 11 counters were distributed at random, and bore no resemblance to the model)?—*Yes.*—(The elements of the model were then spread out.) And now?—*Still the same.*'

Cha (6;0), when he was shown a collection of 12 counters, took 11, one at a time, without making them into a figure, looking at the corresponding elements in the model, then of his own accord added one more. When the elements of the model were spread out, he continued to recognize the equivalence. Same reaction in the case of the series of 4 pairs: he at once took 8 counters and merely made the rows without copying the figure.

And now some examples of categories III–V:

Fav (5;6) had no difficulty in reproducing the figures in categories III and IV. He copied the figure, and also assumed the equivalence of the sets when the configuration was changed. For a figure of type V, he began by copying the model, and then counted aloud: '*I must put 3 more*', etc., then, getting confused, he stopped both copying the figure and counting, and adopted a procedure very typical of this stage, i.e. he made an 'arbitrary' correspondence. He separated the elements of the model, arranged them 2 by 2 in two vertical rows, then did the same with the counters of his own set, but placed these horizontally. He then saw at once that there was one missing and added it.

Maw (6;o) also correctly reproduced complex figures like those of type V, but in order to check them, relied only on the correspondence: 'Are they the same?—(He counted 12 and 13.) *There's one too many* (removing 1, which was wrong as he had merely made a mistake in counting).—Then why is there an empty space here?' He then behaved in the same way as Fav. He destroyed his own figure and put the counters in a row, then, with his finger made the correspondence with the counters in the model, which had remained in position. He then saw that there was one counter missing and added it.

Similarly, when he took 22 matches to correspond to 22 counters arranged in a complex figure, he counted to himself as he did so. 'Are there as many?—*Yes.*—How many?—*I don't know* (having forgotten the last cardinal number).—Then how do you know they're the same?—*Every time I put a match, I pointed to a counter.*—And how do you know you didn't make a mistake?—(He then arranged the counters in a row and put a match opposite each one.)'

It is obvious that Fav and Maw believed in the equivalence of corresponding sets, since they themselves destroyed the figures in order to check their numerical equality.

No examples could indicate more clearly that it is only when the correspondence becomes operational that the child feels certain of his counting. We can therefore distinguish a stage characterized by operational correspondence, with recognition of the equivalence of corresponding sets, and conservation of quantities. This stage is intermediary between mere intuitive correspondence and correspondence between the objects and the numerals used to count them. This last type of correspondence, which is characteristic of a fourth stage, in which practical correspondence is replaced by the ability to use numeration correctly, dose not concern us here, since the object of this volume is the study of the genesis of number, and it is only when operations are logically established on the practical plane that counting becomes truly numerical.

§2. *Single rows*

Before proceeding to discuss the reactions given above, it will be useful to analyse correspondence between single rows. This study will not be a repetition of that in Chapter III, since then we were concerned only with investigating why one-one correspondence, even between objects that are qualitatively complementary, does not entail the notion of necessary and lasting equivalence of corresponding sets. Here, on the contrary, our object will be to place correspondence among the various processes of cardinal evaluation, i.e. to study, making use of like objects, how the child makes two sets of equal value. Moreover, although in the preceding sections we have already seen these processes at work, we feel that it is desirable to simplify the problem, in order to discover whether the same results are achieved when single rows are used instead of complex figures.

Stage I: Global comparison

In the case of single rows, the reactions are very similar to those observed earlier. Instead of making the one-one correspondence, the child bases his evaluations on only one or other of the two global qualities of the row, its length or the density of the elements, without co-ordinating them. Here we have some examples:

Don (4;1) had a sister, Myriam: 'Mummy is giving Myriam all those pennies to go to the fair. Now you take the same number of pennies as Myriam.—(He took a handful at random (5), but arranged them so that his row was longer than the model.) *It's bigger, it's not right!*—Why? Is one of you richer, or have you both got the same?—*Yes, I'm richer.*—Well then, make it so that it's right.—(He put them all back into the box, then took out 4 which he put close together, then 1 more which he put close to the others.) *But this will be smaller* (his row). *I'll have to put some more.* (He added 1 at each end, thus obtaining a row of 7, the same length as the model).—Are they the same like that, or will one of you be richer?—*They're exactly the same.*'

Char (4;4) also began by making a compact row of 11 buttons to equal the 6 spaced out buttons of the model, then, as his row was longer than the other, he removed 3 from the end, thus obtaining the same length: 'Are they the same?—*Yes.*—Exactly?—*Yes.*—(The 6 elements of the model were then put further apart, and the 8 in his copy were put closer together.) And now?—*There are more there* (the 6).'

Boq (4;7): 'Put as many sweets here as there are there. Those (6) are for Roger. You are to take as many as he has.—(He made a compact row of about ten, which was shorter than the model.)—Are they the same?—*Not yet* (adding some).—And now?—*Yes.*—Why?—*Because they're like that* (indicating the length).—(The 6 in the model were then spread out.) Who has more?—*Roger.*—Why?—*Because they go right up to there.*—What can we do to make them the same?—*Put some more* (adding 1).—(The 6 were then closed up and his were spread out.)—*Now I've got more.*'

Finally Boq was shown two rows of sweets, one containing 3 that were spaced out, and the other 4 that were close together, the first row thus being longer: 'Where are there more?—*There* (the 3).—Why?—*It's a bigger line.*'

Arc (4;9): 'Mummy is giving these sweets (8) to Luc. You're going to have some too, exactly the same number.—(He put 13 in a compact row, taking great care to make the row the same length as the model.)—Have you got the same number?—*Yes.*—And now (spacing Luc's 8 rather further apart)?—*No, Luc will have more.*'

Ril (5;2) put 9 pennies to equal a row of 6: 'There.—Are you as rich as Daniel, or have you got more?—*We've both got the same.*—(His 9 were then put closer together and Daniel's 6 were put further apart.) Who will be able to buy more?—*Daniel*.'

Ler (5;3) put 8 pennies close together opposite a row of 6, and then, when the 6 were spread further apart, he thought they were more than the 8 '*because it's bigger here*.'

More rarely, the evaluation is based on the density of the elements, as in the following examples:

Don (4;1), just after the experiment quoted above, put 7 red counters close together under 6 blue ones: 'Are they the same?—*Yes*.— (The model row was then closed up and his copy spaced further apart.) —And now?—*I've got more* (7 red ones) *because it's bigger. No, Myriam's got more* (6 blue ones).—Why?—*Because they're close together; there are a lot*.'

Lin (5;3) also, although most of his estimates were based on the length of the row, said more than once that 6 elements close together were more than *n* elements spread out '*because it's bigger*.'

Although the result of these estimates based on density is the converse of those based on the length of the row, the principle is obviously the same: the criterion of the evaluation is not the number of elements or the one-one correspondence, but perception of a global quality.

This brings us back to the questions raised in §1. What is the nature of this quantification prior to one-one correspondence, and why is one-one correspondence impossible at the level of the first stage?

With regard to the first of these, our conclusions are the same as before: elementary or 'gross' quantities are nothing else than the relationships expressing 'more', 'equal to' or 'less' immediately perceived in the given qualities, but not yet co-ordinated. The two qualities inherent in any row of objects, irrespective of the nature of the objects, are the total length and the density of the elements. Now it is impossible to compare any two rows without relating the qualities of one to those of the other, i.e. without one of the rows being seen as longer, shorter or the same length as the other, or as more compact, less compact or of the same density. It is therefore these relationships, which are as elementary as the qualities themselves, that are used by children at this level in their pre-cardinal evaluations. When Don, for instance, says 'I've got more because it's bigger', and Ler thinks that six pennies spread out are more than eight close together 'because it's bigger', they are directly expressing the length of the rows in terms of quantity. If it were a question of comparing a larger number of rows, or of adding the relationships abstractly, new difficulties would doubtless appear sooner or later (cf. Chapters V and VI), but as long as it is only a matter of immediately perceptible relationships, these two criteria suffice for an elementary evaluation. It is clear that the child is also capable of comparing two rows from the point of view of the intervals separating the elements. He recognizes that in one row the elements are more (or less) compact than in the other, and he can translate this perception into elementary quantitative relationships. For Don, for instance, 'because they're close together, there are a lot', and for Lin, there are more when 'it's bigger' (cf. Chapter III, in which Mou, Lid and Fran used density as the criterion for estimating the larger quantity). Each of these two relationships of total length and density thus constitutes a beginning of what will later be cardinal evaluation, both of them being, from the start, inseparable from the quantity.

For the adult, a row of n spaced-out elements keeps its cardinal value n if its length is diminished by closing up the elements. It is therefore the relation between the length of the row and the intervals between the elements which determines the conservation of the whole, whereas the relationships of length and density are variable. It is precisely this co-ordination, or logical composition of the two relationships in question, that the child of this level cannot make, and that is why the notion of conservation of the sets and even of one-one correspondence is still impossible. The elementary quantitative relationships are merely practical schemata which are still pre-logical because there is not as yet any operation properly so called.

Now why is it that one-one correspondence is not possible during the first stage? We must, of course, distinguish between intuitive and operational correspondence. Operational correspondence presupposes the intervention of special operations which we shall discuss later, but intuitive correspondence, when it is qualitatively correct, is the result of elementary multiplication of the relations, and we have seen that the relationships of total length and density are not susceptible of composition at this first level. It is obvious, for instance, that when Boq prefers three spaced-out sweets to four close together because 'it's a bigger line', he is disregarding both the elements as such and the intervals between them, and that when Don, reasoning in a similar way, uses the other criterion and says 'because they're close together there are a lot', he is disregarding the length of the rows and is therefore incapable of comparing the elements as such. It is only when two rows are of equal length and density that their equivalence implies their correspondence and goes beyond global evaluation. It can be seen, therefore, that correspondence is the expression of a construction in the true sense, even at the level of intuitive qualitative correspondence (i.e. before there is any question of numerical correspondence), the operation then being partially replaced by perception of the figures.

This construction can be analysed as follows. First, there must be a decomposition, so that composition may become possible. If the global relationships of length and density of a row are to be merged in a single whole, it must first be understood that the total length is formed by the sum of the intervals separating the elements, and that consequently, in a compact row the intervals will be shorter and more numerous, while in a scattered row of the same length the intervals will be longer and less numerous. Secondly, when the two rows are compared, the construction on which the correspondence rests will presuppose a multiplicative composition of relationships: the two rows will correspond to one another spatially if they are at the same time equal in length and density, i.e. if each element of the one can be placed opposite an element of the other.

In this connection, the hesitations of the most advanced children of this stage, and the means they finally use to discover the correspondence, are most revealing. Having made their evaluation, like the other children, from the point of view of the length only, they begin to notice the density, hesitate for a moment between the two possible points of view, then, disconcerted by the contradictions involved, attempt to take account of both at once. They are thus led to make a spatial correspondence between both the elements and the intervals in the two sets. Here is an example:

Stu (5;11) was trying to make a row equal to one containing 6 sweets. She took 8, one at a time, and put them in a row: ' *That's more.* —How can you tell?—*You can see by the line.*—(The 8 were then closed up and the 6 spaced out.)—*No, there are more there* (6).—Why?—*There* (the 8) *it's smaller. They're close together.*—But are there less?—*Yes.*— (She was then shown two rows, one of 6 sweets close together and the other of 4 spread out.) Where are there more?—*There* (6).—Why?— *Because there's more* (=close together).—(She was then shown two rows of 6, one compact, the other spread out.) And there?—*There* (spaced out), *because it's longer, there are more sweets.*—(She was again shown two rows of which the shorter contained more elements.) And now?— *There* (the shorter one), *because there are a lot.*—(The original 6 were then put down again.) Put down the same number.—(Stu then made the correct correspondence and thus passed beyond the first stage.)

Thus for Stu, it was the discovery that a compact row of six elements may contain more than a longer row of four elements, that made her try to combine the relationships of length and density, and consequently to decompose the sets, thereby discovering the one-one correspondence.

Stage II: Intuitive correspondence, without lasting equivalence

When children at the second stage are asked to pick out a number of elements equal to those in a model row of six, they react immediately (or almost immediately) by making an optical spatial correspondence with the model, but they no longer accept the equivalence of the two rows when the correspondence cannot actually be perceived:

Jon (4;5): 'Take the same number as there are there (6 counters).—(He put 7 counters close together, and then made the correct correspondence.)—Are they the same?—*Yes*.—(His row was then spread out.)—Are they the same?—*No*.—Has one of us got more?—*Me*.—Make it so that you have the same number as I have.—(He closed his up.)—Are they the same?—*Yes*.—Why?—*Because I pushed mine together*.'

Pret (4;11) succeeded in making the correct correspondence after first putting one too many, but when the elements in the model were closed up, he said: ' *There are more there, because there's a bigger line. It has to be the same line, then they're the same*.—What must we do then?—(He rearranged them so that the rows were the same length.' (Same reactions in the case of the reverse operation.

Hab (5;3) began by putting 9 sweets opposite the 6 of the model, but made the row the same length. ' *That's it*.—Are they the same?—*I'm not sure*.—Where are there more?—*There* (row of 9, close together).—What must we do then?—(She put 6 opposite 6 of the model and removed the rest.)—(The 6 of the model were then closed up.) Are they the same?—*No*.—Are there as many here (model) as there?—*No, there* (copy) *there are more*.—Is there more to eat on one side than on the other, or are they both the same?—*I shall have more to eat*.—Make them both the same, then.—(She removed 2, then made the one-one correspondence, and finally put the 2 back when she found they were missing!)'

Per (5;7) had no difficulty in making a row of 6 sweets corresponding to the model. The model was then closed up: '*I've got more*.—Why?—*Because it's a longer line*.—(The process was reversed.)—*Now there are more there, because it's a big line*.' But a moment later, Per said the opposite: 'Are there more here (spaced out)?—*No*.—Why not?—*Because it's long*.—And there (closed up)?—*There are more there, because there's a little bundle* (=close together).—Then are there more in a little bundle than in a big line?—*Yes*.' After this Per went back to using length as the criterion, made the two rows the same length again, and said: '*Now they're both the same*.'

Plus (5;7) also used correspondence in order to find a set equal to the model, but chose 3 spaced out sweets in preference to 4 close together, because 'there are more'. In order to make 6 closed up elements again equal to 6 that were spaced out, he merely spread out the first set.

These examples clearly confirm our hypothesis as to the origin of qualitative correspondence. Elementary though this form of correspondence is on the purely intuitive plane, it nevertheless constitutes a complex relation involving a system of comparisons, i.e. of logical multiplications or divisions. If, for instance, the child is to compare the sides or angles of two rhombuses, he must decompose the figures in order to abstract the similarities in the position of the sides alone and the angles alone. Such relationships obviously belong to a more advanced level than the undifferentiated, globally perceived relationships of the previous stage. In the case of our two rows, it is the co-ordination of the relationships of length and density of the rows that leads to correspondence. As long as the child judges the quantity by length or density alone, there is no possibility of correspondence. The children quoted above are now able to make a copy of the same length and density as the model, the twofold equality being ensured by the fact that each element of the copy is placed opposite an element of the model. Thus Hub (like Jon, Pret, etc.), who begins, like the children of the first stage, by putting too many sweets under the model, says that she is 'not sure' of the equivalence, and then discovers the correspondence by spacing out her own sweets and thus co-ordinating the relationship of density with that of length. Moreover, when one of the rows is closed up or spaced out, and the child is asked to restore the equivalence in which he no longer believes, the reaction at this stage is different. Children at the first stage usually merely add or remove elements in order to have the same length or density again, whereas Jon, for instance, closes up the elements and gives as his reason for thinking the sets are equivalent: 'because I pushed mine together'. Pret, Per, Plus and Hub also restore the equivalence by remaking the optical correspondence, i.e. by co-ordinating the density and length of the rows.

And yet, although the child begins to make the one-one correspondence as soon as he can think simultaneously of the length and density of the rows, this correspondence does not at once lead to the notion of lasting equivalence of corresponding sets, nor to that of their quantitative constancy. The question then arises: how is it that the equivalence lasts only as long as the correspondence is perceived and ceases to exist when it is no longer perceived? Why is it that the co-ordination of the two relationships does not lead to necessary lasting equivalence? In order to find the answer, we must distinguish two aspects of the matter: that of the general co-ordination, and that of the nature of the operations involved.

As regards the first, it is clear that, while there is here a continuous process of co-ordination, its stages indicate the existence of successive planes of structuration. First there are the elementary, global, perceptual relationships that are inherent in perception of the length and density of the rows. Then, when these perceptual relationships begin to be co-ordinated by means of seriations and logical multiplications, the co-ordination takes place first of all on an intuitive and still perceptual plane, and is only semi-operational. This is precisely what happens during the present stage. The child certainly considers the relationships of length and density simultaneously, since he can produce a copy equal in length and density to the model, but the co-ordination does not go beyond the plane of perception, i.e. as soon as the perceived figure, which made the correspondence possible, is altered, not only does the correspondence vanish, but also the co-ordination between length and density.[1]

Indeed, when one of the rows is contracted or expanded, the child does not say: 'it's shorter, but closer together, so we can't tell', but chooses one of the two criteria at random, and judges the total quantity by it alone. Per provides an excellent illustration. Although this child could make a one-one correspondence between the model and his copy, he was at a loss as soon as the distribution of the elements in one row was changed. He then hesitated again between the two relationships, saying first that the spaced-out elements were more numerous 'because it's a longer line' and then the opposite, because there was a 'bundle'. This clearly proves that although Per could co-ordinate the relationships on the perceptual plane, and thus make a one-one correspondence between the rows when the elements were visually in contact, he was not capable of linking them sufficiently closely for the co-ordination to go beyond the intuitive level and to constitute a system of true operations.

Even at this second level, however, there are signs of a beginning of operational co-ordination. For if, as it is the purpose of this book to prove, an operation is indeed a reversible action, it is clear that the reactions of Jon, Pret, Per, etc., who space out or close up the elements in order to restore the equivalences, are forerunners of the construction of true operations.

Coming now to the second aspect, we find that the global relations 'more or less long', 'more or less close together', which characterize the rows themselves and not the detail of the relationships between the elements, correspond to the first level, that of unco-ordinated perceptual relationships. The co-ordination between these two kinds of relationships, which takes place during the second stage on the intuitive plane only, is both additive (seriation) and multiplicative (correspondence), and thus corres-

[1] We shall see later that the conservation of correspondence presupposes numerical, and not merely qualitative, operations.

ponds exactly to the beginnings of operations which we described in Chapters I and II in connection with the second stage of conservation of quantities. Indeed, on the one hand, the density of a row is nothing more than the succession (perceived or grasped) of the intervals separating the elements, and the sum of these lengths is identical with the total length of the row. Hence, to co-ordinate total length and density is merely to decompose the former into segments which define the latter, and this constitutes an additive seriation. On the other hand, to make the one-one correspondence between two rows is to construct two series whose elements are exactly opposite one another, i.e. to multiply the relations 'situated at a certain distance along' by the relations 'situated above'. What the child discovers in making the perceptual one-one correspondence is the beginning of seriation and of multiplication of the qualitative relations of position, but nothing more. When the density or total length of one of the rows is altered, he ceases to believe in the correspondence, because he cannot understand that the displacements compensate one another and that the differences can be equated, an understanding which requires a higher level than that of mere qualitative grouping. All that the child can do is to restore the equality of the two rows, but he does not as yet deduce from this empirical return to the initial position that operational reversibility is always possible.

Stage III: Operational correspondence and lasting equivalence

At the third stage, on the contrary, we find correspondence freed from perceptual or spatial limitations, and persisting in spite of any displacement of the elements. One-one correspondence thus becomes really quantifying, and from now on, expresses numerical equality and not merely qualitative equivalence. Here are some examples:

Fet (5;5): 'Take the same number of pennies as there are there (6).' He made a row of 6 under the model, but put his much closer together so that there was no spatial correspondence between the rows. Both ends of the model extended beyond those of the copy. 'Have you got the same number?—*Yes.*—Are you and that boy just as rich as one another?—*Yes.*—(The pennies of the model were then closed up and his were spaced out.)—And now?—*The same.*—Exactly?—*Yes.*—Why are they the same?—*Because you've put them closer together.*'

Cran (5;8) was shown 6 beans spaced out, and began by putting one opposite each one of the model. His copy was then closed up: 'Are they the same?—*Yes.*—The same amount to eat?—*Yes.*—How do you know? —*I can see.*' Yet when he was asked to evaluate quantities numerically, he was never sure of his answers above 6.

Lan (6;2), to reproduce a row of 6 matches, picked up 4, without counting, but looking at the corresponding elements. Having reached this point, he put his finger on the fourth match of the model, took 2 more, then put his 6 matches in front of the model row, but in a heap, so that there was no spatial contact. We then spread out his matches in a row and made the others into a bundle: 'Are they the same?—*Of course.*—Why?—*Because before, those* (his own) *were in a bundle, and now you've put them like that* (spread out), *and these* (the model) *were spread out before, and now you've made them into a bundle.*'

The contrast between these children and those of the preceding stage is obvious. In the first place, they do not rely on the perceptual contact between the elements, even when they make the one-one correspondence. Fet, for instance, at once made a series that was more compact than the model, and Lan put his six matches in a heap opposite the model row. What is more important, however, is that these children can relate the successive configurations of the corresponding sets by correctly co-ordinating their relationships. For example, in order to prove that the pennies in the model are still equivalent to those in his copy, Fet uses the same argument that the younger children used to prove the contrary: 'because you've put them closer together'. This justification can have one meaning only: when the pennies are put closer together, if none are added or removed the total length decreases but the density increases. The child is therefore now capable of considering simultaneously the relationships of length and density, not only when the series to be compared are similar, but also (and this is the progress over the second stage) when they differ in both length and density. In other words, if we consider the total length and density of the rows as two distinct relationships, as the child does before he co-ordinates them, or when he determines the density by the length of the intervals between the elements, we can say that the third stage indicates the completion of the multiplication of these two relationships. Even at the second stage, there is already a beginning of this multiplication, but at that level the child either compares two corresponding rows correctly because they are equal in length and density respectively, or, when one of these qualities is the same in both, concludes correctly as to the other. When the two qualities vary together, at the second stage the child's estimate is wrong, while at the third stage, by multiplication of the two relationships, he grasps for the first time that a row which is both shorter and more compact than another can be equal to it.

It is by the inclusion of each perceptual situation in the system of all the possible perceptual situations that from now on multiplication of the relationships is independent of actual perception of the rows. There is therefore, in reality, a freeing from perception in general, since each perception of the configuration takes its place in a coherent system of transformations governed by the logic of relationships, each composition corresponding to a possible perception of the sets.

It is this freeing from perception that marks the beginning of operations properly so called, which are thus seen to be the result of the progressive reversibility of thought. The terms used by Lan to explain the relationships between the two corresponding sets might be translated as follows: heap becomes row = row becomes heap. In other words, the two sets are still equivalent because their transformations are only reversible changes of position, i.e. they are the result of operations that can be reversed.

We must, however, point out that logical multiplication of qualitative relations is not in itself sufficient to account for numerical correspondence, with lasting equivalence, just as it was not sufficient to lead the child to the notion of conservation of continuous and discontinuous quantities (Chapters I and II). In the case of correspondence, as in that of the relationships inherent in conservation of quantities, the transition from the qualitative to the arithmetical operation is explained by the equating of the differences, i.e. by the implicit or explicit introduction of the notion of the unit.

The assumption that a short, compact row corresponds term for term with a longer and less compact row, involves the understanding of two facts essential to the construction of number. Hitherto, the elements of the corresponding rows have been considered by the child as being determined by their intuitive spatial qualities: the first counter on the left in the upper row, the counter next to it on the right, and so on. But once the correspondence is accepted as lasting irrespective of these positions, the elements merely become units, each equivalent to the others, and the correspondence then rests only on the notion of equal units, differing one from the other only by their relative order of enumeration. In other words, the correspondence is now the application of the same order of enumeration to two sets of equal units. From the point of view of the intervals between the units, we find the same mechanism. Up to the third stage, the child accepted the one-one correspondence between two rows of elements only if the total lengths and also the density, i.e. the intervals between the elements, were both equal. From the third stage onwards, however, he recognizes that the correspondence persists when one of the rows is more compact, the difference in length being compensated by the difference in the intervals. The discovery of truly arithmetical correspondence thus always presupposes a new operation as compared with mere qualitative logic, this operation being the equating of the differences, or to put it more concretely, the seriation of units seen as equal in all respects except the temporary relative position of each one in the series.

§3. Conclusions

The facts contained in this chapter are remarkably in agreement one with another and with those of the previous chapter. They provide us with the general picture of the stages through which correspondence passes, and thereby enable us to attempt a general explanation of the successive methods of quantification.

We have seen, in the course of our analysis, that the problem has gradually become more and more precise. In Chapters I and II we saw that the child does not at first assume conservation of either continuous or discontinuous quantities when the perceptual configuration is changed. We then examined the question of whether one-one correspondence, in its more familiar forms (correspondence between container and content, and one for one exchange) was sufficient to ensure conservation, i.e. necessary lasting equivalence, of corresponding sets. Chapter III led us to give a negative answer to this question. There is a level of perceptual correspondence which is characterized by the disappearance of the equivalence as soon as the corresponding elements are no longer in contact. Reactions of this kind are a relic of a first stage during which the one-one correspondence is not grasped even when it is imposed by the external situation, the equivalence resulting from a global estimate of the space occupied. We found it necessary, therefore, to study the spontaneous processes of quantification used by the child in order to determine the cardinal value of sets, and we therefore devoted Chapter IV to the question of spontaneous correspondence.

The tests used in Chapter IV involved the children in an activity which was a direct continuation of their everyday experience, and this activity yielded a rich crop of spontaneous procedures following a regular order: global evaluation, correspondence without lasting equivalence, and numerical correspondence with lasting equivalence. Three questions then arose. Why does the child not feel the need, from the beginning, to decompose the global totalities that he thinks he can evaluate? How does the first form of decomposition or intuitive qualitative correspondence make its appearance? In what conditions does operational qualitative correspondence become numerical correspondence?

In §2, we outlined the answer to these problems in the case of rows, but we must now generalize it. In so doing, we shall distinguish between (I) psychological analysis, which is causal and genetic, and (II) analysis of the logical construction of operations, though, as will eventually appear, the two kinds of interpretation are parallel.

I. All the preceding experiments have shown that at a first level (usually at about the age of $4\frac{1}{2}$–5), the child evaluates discontinuous quantities as if they were continuous, i.e. extended, quantities. His quantitative judgements are thus based only on the general shape of the set and on global relationships such as 'more or less long', 'more or less wide', etc.

There are two possible explanations of this initial reaction. Either the child does not feel the need to decompose the wholes he can perceive and is trying to evaluate, or he is incapable of such decomposition. Psychologically, the need and the capacity are of course closely linked, but for the moment we shall assume that they are distinct. That the child should begin by considering non-analysed wholes, without feeling the need to decompose them as long as experience does not compel him to do so, is perfectly consistent with what we know of the psychology of thought at this level.[1]

Hence the child who is asked to pick out 'as many' counters as there are in a given set is in no way equipped by his intellectual structure to consider the set as being a union of units, i.e. $1 + 1 + 1$ . . . etc., which would imply that he already possessed the notion of whole number. For the child, therefore, 'as many' merely means a set similar to the model with respect to its overall qualities. But if he does not feel the need for decomposition, does this mean that he is incapable of it? To our mind, the preceding reactions have given a decisive answer to this question.

The only principle of synthesis at the disposal of the child at the first level is the intuitive global preception of the general configuration itself, in the absence of 'operations' which would enable him to put together again the various parts of the perceptual intuition if it were broken up. That is why, as soon as there is an alteration in the data, children of the first stage apparently base their evaluations on one criterion only: length of the rows, width of the figures, density, etc.

But might it not be said that in the very action of copying there is co-ordination of the global qualities, and therefore at least a suggestion of decomposition, since the model is roughly reproduced? There precisely is the point: the copy is only roughly

---

[1] In *The Language and Thought of the Child* we have already shown that what Decroly calls the 'global', and Claparède the 'syncretic', character of children's perceptions, is a general attribute of the whole of the young child's thought.

correct. Closed figures depending on a given number of elements are well reproduced, because they involve a 'good' configuration, but collections, rows, open figures, and even closed figures with an arbitrary number of elements, are not correctly copied. Linear series, in particular, are evaluated by their total length only, irrespective of their density.

Although the method of global comparison allows of a rough comparison between two sets of the same form, covering the same area, and having approximately the same density, it becomes inadequate as soon as these properties differ substantially. Two sets which the child has stated to be identical by global comparison, are no longer considered equivalent when the elements of one set are spaced out. He cannot understand that when there is a change in the shape, and therefore in the distribution of the parts, something remains invariant, namely, the number of elements. The reason is that he has not yet acquired the notion of number, but only of perceptual wholes. Hence, in our view, the notion of conservation of the set is lacking because the elementary relationships inherent in the global perceptions are merely juxtaposed instead of being co-ordinated.

The method of global comparison is therefore not only vague, but lacking in mobility, since there is no operational mechanism by which the various successive states can be linked into a dynamic whole or system of relationships. Hence the characteristic feature of this first stage is the almost complete irreversibility of thought. It is true that each of the global qualitative relationships established by the child, e.g., 'longer', etc., is capable of giving rise to an inverse relationship, 'less long', etc., but as these relationships are not decomposable into units and are not co-ordinated one with the other, but merely put together in a non-structured whole, they cannot yet form a reversible system, and perceptual intuition therefore holds sway, operations being as yet impossible.

The second method, which is characteristic of the second stage, and which consists in comparison of figures by intuitive qualitative correspondence, indicates some progress, but this is less than might at first appear. The progress lies in the precision brought to the analysis of shapes and qualities, which results in a deeper understanding of the intuitive data. At the previous level, the only details noticed are those necessary for the construction of the overall shapes: angles, ends of rows, etc., but from now on there are no privileged details. Each part of the whole is perceived and taken into account, and the child begins to co-ordinate the various criteria. It is because he is puzzled at finding that he arrives at different evaluations according as he stresses one or other of the criteria, that he eventually comes to co-ordinate them.

G

The child's success in thus reproducing the various geometrical configurations of the sets is achieved through a new semi-operational method, or rather through the development of a schema which already existed within the global comparison, but which comes to the fore at this level, i.e. intuitive qualitative correspondence. Psychologically, to make a correspondence is merely to systematize judgements of resemblance and difference. In fact, the child perceives the details of one figure only through their resemblance to, or difference from, those of the other to which he is comparing it. He therefore works out the correspondence between all the analogous parts, and no longer concentrates only on certain outstanding details and the general configuration. This qualitative correspondence, or 'comparison of the parts' is the tool used by the child for the reproduction of all the figures whose shape depends on the number of elements, and although it is not always successful in other cases, it constitutes a new and much more efficient method of reproducing the sets.

Yet this second method, although more precise than the first, is not much more mobile. It enables the child to compare only certain privileged static states of the sets in question, i.e. those which give the figures their particular shape. Ba, for instance, was doubtful as to the equivalence of two sets of twelve counters arranged as similar rectangles, because in one, the longer side was horizontal, and in the other, vertical. Similarly, Nil was not prepared to accept the equivalence of the counters in two concentric circles in spite of the fact that each element in the outer one was opposite an element in the inner one. While it is true that precise comparison of figures has more possibilities than global comparison, since there is an infinite variety of figures, from the point of view of co-ordination of relationships and conservation of quantity, there is only a slight progress, since displacement of the elements, resulting in a change in the figure, is sufficient to make the child think that the total number of elements has changed.

There is, indeed, a beginning of co-ordination of the relationships of length, width, density, etc., but it takes place only on the purely practical or intuitive plane. The tool used for the co-ordination of these relationships is not yet the operation as such, but the configuration itself. In order to make his own figure correspond to the model, the child must of course take into account simultaneously dimensions, density, shape, etc. As compared with the first stage, the progress lies in the fact that in the actual construction of the figure these relationships are co-ordinated, but as soon as the figure is changed, the child is incapable of abstract operational co-ordination of the relationships involved, and has recourse to the only available principle of unification: the figure he perceives. This explains why the child at this stage ceases to believe in the constancy or correspondence of the sets when the configuration of one is changed, and why he then again bases his evaluation on one criterion only, forgetting the others.

To sum up, the second method is merely a continuation of the first. It is more precise, slightly more mobile, but still restricted to sensory intuition, and not yet capable of truly logical and operational dissociations and compositions. It can be described as semi-operational, since on the practical plane it allows of qualitative correspondence, which implies intuitive co-ordination of relationships. With this semi-operational character goes progress in reversibility of thought, reversibility being the psychological expression of the operation. This can be seen from the fact that although children at this level think that the number of elements changes with a change in the configuration, they nevertheless assume that a return to the original figure is possible. Thus in order to restore the equality between two rows, they merely space out or close up the elements of one of them, and do not add or remove any elements. But obviously this reversibility is incomplete and the relationships still do not constitute a reversible system. In other words, they are not yet independent of perception.

The third method, on the other hand, represents a definite progress: correspondence leads to necessary and lasting equivalence. The sets are now assumed to be equivalent, whatever the configuration or the distribution of the elements. The progress takes place gradually as a continuous process, the correspondence depending less and less on the figure itself, i.e. on perceptual intuition. As soon as qualitative correspondence is to any extent independent of the precise form of the respective parts of the two figures, the elements become interchangeable units, and the correspondence thus acquires a numerical character. But this freedom presupposes lasting co-ordination between the relationships, without recourse to the figure, i.e. correlation of successive perceptions hitherto assumed to be irreducible.

The fundamental factor of this development is, in our view, the complete reversibility of the action involved in the child's procedure. The operation he performs is no longer immediately absorbed in the intuitive result obtained. It frees itself, as it were, and becomes capable of moving in reverse. Each transformation can be compensated by its inverse, so that any arrangement may give rise to any other, and conversely. Thus instead of relying on an all-important figure, the child proceeds exclusively by reference to the one-one correspondence, and thereby succeeds for the first time in decomposing the wholes and co-ordinating the relationships. From now on, therefore, his actions constitute a reversible system involving constancy of the set. This system serves as the principle for generalization of qualitative correspondences or logical co-ordinations of relationships into numerical correspondence, in which each element, irrespective of its qualities, is considered as a unit equal to the others and differing from them only by its temporary position in the series.

II. We shall now consider, in its broad lines, the logical structuration of the child's judgements, as it develops, by a series of transformations, from the elementary, unanalysed relationship to general one-one correspondence.

The logical construction of correspondence which takes place during the three stages analysed in Chapters III and IV finds a natural place within the framework of quantification which we described in relation to conservation of continuous and discontinuous quantities. Global evaluation corresponds to 'gross quantity', qualitative correspondence to 'intensive quantity', and numerical correspondence to 'extensive quantity', it being understood that the logical multiplications which give rise to qualitative correspondence merely begin at the second stage and only on the intuitive plane, and that they are generalized during the third stage when they combine with those that give rise to numerical correspondence.

At the level of global quantification, the child is incapable of multiplying the relationships logically. He is also incapable of decomposing and re-combining them. Since therefore, they can neither be added nor multiplied logically, they are not as yet relations. They merely express qualities perceived in the comparisons made, as 'more', 'less', or 'equal', and are therefore what we called in our analysis in Chapters I and II 'gross quantities' or relationships between 'gross qualities'.

The transformation of these global relationships into relations proper, and the construction of qualitative correspondence, are characterized by the following operations (semi-operational or intuitive at the second stage, and abstract at the third): additive seriation, and multiplication of additive series, this multiplication constituting the correspondence.

In the present case, this additive seriation and multiplication of relationships are the complementary operations of decomposition into parts and reproductive composition, as we showed in §2 in the case of linear series. Additive seriation of relationships here consists in establishing that the total length of a row is formed by the sum of the intervals separating one element from the next, while multiplication of relationships, which makes qualitative correspondence possible, consists in the construction of a new row having exactly the same length and the same intervals as the first.

In terms of classes rather than relationships, the correspondence of two sets will consist in the distribution of the second set in such a way that the elements of the two sets are similarly placed, and that they can also be paired to form similar sub-sets which are also similarly placed.

When two rows of elements are in qualitative correspondence, the second series has the same total length and the same intervals as the first. From logical multiplication of the relationships it follows that in the case of

(1) equal length and equal density, the sets are the same;
(2) greater length and greater density, or smaller length and smaller density, one set has more, or less, elements than the other;
(3) equal length and greater density, or equal length and smaller density, one row contains more, or less, elements than the other;
(4) inverse lengths and densities in (3), the conclusion is the same as in (3);
(5) greater length and smaller density, or greater density and smaller length, the number of elements in one series is larger and smaller than in the other, and therefore equal.

The child at the second stage has no difficulty in grasping intuitively the first four of these compositions. The first merely expresses qualitative correspondence; the second states that if a row is both longer and denser than another it contains more elements; the third states that equal length and greater density implies more elements; the fourth states that equal density and greater length also implies more elements. None of these multiplications requires an abstract operation, since perception is sufficient. The child at the second stage is incapable, however, of grasping the fifth composition, although it is implied by the earlier ones: if a row is both shorter and denser than another, it may contain more, less, or as many elements. It might be suggested that it is the uncertainty which is the obstacle to understanding, but the relation (5) could be expressed as follows, in which case there is no longer uncertainty:

(6a) equal number multiplied by greater length implies smaller density, and equal number multiplied by smaller length implies greater density, or
(6b) equal number multiplied by greater density implies smaller length, and equal number multiplied by smaller density implies greater length.

How is it then, that the child at the second stage who has just established the equivalence by one-one correspondence, and who understands the compositions (1) to (4), does not grasp the multiplications of (6a) and (6b)?

At the second stage, the child is still on the intuitive plane. He sees that the length and density of the rows are variable and he is perfectly coherent from the point of view of perception in assuming that this variation involves variation in the number, and this prevents him from attempting composition (6). Where he ceases to be logical, however, is in failing to grasp that in a contracted series the decrease in length carries with it increase in density. Instead of deducing that the result of composition (5) is uncertain, he then dissociates length and density and makes the mistake of assuming that the number of elements depends on one of the two only.

How then does the child at the third stage succeed in overcoming this difficulty and discovering the constancy of number? Here there is a distinction to be made. On the one hand, if the comparison of two sets is merely a matter of 'more or less numerous' (e.g. all the blue counters that correspond to the red counters), it is obvious that generalization of logical multiplications will suffice to establish the constancy of the sets, because of the operational reversibility of qualitative correspondence. The correspondence can be made and unmade, i.e. the two sets, which are two series of relationships, can be multiplied by another relationship which links them together and which can then be disregarded. Through this relationship, the two sets become, and remain equivalent, which constitutes a certain constancy. When, for instance, a set of blue counters has been placed term for term below a set of red counters, the two series remain linked by the relationship 'below' or 'above', which ensures their equivalence from this particular point of view.[1]

But this constancy of classes or series of relations is not as yet constancy of number, and the equivalence to which we have just referred is not numerical equality. For example, there will be qualitative correspondence between three blue counters forming a triangle and three red counters also arranged in a triangle. If the red counters are then arranged in a row, the possibility of arranging them in a triangle still remains, and from that point of view, and that only, they are still equivalent to the blue ones. This equivalence is therefore of a special kind, depending on the same

[1] Is the notion of number essential before this first form of constancy can exist? Logically the notion of extension of classes or sequence of relations, and that of number are equivalent; psychologically the two notions appear synchronically (cf. Chapters VII and VIII).

configuration. This is understood by the child in the third stage when, like Lan, he says that two sets which formerly corresponded are still 'the same' because the heap can be made into a row as easily as the row can be made into a heap. A further step involves the assumption that the three counters in a row still correspond to the three in the triangle, and to any other set of three counters, whatever their distribution. This also is grasped by children at the third stage, since they frequently succeed in making the correspondence without troubling about the shape of the sets.

This brings us to the third stage in the logical construction of correspondence, that of numerical correspondence proper, which is parallel to what we called 'extensive quantities' in Chapters I and II and reaches its apex at the same time as the operations of logical multiplication, i.e. at the same time as the discovery of the constancy of classes and series of relations takes place.

The explanation of the transition from qualitative to numerical correspondence can perhaps best be given in terms of classes. Let us again consider the case of the three blue counters in a triangle with a corresponding set of three red counters also in a triangle. Obviously any one of the counters can be used to start the correspondence, but once it is in the figure, its position is defined absolutely, and the correspondence is defined by the spatial properties of the counter chosen. Order in no way intervenes in the definition of the total classes formed by the corresponding elements. Such is the qualitative correspondence used by the child (and also frequently by adults). If, instead of making a triangle with the red counters, the child puts them in a heap or a row, or distributes them at random, the one-one correspondence he makes is of a new type, since each counter no longer carries with it qualities that distinguish it from the others, but becomes a unit equal to the others. Each red counter can then correspond to any one of the blue counters, but to one only. Hence the set of red counters acquires its quality of number three, and is no longer the class of counters forming a triangle, just as a pair of counters acquires the number two and is no longer the class of counters forming the ends of one side of the triangle. Moreover, any union of a pair of counters will produce the same class containing two elements irrespective of their qualities.

In this numerical correspondence, how are the elements distinguished one from another? It is merely by the order in which they appear in the correspondence, an order which is relative, and varies from one operation to another, and which we shall therefore call 'vicariant'. For instance, in order to find the number of red counters corresponding to the blue ones in a complex figure, one child will point to each blue counter in turn, in any order (provided he does not count any element twice and does not omit any) and each time he will add a red counter to his row; another child will make a pile of red counters, and a third will merely take one each time from his reserve pile and put them aside at random, and so on. The only order common to all is in the act of pointing, but this order is essential if the correspondence is to be correct.

The correspondence therefore ceases to be qualitative and becomes numerical when the elements are grasped as being equivalent in all respects, and when the differential properties that distinguished them within the set are replaced by the only difference compatible with their equality, i.e. their relative position in the order of the correspondence. Once again, therefore, we find that it is the equating of differences that is the origin of the unit, and consequently of number.

We find the same mechanism of arithmetization when we examine the evolution of relationships. Children at the third stage accept the fact that there is equivalence in spite of the distortion of one of the corresponding rows, without feeling the necessity for a return to the initial state. This means that they replace qualitative correspondence by mathematical correspondence, and that they understand that the decrease in length is exactly compensated by the increase in density. The multiplication of qualitative relationships is thus from now on completed by a higher operation, that of the equating of differences. This being so, the length of the row and the size of the intervals lose their significance, and it is only the constant relationship between the two which counts for the child. Each interval becomes a unit equivalent to the others and the relation that represents the shift caused by the interval is then equivalent to 'plus one'.

It is clear therefore, that whether it be the elements as such or the relations that are being considered, in order that there shall be the transition from qualitative to numerical correspondence, a process of reasoning that goes beyond mere qualitative logic is necessary. It is the construction of units which are at the same time equal to one another and susceptible of seriation, and this construction takes place through the equating of differences. A class is, in fact, a union of terms seen as equivalent irrespective of their differences. For instance, all the counters of a series form a class to which those at the ends belong on the same terms as the others; red and blue counters are counters irrespective of their colour, i.e. two classes are united to form a third by disregarding their difference, in this case the colour. An asymmetrical relation, on the other hand, is the expression of a difference, e.g., when counter B is on the right of A and a certain distance away, A and B are conceived as different. To unite two asymmetrical relationships in one is to add the differences. Symmetrical relationships are those which unite the elements of the same class, without thereby adding anything. None of these qualitative compositions, therefore, would make it possible to define units properly so called. The union of two classes in a third does not constitute two units, because their union results from their common qualities, and in the new class their differences are disregarded. The union of two asymmetrical relationships also does not produce two units, since the partial differences which are composed are not necessarily equivalent. The construction of number, however, consists in the equating of differences, i.e. in uniting in a single operation the class and the asymmetrical relationship. The elements in question are then both equivalent to one another, thus participating of the class, and different from one another by their position in the enumeration, thus participating of the asymmetrical relationship. Moreover, since these differences are differences only of order, they are all equivalent one to the other. It therefore follows that the criterion for the transition from an arbitrary qualitative series to the corresponding numerical series is that each elementary relationship shall be considered as equivalent to the others.

CHAPTER V

SERIATION, QUALITATIVE SIMILARITY
AND ORDINAL CORRESPONDENCE

THE various forms of correspondence and equivalence
examined in chapters III and IV are both ordinal and
cardinal in character, but we have so far insisted on their
cardinal aspect only. We shall now examine the question of
seriation, of correspondence between two series of asymmetric
relations, or 'qualitative similarity', and of ordinal correspondence, i.e. similarity that has become numerical.

The making of a one-one correspondence between the elements
of two series does not *a priori* involve primacy of the cardinal over
the ordinal. It is indeed possible, as we stated in the conclusion of
the previous chapter, to maintain that, in order that the correspondence shall be exact (i.e. each term being counted once and
once only), the different terms must be ordered in a sequence in
which each element is distinguishable from all the others. When
it is a matter of arbitrary sets formed of equal elements only distinguishable by their position, the elements can be arranged in any
order, provided that there is an order and that it permits of each
element being counted once and once only. This is what in the
previous chapter we called 'vicariant' order, which means that
either of two elements can be the first or the second, provided that
there always is a first and a second. In such a case the order can
be disregarded and the significance of the correspondence
becomes primarily cardinal, since the equivalence between the
sets can be established irrespective of the order. On the other
hand, the ordinal aspect of the correspondence is more marked
when the elements of the sets in question differ one from another
by characteristics capable of seriation, and when these characteristics determine the position of the elements in each of the two sets,
the order thus no longer being vicariant. Let us take, for instance,
a sequence of wooden figures of varying heights and a series of
sticks of varying lengths. The sticks and the figures can be made to
correspond according to their various sizes and the correspondence
between the positions will be easily recognizable when the
elements of the two sets are mixed. Thus there are three possible
operations: simple qualitative seriation, qualitative corres-

pondence between two seriations (similarity) and numerical correspondence (ordinal) between the two series.

We shall now examine the reactions of the child with regard to these three operations. Will the intuitive character of the series that are to be correlated make for a more stable correspondence? Shall we find that the correspondences will produce more lasting cardinal equivalences? If this is not so, will the child at least achieve a notion of permanence of order, the understanding that even when the elements are disarranged a given position in set B always corresponds to a given position in set A? It is clear that the problems that arise in connection with ordinal correspondence are exactly parallel with those of cardinal correspondence discussed in the previous chapter, and we shall find that the reactions are the same and that the evolution of ordination goes hand in hand with that of cardination.

§1. Technique and general results

Ten wooden dolls of the same thickness, which can stand up or lie down, of clearly differing heights, the tallest being at least twice as big as the shortest, and ten sticks, also varying in size, but with less difference between them, represent the material. Ten balls of plasticine, also of clearly differing sizes, represent the rucksacks corresponding to the dolls, and are to be used as control material.

The first problem (Question I) is to find the correspondence between the dolls on the one hand and the sticks or balls on the other when the sets are not in order. The child is told that the dolls are going for a walk, and the correspondence is suggested, but without explicit reference to size. For instance, he is asked to arrange the dolls and sticks so that each doll can easily find the stick that belongs to it. The experiment is continued until the child understands the principle of serial correspondence.

Once the two rows have been arranged in correspondence one with the other, the following modification is made before the child's eyes: the rows are left parallel, but the dolls are brought closer together and the sticks or balls are spread more widely, so that the corresponding elements are no longer opposite one another (Question II). Touching one of the dolls, we then ask the child: 'Which stick will this one take?' The question is repeated, the dolls and sticks being taken either in order or at random according to the child's answers.

When a number of experiments of this kind have been made, the order of one of the series is reversed and the same questions are put (Question III). A fourth problem with which the child is confronted is that of discovering the stick or ball corresponding to one of the dolls when one or both of the series are disarranged (Question IV).

The exact level of the child's understanding can be discovered by way of a fifth question. All the elements of the two series are mingled and one of the dolls, number 6 for instance, is picked out. The child is then told that some of the dolls are going out for a walk, but not all, only those that are bigger (or smaller) than the one chosen, and he is asked (Question V) to find the sticks belonging to the dolls that are going out and those belonging to the dolls staying at home.

These five questions, which must be kept separate in questioning the child, can be reduced to three problems as far as systematazation of the results is concerned: (1) that of constructing a serial correspondence or similarity (Question I); (2) that of determining a serial correspondence when it is no longer directly perceived, i.e. of making the transition to ordinal correspondence (Questions II and III); and (3) that of reconstructing the ordinal correspondence when the intuitive series are destroyed (Questions IV and V). The solution of each of these problems involves three stages which are almost synchronic, and are also synchronic with the stages of cardinal correspondence and with those that we shall find, in the next chapter, in the relations between cardination and ordination.

The three stages in the construction of serial correspondence are: global comparison, without either exact seriation or spontaneous one-one correspondence, then intuitive, progressive seriation and correspondence, and finally immediate, operational seriation and correspondence.

In finding the correspondence when the intuitive series are disarranged (Questions II and III), three stages are again noticeable. During the first stage, the child does not find the correspondence between a given doll and its stick or ball once the two elements are no longer opposite one another. In the second stage, he either tries to count or falls back on a new one-one correspondence suggested by the semi-intuitive arrangement of the rows to be compared. In both cases he makes various systematic errors, of which the most obvious is confusion between the right position and that of the preceding element. In the third stage, he finds the correspondence by combining ordinal and cardinal notions.

In the reconstruction of a correspondence when one or both rows are disarranged (Questions IV and V), we again find three stages. In the first, the child is incapable of reconstructing either one or other of the series and answers immediately and arbitrarily. In the second stage, he counts, but pays no attention to the order, or else confuses the right position with that of the preceding element. In the third stage, he succeeds in finding the correct correspondence through co-ordination of seriation and cardination.

As the facts to be analysed are very complex, we shall examine the three problems separately instead of proceeding by general stages, the uniformity of the latter being sufficiently clear from the general outline we have just given.

§2. Construction of serial correspondence (Qualitative similarity)

One of the most interesting problems that arise in the construction of serial correspondence is the following. Is it easier for the child to construct a single series of objects, arranged, as in the present case, in order of increasing size, or to construct two corresponding series, each element of the first thus being in relation not only to the larger or smaller elements of that series but also to those of the parallel series? It might be thought that it is simpler to construct a single series, without external correspondence, since the combination of relationships involved in one series might become twice as complex in the case of two parallel series. This would be true if the correspondence resulted from logical multiplication and not merely from additive composition. On the other hand, it might be thought that, as in the case of cardinal correspondence, the finding of any correspondence is an analytic tool for the child and that therefore the construction of two similar series may be psychologically simpler than the construction of one.

It is interesting to find that experiment proves that the construction of a single series and the finding of a one-one correspondence between two series amount to the same thing, the difficulty involved in co-ordinating relationships in a single series being equal to that involved in finding a correspondence. The examples that follow show that at the level at which the child is unable to make dolls and balls correspond he is also unable to form correctly isolated series and that when seriation becomes possible, correspondence also becomes possible.

The following are examples of the first stage:

Gui (4;6) began by arranging the dolls of his own accord in the following order: 2, 7, 1, 6, 9, 5, 8, 3, 4, 10. 'Can you put them in order, the biggest first, then the one that's a little bit smaller, then getting smaller and smaller till you come to the smallest?—*Yes* (he arranged them thus: 7, 6, 1, 10, 2, 9, 8, 4, 5).—Which ball will this doll have (10)?—*That one* (10).—Yes, and this one (1)?—*That one* (1). —Yes. And now can you put the dolls in order so that they can easily find their balls? Put the smallest here, then the next biggest, then the next until you get to the biggest of all.—(He put 1, 3, 2, 4, 5, 6, 10, 9, leaving out 8 and 7 at first and then putting them between 5 and 6.)'

We then helped him to make the correct series by disarranging the whole set and discussing each doll in turn until he succeeded. 'Now you must give them their balls. The small dolls must have the small ones and the bigger dolls the bigger ones and so on. Which balls will you give to these two (1 and 10)?—*Those* (1 and 10).—That's right. Now, go ahead.—(He then arranged the balls, each one opposite a doll, but in the following order: 1, 5, 6, 7, 8, 9, 4, 3, 2, 10).—But these dolls will cry because you've given them balls that are too small!—(He at once removed balls 4, 3 and 2, but in trying to fit them in, disarranged the first balls, which he then rearranged in the order: 1, 3, 4, 2, 5 . . .)— Is there the same number of balls and dolls?—*Yes.*—How many balls? —(counting) *10.*—And how many dolls?—(he had to count again) *10.*'

Val (5;6): 'Show me the stick belonging to this doll (D10).[1] (He pointed to S10.)—And to this one (D1)?—(He pointed to S1.) Good. And what about the other dolls?— . . .—Arrange the dolls.—(7, 9, 6, 5, 2, 3, 1, 10, 8, 4.) Which stick will go with that doll (D8)?—*That one* (S6).—And with D4?—(He pointed to S4)—How must we arrange them so as to find the right ones?— . . . —Arrange the dolls: the biggest here, then the one that's a little bit smaller, then the next smallest, until you get to the smallest of all.—(10, 9, 7, 4, 6, then 10, 9, 6, 7, 4, 8, 5, 2, 3, 1.)—Try to put the biggest first; you've got it, look (10), then the one that's a little bit smaller; that one's right too, look (9), then the next smallest; is that one (7) right? etc.—(In this way he managed to get 10, 9, 8, 7, 6, 5, but then put 3, 1, 2, 4, then 4, 1, 2, 3, then 4, 2, 3, 1.)—In that right (2, 3)?—*No* (correcting it). Now put the stick belonging to each doll.—(He put 9, 10, 8, 7, 4.)—Is that right?—(He changed 9 and 10.)—And what about that one (4)?— (He inserted 5.)— . . . —etc.'

Clan (5;8) tried to make the correspondence without previous seriation of either of the rows: D6 for B10 and D1 for B1. 'Where's the biggest doll?—(He put D9 with B10, then D3 with B4, D2 with B2, made the correction B10 with D10 and B9 with D9; D4 with B6; etc.)—How can we be sure that each doll has his right ball?—(He made a few changes but without forming the series.) Suppose you begin with the biggest, then put the next size and so on.—(He then tried to form the series, but experienced the same difficulties as the earlier children.)'

Ros (5;6), after having the same difficulties in forming the series of dolls, put B1 opposite D1, then B3 with D2, B4 with D3, B8 and then B6 with D4, B8 with D5, and B9 with D6. He then took B5 and said: '*I don't know where to put this one.*' He removed B4 and put B5 in its place, opposite D3. Having looked at the whole row, he was not satisfied, removed all the balls and then arranged them thus under the row of dolls 10–1: B10,—,9, 7,—,8, 6, 5, 4, 1, balls 2 and 3 being left out and dolls 9 and 6 having no balls.

It is obvious that there are three methods, and three only, of

---

[1] D=doll, S=stick, B=ball.

solving this problem of correspondence. The first is to seriate the dolls, then make a separate series of balls or sticks in the same order, and then make each term of the first series correspond with the term having the same position in the second series. We shall call this the method of *double seriation.* The second method consists in forming one of the sets into a series and then putting the elements of the other set directly in correspondence with them, taking them one by one according to their position and in the same order. This is *simple seriation with correspondence.* By the third method there is immediate one-one correspondence between balls and dolls without previous seriation, the seriation taking place, of course, either in fact or by visual judgement, simultaneously with the correspondence itself. *This is direct correspondence.*

A first point to notice is that not only were all the children at this stage unable to use the method of double seriation correctly, but they were even unable to conceive of it. The idea of double seriation does in fact presuppose that the problem has already been solved, that is to say it requires the ability to imagine as it were in the void the set of relationships involved in the series and the correspondence. Now since at this stage the child cannot at once even make the correct series of dolls, when making balls and sticks correspond with them he obviously will not try to seriate them, but will deal with them individually in succession.

A second observation to be made is that when children at this stage use the method of simple seriation with correspondence they are not capable of exact spontaneous seriation. The first attempt of Gui, for instance, produced 2, 7, 1, 6, 8, etc., and that of Val 7, 9, 6, 5. The interest of this first reaction, as compared with those of older children, lies in the fact that it is indicative of an attitude that is still global and contrary to the analytic approach required for seriation. Indeed, when the child has produced his spontaneous series and is then asked to form a true series, he is no more successful. The seriation of a set of elements according to size requires awareness that each term is both greater than the preceding terms and smaller than those which follow, and it is obvious that Gui and Val forgot the latter condition. Gui first produced 7, 6, 1, regardless of the other terms, then added 10, 2, and finally 9, 8, 4, 5, while Val, after several corrections in his attempt to form a decreasing series, put 10, 9, 7, 4, 6, and then added 8, 5, 2, 3, 1.

The third fact that emerges is that the correspondences made by the child do not go beyond the level of these seriations, i.e. they are still global and pre-serial. There are two distinct cases, that in which, like Gui, Val and Ros, the child makes the balls and sticks correspond to dolls that have previously been seriated, and that in which, like Clan, he makes the correspondence without previous seriation. In the first of these, we find that although with the help of the experimenter he achieves a correct series of dolls, he proceeds when he is establishing the correspondence between balls and dolls in exactly the same way as when making his spontaneous series of dolls prior to adult suggestion. Gui, for instance, put opposite dolls 1–10 balls 1, 5, 6, 7, 8, 9, 4, 3, 2, 10, and in spite of our suggestions failed to find the correct correspondence and finally inserted ball 2 between balls 4 and 5. Val made sticks 9, 10, 8, 7, 4, etc., correspond to dolls 1–10, while Ros went so far as to make sticks 1, 3, 4, 6, 8, 9 correspond to dolls 1–6 and then for the series of dolls 10–1 finally produced balls 10, –, 9, 7, –, 8, 6, 5, 4, 1, two balls remaining without dolls and two dolls without balls. As for Clan, he only succeeded in forming the following pairs: 6-10, 1-1, 2-2, 9-10, 3-4, then 10-10 and 9-9, but finally 4-6, 7-7, 5-3, 6-5, followed by 5-4, 6-5 and 3-3.

All this is a clear indication that the difficulties of serial correspondence are of the same kind as those of seriation itself and that the characteristic feature of this correspondence, i.e. its double seriation, in no way affects, either favourably or otherwise, the understanding of seriation. Are we then to conclude that in serial correspondence seriation has primacy over correspondence and that the latter notion is merely an external addition involving nothing new? By so doing we should ignore the fact that seriation itself implies a kind of correspondence, that which links any one element to the next. In other words, seriation is an intrinsic correspondence and serial correspondence is an extrinsic correspondence between two series. Moreover, conversely it can be said that all correspondence presupposes seriation, and when spontaneous seriation is not possible, neither is serial correspondence, and vice versa. It will be remembered that at this level cardinal correspondence and even non-serial qualitative correspondence are also impossible and that instead of operations we find global evaluations. In the following pages we shall try to show the connection between ordinal and cardinal correspondence, but for the moment we shall merely point out how little understanding of cardinal correspondence was shown by the children quoted above. Ros, for example, finally made eight balls correspond with ten dolls, while Val first put nine balls opposite ten dolls and later, when he had arranged two rows of ten elements, did not at once infer that there were ten dolls when he had counted ten balls.

Coming now to a consideration of the reactions of the second stage, we find a two-fold progress. On the one hand, the child is capable of spontaneous construction of correct series after a certain amount of trial and error, and on the other, he can successfully solve the problem of serial correspondence, in particular by the method of double seriation.

We give three examples of this level:

Tis (5;6) was looking at the dolls and sticks which were all confused. 'Are all the dolls alike?—*Oh no, they get smaller and smaller, and that's the smallest.*—Do you know which stick belongs to which doll? How can we find out?—*We must arrange them smaller, smaller, smaller.*' Of his own accord, Tis then began to arrange the sticks in the following order: 9, 10, 8, then said '*No, I've got two the same size.*' He then measured 10 and 8 and put 10 in position, then compared 9 and 8, put down 9, 8, 7. (He had not compared 10 and 9 and had corrected his original mistake by chance.) He then picked up 6, 5, 4, measured them one against the other, then continued the series 6, 5, 4, 3, 2, 1. After this he looked at the dolls and without any suggestion from me put the 10 and the 1 opposite sticks 10 and 1. He then correctly placed doll 9, then 7, 8 (correcting himself after comparing them) and finally completed the series 6, 5, 4, 3, 2, the whole series of dolls thus being opposite the sticks. In spite of this brilliant beginning, however, Tis lost himself, as we shall see in §2, as soon as the sticks were moved rather closer to one another while the row of dolls remained untouched.

Chou (7): 'Which doll goes with that ball (the biggest)?—*The very big one.*—Now put the balls with the dolls they belong to.' He arranged the dolls in the order 4, 6, 7, 8, 3, 10, 9, 5, 2, 1.—Is that right?—*No.*' Without further suggestion he then produced 1, 2, 3, 5, 6, 7, 9, 10, and after some trial and error finally added 4 and 8. 'And now?—*I must put the balls.*' He began by making the correspondence with the preceding term in the row of dolls, 6 with 5, 7 with 6, 9 with 8, etc., but corrected himself when he saw the whole set.

Cha (6;6). 'How can we find the ball belonging to each doll?— ... —Which ball will that one have (10)?—(He pointed to 10.)—And that one (5)?—*That one* (7).—How can we be quite sure?—*I'll put them like this* (seriating): 10, 8, 9, then 10, 9, 7, 8, then 8, 7, 5, 6, then 6, 5, 4, 3, 2, 1.' After this he put the balls opposite the dolls, but making an error of one position in each case so that finally there was one ball without a doll and one doll without a ball. 'Is there the same number of balls and dolls?—*There are more dolls.*—How many?—(He counted the 10 dolls.)—And how many balls?—(Counting) *10.*—So it's the same number?—*Yes* (correcting the correspondence).

There is no need to quote further examples to see the significance of this second stage. The difference between it and the first stage, i.e. the appearance of correct and spontaneous seriation and serial correspondence, is obvious. It is however,, less easy to distinguish it from the third stage, to which it is connected by all the intermediate stages. The difference of principle, which is evident in the clear cases, is that seriation and serial correspondence are still intuitive and perceptual in the second stage, whereas they become operational in the third, when the corres-

H

pondence is truly ordinal, i.e. numerical. The distinction becomes more evident by comparison with the results of the experiments in §§3 and 4, which show the mechanism of serial correspondence, but for the present we shall confine ourselves to discovering differential criteria used by the child at the intuitive and operational levels in constructing his series and correspondences.

In the first place, at the second stage all the subjects can form a series without intervention from the experimenter. The child is capable of arranging an element in a series in such a way that it is both the largest (or the smallest) of those still to be seriated and the smallest (or the largest) of those already seriated. But is this operational logic or mere perception of practical relationships? An examination of the method followed by the child provides us with a certain number of clues which gain in significance when viewed in connection with other features of the same level. To put it briefly, the child at the second stage does not immediately master the whole set of relations necessary for seriation, but discovers them gradually by dint of empirical trial and error. Thus Tis, the most advanced of the children quoted above, begins with 9, 10, 8, then measures 10 and 8 against one another, then 9 and 8 (but not 10 and 9). Chou begins with an arbitrary sequence, then tries to grade the series, but forgets and has to make corrections. Cha also is hesitant with regard to the dolls, constantly inverts the order and then corrects himself, and seriates the balls but forgets the first. It is not the hesitation itself that is important, but the attitude of which it is an indication. When there is primacy of intuition over operation, although the child knows he is constructing an increasing scale, he compares the elements by small groups, or even by pairs, whereas when there is primacy of operation over intuition he feels the need continually to compare the whole set of data, i.e. to choose, for instance, first 'the smallest of all', then 'the smallest of those that are left', and so on. These gradations are obviously difficult to distinguish and it is only by considering the whole set of the subject's reactions that we can arrive at a correct interpretation of his behaviour. It will, however, become clear that our suggested interpretation is correct when we see (in Chapter VI, §1) that the child at this level is incapable of inserting new elements into a series correctly and (in §3 of the present chapter) of mentally reconstructing a seriation when the perceptual order of the correspondence is evenly slightly changed.

As for serial correspondence, again at this stage we find it developing in close connection with seriation, but without being identical with it, since the two operations are interdependent and yet distinct. In the case of each child, there is a close analogy

between the way he seriates and the way he makes a correspondence. Chou begins with arbitrary correspondences just as he began
with an arbitrary seriation; Cha, who puts 9 instead of 8, 8 instead
of 7 and 6 instead of 5 in his seriation, has a lag of one place in
his correspondence, and Tis, who seriates more systematically,
obtains his correspondence by double seriation.

The fact is that the construction of a series or of a serial correspondence involves co-ordination of the relations $A \rightarrow B \rightarrow C$ . . .
so that when $E \rightarrow F$ then at the same time $E \leftarrow A, B, C$ . . . and
$F \rightarrow G, H, I$ . . . etc. Now a comparison of the reactions of this
second stage with those of the first shows that the main difference
is that in the first stage the child does not proceed by means of such
relations, but by 'pre-relative' qualities. Either his seriations and
correspondences are still arbitrary, or he puts the 'small' elements
on one side and the 'big' elements on the other in groups of two or
three. In the latter case he is using the qualities 'big' and 'small'
(with the perceptual relations that connect them), and not the
relationships 'bigger' and 'smaller', much less the co-ordinations
'both bigger than X and smaller than Y' which are the true
criterion for the relation. By such a method, both seriation and
serial correspondence are clearly impossible, but as soon as the
relations established between the elements acquire true relativity,
the resulting co-ordination leads both to simple seriation and to
serial correspondence. Once two relations are co-ordinated, i.e.,
once at least three elements are related, further co-ordination
offers no new problem. The difficulty lies in the transition from
quality to relation, but once this is overcome, both corresponding
double seriations and isolated additive series are possible.

One reservation must however be made. As we pointed out
earlier, the relations discovered during the second stage are only
developed on the intuitive, experimental plane, i.e. they are only
semi-operational and do not as yet constitute true operations
susceptible of being manipulated in abstract apart from perception. This final progress is achieved in the third stage, which is
illustrated by the following examples:

Shen (6;6), without preliminary seriation, at once made the biggest
ball (10) correspond with the biggest doll (10), then B9 with D9, B8
with D8, and so on. In each case he looked for the biggest doll and ball
of those that were left, and did not even feel the need to put them in a
row, but placed them in pairs on the table. 'Put the dolls in a row.—
(He arranged them 10—1).—And now the balls (these had all been
mixed).—(He at once formed the series opposite the dolls).'
Derc (6;10) also proceeded by direct correspondence. 'How can we
find at once the ball belonging to each doll?—*I don't know.*—Think
hard. What must we do?—(He put D10 with B10, D9 with B9, D8

with B8, etc., each time looking for the biggest of the elements that were left and putting them into the series.)—Are there as many balls as dolls? —*Yes* (He then changed B7 with B6 and said: *If it was like that it wouldn't be right.*')

Pot (7;2) first seriated the dolls, making a single transposition which he immediately corrected, and then formed the series of sticks opposite them.

What is new at this stage is that the child is all the time considering the set of relationships between all the elements, since with each new step he looks for the biggest (or the smallest) of the remaining elements. The series is thus built up without any hesitation or trial and error. It is noteworthy, and is moreover a confirmation of our earlier interpretations, that children of this stage find it as easy to operate by immediate correspondence, like Shen and Derc, without previously seriating first dolls and then balls, as to begin by simple seriation and then make the correspondence.

The construction of serial correspondence, or qualitative similarity, is thus completed through a system of operations properly so called, capable of co-ordinating both direct and inverse relations. We have so far confined ourselves to the purely logical or qualitative aspect of this evolution. Now we shall see that as soon as the operation is no longer linked with perception, there is a second aspect to be considered, i.e. the arithmetical aspect which constitutes ordinal correspondence or generalized similarity.

§3. *From serial correspondence to ordinal correspondence*

Once serial correspondence has been built up in the manner we have just described, the intuitive order of the series and correspondences can be disarranged in order to show the mechanism at work. The two experiments we shall study concurrently consist in (1) displacing one of the series with respect to the other (e.g. by moving the balls closer together but leaving the dolls untouched), and (2) reversing the order of one of the series. In both cases one of the dolls is indicated and the child is asked which ball corresponds to it, and vice versa. (The test takes place immediately after the child has succeeded in forming the series.)

Here again we find the three stages described above, but with certain interesting additional points of detail. In the first, the child loses all idea of correspondence as soon as one of the series is displaced and merely chooses the elements that are opposite one another. In the second stage, he tries to discover the correct correspondence either by empirical means or by counting, but he constantly confuses the right position with that of the preceding term. In the third stage, however, he solves the problem by co-ordinating his estimate of the required position with that of the cardinal value of the sets in question. In the latter case, both qualitative serial correspondence and ordinal numerical cor-respondence are involved.

Our first examples illustrate the first stage:

Gui (4;6) had succeeded, with some help, in forming the series of dolls and balls. 'Watch. We'll put the balls a bit closer together but you'll still be able to tell me which ball each doll will have. (This was done in such a way that ball 10 was opposite doll 9 and ball 1 opposite doll 1, the order remaining unchanged and the correspondence still being clearly visible.) Which ball will this doll (7) have?—*That one* (8) which was opposite doll (7). And that one (D8)?—*This ball* (B9).—And that one (D9)?—*This ball* (B10).—And that one (D10)?—*That one* (B10 again).' The balls were then moved still closer together so that B1 was still opposite D1 but B10 was opposite D8. Gui then allotted B9 to D7 which was opposite, B10 to D8, and so on. When however we took them in order from D10 to D5 he gave the correct correspondence, but as soon as a random choice was made he again went wrong.

Ros (5;6), when the balls had been moved closer together was told: 'Show me the ball belonging to this doll (D10).—(He pointed to B10.) —And to this one (D9)?—(He pointed to B9.)—And to this one (D5)? —(He pointed to B6.)—And to this one (D8)?—(He pointed to B8, 7, 8, and then 7 again.)—And to this one (D9)?.—(He pointed to B8).' etc.

The balls were then moved slightly closer together and we proceeded systematically from D10 to D1. Ros found the right ball in each case, with two exceptions. When however dolls were picked out at random he could not seriate mentally and again chose the balls that happened to be opposite.

We then went on to Question III. Before the child's eyes the order of the series of balls was reversed while the series of dolls remained un-changed, the order of dolls being from D10 to D1 and that of the balls B1 to B10. Ros's first reactions showed that he understood the position. 'Which ball belongs to this doll (D10)?—(He first pointed to B1 which was opposite and then went to B10.) And to this one (D1)?—(He first pointed to B10 and then asid: '*No, that's the one* (B1).' But as soon as dolls were picked out at random he merely pointed to the ball opposite and ignored the inverse relations.

Val (5;6) was asked, when the sticks had been moved closer together: 'Which stick belongs to this doll (D10)?—(She pointed to S10.)—And to this one (D1)?—(She pointed to S1.)—Is there the same number of dolls and sticks?—*There are more dolls* (because the row of dolls was longer: see Chap. IV §1).—Hang all the sticks on the dolls.—(She did so.)—Are there more dolls?—*There are just as many.*—(The sticks were removed and placed as before and Val again allotted S10 to D10 and

S1 to D1.) Now show me the stick belonging to this doll (D7).—(She pointed to S6 which was opposite.)—And to this one (D9)?—(She pointed to S10.)—And to this one (D8)?—(She pointed to S6.)—And to this one (D6)?—(She pointed to S4.)—And to this one (D4)?—(She pointed to S2.)'

The order of the sticks was then reversed (Question III). Val understood the position since she made S10 correspond to D10, and S1 to D1, but then failed completely, making S8 correspond to D7, S3 to D2, S4, 5, 6, 5, and finally 6 to D4, etc.

These three examples are sufficient to provide an easy interpretation of this first stage. We have already seen that at this level the child is incapable of achieving spontaneously correct seriation and serial correspondence, but that when helped by questions he can succeed. The question that thus arises is whether the child is not after all capable of seriating. The results of the above experiments provide a definite answer: at this level the child is so far from real understanding of seriation that he no longer sees the correspondence once the elements are no longer directly opposite one another, even when the two series are parallel and there has only been a slight displacement of one series.

And yet the child clearly understands the questions put to him, as is proved by the fact that when the dolls are taken in order, from 1 to 10 or from 10 to 1, he can point out each time the corresponding ball. He also never fails to find the correct corresponding element for the two ends of the series. But as soon as one of the middle elements is chosen, and the intuitive order of the series is no longer followed, the child is lost. Instead of starting from the ends and working out the correspondence with his eyes or his fingers, he merely points to the element opposite. Thus the series and the correspondences that he makes with the help of the adult are for the child at this stage only global figures which he cannot yet analyse systematically. His apparent ability to understand the correspondence when the order of the series is followed arises from the fact that he keeps the whole figure in mind, but with no real perception of the relationships, so that when elements are picked out at random any correct analysis is impossible. To sum up, at this first stage the child is at the same level with respect to serial correspondence as the one we described in Chapters III and IV in the case of cardinal correspondence, that of global comparison without even intuitive grasp of the relationships between the different elements.

We come now to some examples of the second stage, that of intuitive or empirical seriation and serial correspondence.

Lie (5;6) had succeeded, after some trial and error (transposition of 5 and 6, 7 and 8, etc.) in seriating the dolls and finding the correspondence with the balls. He was then asked to find the corresponding elements when the balls were spaced (before his eyes) so that ball 9 was opposite doll 10 and ball 6 opposite doll 1. 'Are there as many balls as dolls?—*There are more balls.*—How many balls are there?—(counting) *10.*—And are there 10 dolls?—*No.*—Count them.—(counting) *Ah yes! There are ten of them too.*—Well then, which ball goes with this doll (D5). —(He pointed to B7.)—And with this one (D1)?—(He pointed to B1.)' He then pointed to B10 for D10, B9 for D9, B8 for D8, B7 for D7, but when I picked out dolls at random he systematically made B8 correspond to D7, B2 to D3 (because he had pointed already to the two preceding elements D1 and D2), B4 to D3 (this time pointing to the three elements preceding B4 in order to find the correspondence with D3), etc. When we went back to the regular series from D10 to D1 he answered correctly (still pointing with his finger), but as soon as the elements were again picked out at random, he fell into the same error.

With regard to Question III (the order of the dolls reversed), he answered correctly when the order D1 to D10 was followed, but was wrong by one position every time when it was not.

Kel (6;6). When the sticks were moved closer together, Kel made S1 correspond to D1 and S10 to D10, but at first put S7 with D6, correcting himself later.

The order of the balls was then reversed. Kel cried: '*Ah! I understand the game*', and wanted to reverse the order, but was prevented from so doing. He found the correspondence between D9 and B9, D7 and B7, but pointed to D6 for B5. 'Are you sure?—(Using his finger he made the correspondence term for term between the two series from D10 to D5 and from B10 to B5.)—Then which doll does this ball (B5) belong to?—(He again pointed to the sixth doll, confusing its position with the number of preceding elements.)—And this one (B4)?—(He pointed to D7, mistaking the direction.)—And this one (B5)?—(He pointed to D6, confusing its position with the number of preceding elements.)— And this one (B4)?—(He pointed to D8, going in the wrong direction and confusing its position with the number of the preceding elements B1, B2 and B3.)' Similarly he pointed to D4 for B3, and D3 for B2 as a result of the same systematic mistake. Then all the balls from 1 to 10 were pointed at one after the other and Kel found the corresponding doll in each case. Doll 6 was then indicated, and Kel again pointed to ball 7.

Pel (6;10), when the sticks were moved closer together, at once found the correct correspondence between sticks 1 to 10 and dolls 1 to 10.— And which stick belongs to this doll (D8)?—(He pointed to S8.)— How did you find out?—*Because I saw that there were two there* (D10 and D9, which were in front of D8) *and there were two there as well* (S10 and S9).—And what about that doll (D4)?—(He pointed to S3.)—And that one (D1)?—(He pointed to S1.)—And that one (D4)?—(He again pointed to S3, after trying to put it opposite.)—And that one (D6)?—(He pointed to S6 and then changed his opinion.) *No, it's that one* (S5).—And for this one (D4)?—(He pointed to S3.)'

When one series was reversed (Question III) and Pel was asked to find the ball corresponding to D6, he used his finger to make the correspondence: he touched D10 and B10; D9 and B9; D8 and B8, but then D7 and B6 and lost his direction. He began again, lost himself once more, and then counted 1, 2, 3, 4, 5 for D6, counted the balls 1 to 5 and pointed to ball 5, etc. 'How many balls are there?—*10.*—And how many dolls?—*Ten of those too. Oh no, eleven, because that row is longer.*'

Chou (7;0), when the sticks were moved closer together was asked: 'Whose is this stick (S1)?—(He pointed to D1.)—And this one (S10)?—(He pointed to D10.)—And this one (S4)?—*It belongs to this one* (D3). Why?—*Because there* (D1 and D2) *there are 2 and there as well* (S1, S2 . . .) *Oh no!* (He then pointed to D4.)—And that one (S7)?—(He pointed to D8.)—And that one (S10)?—(He pointed to D10.)—And that one (S7)?—(He again pointed to D8.)—How do you know?—*Because there* (S10, S9 and S8) . . . *Oh no, it's that one* (D7), *because there* (S10, S9 and S8) *there are three, and there too* (D10–8.)—And this one (S6)?—He pointed to D7.)—Why?—*Because there* (S10 to S7) *there are four, and there are four there as well* (pointing to D10–D7).'

In the case of Question III, the reactions were the same. Chou pointed to B10 for D10 and B1 for D1, but to B5 for D6. 'Why do you think it's that one?—*Because there's the same number* (pointing to dolls 1 to 5, but counting balls 1 to 5 and then pointing to B5).'

These examples illustrate the first attempts at reconstructing the correspondence when one of the series is modified with respect to the other. As we saw earlier when considering the question of cardinal correspondence, in a similar situation children fail to see that numerical equivalence is maintained. Here the position is the same. Lie thinks there are more balls than dolls because the dolls are closer together, Pel thinks there are more dolls because they are further apart, and so on, in spite of the fact that the children themselves have just made the correspondence between the two sets not only with respect to size but also to position. It is therefore clear that like the qualitative correspondence of this stage, serial correspondence also does not involve understanding of cardinal equivalence. This does not prevent the child from attempting to discover corresponding positions, since at this stage, although he cannot see the cardinal equivalence when the elements are no longer opposite one another, he believes it can be restored by a return to the original position. This attempt at finding the corresponding position is of the nature of reversibility, and will lead in the third stage to the notion of lasting equivalence, both cardinal and ordinal. For the moment, however, the child is not in a position to construct such an operational system. How does he in fact proceed in order to discover the corresponding positions?

The simplest reaction, once the idea of merely pointing to the elements that are opposite one another has been abandoned, is to start from the ends of the series and make the correspondence

term for term either with the finger or the eyes. This is the procedure adopted throughout by Lie and Kel, and by Pel for
question III. But in the case of children who are not used to
counting, this method frequently leads to omissions or to the
counting of one element twice. Moreover, when one of the series
is reversed, there are often mistakes in direction. Hence at a given
moment the child sometimes adopts a second method, that of
counting aloud: he starts from the first or the tenth doll, going on
until he reaches the one whose corresponding element is to be
found, and then counts the sticks or balls up to that number
(cf. Chou).

Whichever method is used, the examples we have given, and
which are typical of this level, show that the children constantly
make a mistake of one unit. The explanation of this fact is provided by the children themselves, although it remains for us to
examine the justification for it. When it is a case of finding the
element corresponding to an element n, the child counts the preceding $n - 1$ elements, then goes to the other series, finds $n - 1$ and
stops there. According as he starts from one end or other of the
series the position found will be one unit too high or one unit too
low. For instance, Chou chose ball 5 for doll 6 'because there's the
same number'; he had counted the dolls 1–5 before coming to the
sixth, and then pointed to the fifth ball. But he also chose doll 7
for stick 6 because after stick 6 'there are 4', and doll 7 is the
fourth starting from 10. Yet this child, at the beginning of the
interview, had several times corrected this same mistake of his
own accord. Similarly Pel, who began by choosing stick 8 for
doll 8 'because I saw that there were two there and two there',
afterwards chose stick 5 and ball 5 for doll 6 through counting
dolls 1 to 5. In the case of Kel and Lie, who did not count aloud
but made the correspondence with their fingers, the phenomenon
was the same. Lie, for instance, gave ball 2 to doll 3 even when
he showed with his finger the correspondence between ball 1 and
doll 1, and ball 2 and doll 2!

What then is the explanation of this type of mistake and its
inevitability? As long as the corresponding elements are opposite
one another, there is no difficulty, since the correspondence
results from the qualitative similarity. The problem arises once the
perceptual schema is destroyed. The child who is asked which
stick goes with doll 5 has to characterize doll 5 by its position,
but in order to determine this position in relation to that of the
sticks, it is not enough to focus on the element in question. Its
relative position must be calculated, and this can only be done
by estimating the number of elements that precede it. This results
in a dissociation, in the child's mind, between the position to be

found (that of doll 5) and the number of preceding terms (dolls 1-4). When therefore, in determining the position, he counts not 5 but 4, it is because the numbers 1 to 4 and the number 5 do not perform the same function for him in this particular case. The numbers 1 to 4 represent the set separating D5 from the beginning of the series, whereas the number 5 represents the position characterizing the doll. This explains why the child says 'there are four in front', or merely 'there are four', since for him the position does not as yet possess a number of the same nature as those he uses to count the preceding terms. In the same way, when he estimates the numbers by pointing to each element with his finger, he dissociates the set of the first four elements from the fifth, whose position he is trying to determine. When, however, he then tries to determine the position of the corresponding element in the other series, the reverse phenomenon occurs. As this element is not already given, as was the doll pointed out by the experimenter, it remains throughout on the same level as the others, and there is no separation. Thus the child who counted four, either verbally or with his finger, before coming to doll 5, will apply the number 4 to the corresponding series of sticks, but in a different way, since there is no *a priori* distinction between the element whose position is to be found and those which precede it. Thus when he applies to the successive sticks the numbers 1, 2, 3, 4, these numbers bear both a cardinal and ordinal meaning for him, so that on reaching number 4 he is under the impression that he has arrived at the corresponding term and couples stick 4 with doll 5.

Although from the point of view of logic and arithmetic this lack of co-ordination between the cardinal and ordinal mechanisms may appear to be the result of a temporary dissociation, it is in fact an indication of the beginnings of co-ordination. There is a definite progress over the first stage, when the problem did not even arise, since the child was capable neither of correct seriation nor serial correspondence. With the progress in seriation, we find the first link appearing between position and cardination, since in order to discover the position of an element in the case of optically displaced series it is necessary either to count the number of preceding elements or to find it by one-one correspondence. As however the seriation of the second stage is still intuitive and not yet truly operational, it does not include cardination. The position of an element is still only its situation in a qualitative scale and there is not as yet correlation with a cardinal value. Hence the lack of co-ordination found at this level.

But this is not all. The hesitation characteristic of this stage is an indication of the beginnings of dissociation between qualitative and numerical relations, i.e. between serial and ordinal correspondence. There is qualitative similarity between two series of relations when two sets of objects are seriated according to the same sequence of asymmetric, qualitative relations, the position of each element in the first series corresponding to that of a given element in the second. Thus when the child does no more than seriate the sticks and dolls according to their size, making the two series correspond, it is a case of mere qualitative similarity. But in such seriations each element is different from all the others ('larger' or 'smaller' in this particular case), and moreover each relation is different, since the difference in size between one doll and the next is not necessarily constant. In ordinal seriation, on the contrary, each element counts as one unit, equivalent in all respects to the others except for its position in the series, and each relation of order linking two elements is equivalent to any other. When therefore the child at the second stage is confronted with two optically displaced qualitative series, he is compelled to combine ordinal correspondence with mere serial correspondence, i.e. to consider the dolls and sticks as units to be counted as well as seriated. He is thus faced with the problem we considered a moment ago: if each element of an ordinal series counts as one unit equivalent to any other, the only difference between the element n and the element $n + 1$ is that the element n comes after $n - 1$ other elements, while the element $n + 1$ comes after n others. Ordinal position thus presupposes cardination, and the converse is also true, as we saw at the end of Chapter IV. It is at this point that children at this level fail. They understand that in order to find the position of a given element the preceding elements must be counted as equivalent units, but they cannot conceive of the element in question as being a unit comparable to the others. We find therefore that in determining a given position by numeration, the child separates the qualitative position of the element in question from the cardinal number of the set of preceding elements. He fails to understand that each position is itself a number and that this number is inseparable from the whole aggregate of which it is a part.

We now come to some examples of the third stage, showing the progress made in operational construction of both serial and ordinal correspondence.

Bos (6;6), Question II: 'Whose is this ball (B8)?—(He pointed to D8.)—How do you know?—*I can see 3 there* (B10, 9 and 8) *and there* (D10, 9 and 8).—And this one (B6)?—*It belongs to that one* (D6) *because before there were 3 and now it's jumped to 6* (so he had counted balls 1-6). —What did we do?—*Before, there were 3* (10, 9, 8) *and now we've jumped to 5* (this time counting balls 10, 9, 8, 7, 6 and dolls 10–6 and again pointing to D6 and B6).'

When one series was reversed, he pointed to D7 for B7, D4 for B4, and so on. He then counted the preceding elements each time, but without making a mistake in the corresponding series. For example, in the case of B4 he said: '*There, there are 3 at the side* (B1, 2, 3)' then counted D1, 2, 3 and pointed to D4.

Vig (6;6), Question III: 'Whose is this ball (B10)?—(He pointed to D10.)—And that one (B8)?—*It belongs to that one* (D8).—How did you find out?—*There are 3 here* (D10, 9, 8).—And that one (B5)?—*That one* (D5).—Why?—*I looked to see if there were 4* (counting the preceding ones).' He also pointed to B6 for D6, etc.

Question II: 'Which stick will this doll (D6) have?—(He pointed to S6.)—How did you find out?—*I looked to see how many were left* (S7, 8, 9, 10).' etc.

Nel (7;0), Question III: 'Will every doll have its stick all the same? —*Yes.*—Which doll will have this stick (S6)?—*That one* (D6).—And this stick (S3)?—(He first pointed to D8, then to D3).'

Question II: 'Which stick must we give to this doll (D5)?—*That one* (S5) *because there are 4 dolls here* (D 1–4) *and 4 sticks here* (S1–4).—And this stick (S7)?—*That one* (D7) *because there are 6 sticks in front* (S1–6) *and 6 dolls in front too* (D1–6).'

From the cardinal point of view, there is no longer hesitation on the part of the children in stating that the number of sticks or balls is still equal to the number of dolls even when the order is inverted or the series is displaced. This new progress constitutes a fact of capital importance for the arithmetization of serial correspondence. Moreover, in determining a position *n*, all the children use numeration whether they count from 1 to *n* or from *n* to 10. When, like Nel, they only count the preceding terms, they do the same thing in the corresponding series. In some cases, like Vig, they count the remaining terms (e.g., 7–10 for 6); in others, like Bos and Vig, they count the element whose position they are finding as well as the preceding elements, whether they start from the beginning or end of the series. In a word, the two mechanisms of cardination and ordination are now correlated, the former having become independent of the parts and being applied to all the terms as equivalent units, and the latter being no longer dependent on quality. From now on, the element *n* represents for the child both the *n*th position and the cardinal value *n*.

§4. *Reconstruction of cardinal correspondence*

The accuracy of the foregoing interpretations can be tested by carrying the experiment further and completely or partially disarranging the series. We shall then see how much of the correspondence the child retains and how he sets about reconstructing it.

As before, the same three stages can be identified. In the first there is no longer correspondence, the series are not reconstructed, and elements are chosen at random. In the second stage there is an effort to solve the problem, but without systematic reseriation or cardination, while in the third the reconstruction is achieved by co-ordination of ordination and cardination.

Here are some examples of the first stage:

Gui (4;6). The series of dolls and sticks had just been mixed up. 'Look. All the dolls smaller than this one (D6) are going to bed now. Put them over there.—(He took D4, 1, 3, 2, 6.)—So which sticks will stay in the cupboard?—(He began by adding doll 7 to the set that were staying at home, then put sticks 1, 2, 4, 6, 3 into the cupboard and left sticks 5, 7, 8, 9, 10 on the table.)—And which dolls are going for a walk?—(He pointed to the set that was left, D5, 8, 9, 10.)—How many sticks are staying in the cupboard?—(He counted) 5.—And how many dolls are staying at home?—6.—Well then?— . . .—(He seemed in no way disturbed by this lack of correspondence.)'

Val (5;6). 'Look. All the dolls smaller than this one (D7) are going for a walk. So which dolls will stay at home?—(He pointed to D9 and 10.)—And which sticks will stay in the cupboard)—(He pointed to S10, 8 and 9.)—And now all the dolls smaller than this one (D5) are going for a walk. Which sticks will stay at home?—(He made the series S10, 9, 8, 7.)—Which sticks will go out?—(He pointed to the rest.)—Which dolls will stay at home?—(He pointed to D9, 10, 8, 7, 6.)'

Rei (5;6). 'All the dolls bigger than this one (D6) are going for a walk. Which sticks will they take?—(He pointed to S10, 9, 8.)—Which dolls are going for a walk?—(D10, 9, 6, 7.)—Now the dolls that have stayed at home are going to play with their balls. Get them ready.—(He made a row of B4, 1, 3, 2, 5, 6.)'

Question IV naturally gives us nothing new at this stage, since neither seriation nor correspondence is as yet spontaneous. With respect to Question V, however, the above reactions provide new confirmation of the evidence we already have as to seriation and serial correspondence on the one hand and the relationship between ordination and cardination on the other.

In the first place we see that when the child is asked to pick out dolls larger or smaller than a given one (D6, for instance), instead of comparing or seriating the other elements so as to divide them into two groups, he makes a general division into two classes, those larger and those smaller, without paying any attention to detail. Thus Gui includes D7 in the set of those smaller than D6, and D5 in the set of those larger than D6, while Val forgets 8 between 7 and 10, and so on. Moreover, when the same children are trying to find the sticks corresponding to these sets, instead of making the correspondence or counting, they again merely make a rough estimate, putting the bigger sticks with the big dolls and the smaller sticks with the small dolls. These reactions fully confirm our earlier findings with regard to seriation and serial correspondence at this stage.

We find, however, in these reactions new and interesting facts with regard to the relationship between cardination and seriation, facts which support our interpretation in the previous paragraph. When the child is required to find the same number of sticks and dolls, the problem is both cardinal and ordinal, which was not the case in the earlier questions, when the series were to be constructed with a given number of sticks and dolls or when the correspondence could be discovered optically. What is most revealing in the present experiment is that although the children are content to make global seriations and serial correspondences they completely disregard cardination and cardinal correspondence. Thus Gui allots five sticks to the six dolls staying at home, and leaves five sticks on the table for the four dolls that are going for a walk. Similarly Val keeps three sticks for two dolls and puts four sticks in the cupboard for the five remaining dolls, while Rei gives three sticks to four dolls, and so on.

It is therefore obvious that absence of spontaneous seriation implies absence of spontaneous cardinal correspondence. We have already seen that absence of seriation implies absence of the notion of preservation or lasting equivalence, and now we find that at this level there is not even spontaneous cardinal correspondence when the child is confronted with a problem of double seriation.

We now come to some examples of the second stage:

Tis (5;6), Question IV: 'Can you tell me now which stick this doll will have (D6)?—*Yes, we must do what we did before* (making the series of dolls, but not of sticks, and immediately giving S5 to D6).—And what about this one (D3)?—*This one* (S3),' etc.

Question V. 'All the dolls smaller than this one (D6) are going for a walk.—(He collected D10, 9, 8, 7, 6, 5, and pointed to D1, 2, 3, 4), saying: *They've gone for a walk*—(he then added D6 and 5 to the set D1–4.)—Now show me the sticks they've taken with them.—*Oh! that's difficult* (he then put S5 with D6, S4 with D5, S3 with D4, S2 with D3 and S1 with D1).—*Oh, there's one missing* (adding S6 and gradually correcting the correspondence by trial and error.—(The sticks were then retrieved, and mixed with the others.)—Now put into the cupboard the sticks of the dolls that are staying at home.—(He put in S10, 9, 8, 7.)—Are you sure?—*Yes, it's all the big ones.*'

Tal (5;5). The dolls were in a series, but the sticks were disarranged. Question IV. When asked for the stick belonging to D7, Tal chose S5, without seriating the sticks. For D10 he chose S10, but again for D7 he

counted 4 (D10, 9, 8, 7), made a row of 4 sticks (S10, 8, 5, 9), and then
pointed to S9 as corresponding to D7!

Question V was however successfully solved, since the dolls were still
seriated. 'How many sticks will stay in the cupboard?—(He counted)
5.—And how many dolls will stay at home?—(Without counting) 5.'

Cha (6;0). The sticks were seriated, but the dolls disarranged.
Question IV: 'Which stick will go with this doll (D6)?' Cha put D10
some distance from the series of sticks, then arranged D9, 8, 7 and 6
after D10, without paying any attention to the sticks. D6 happened
to be opposite S4 and Cha cried: '*It's that one!*—Where's the stick of
this one (D10)?—*There* (S10).—Then where must we put this one
(D10)?—(He put it opposite S10 and then completed the series correctly from D10 to D1.)'

Ora (6;0). The dolls were seriated and the sticks disarranged.
Question IV: 'Can you find the stick belonging to this doll (D4)?—
(He counted 7 dolls, beginning from the 10th, made a row of sticks
1–7, and then pointed to S7.)—And to this one (D6)?—(He counted
the 4 preceding dolls and pointed to the 4th stick from the end, S7).'

Question V: 'Look, All the dolls bigger than that one (D6) are going
for a walk. Which sticks will stay in the cupboard?—(He made the
correspondence from S6 to S10 with D6 to D10 and pointed to the
other sticks.)'

Chou (7;0), Question V: 'All the dolls bigger than that one (D6)
are going for a walk.—(He seriated dolls D6 to D10.)—Put into the
cupboard the sticks that will stay at home.—(He put on one side
S1, 5, 4, then, separately, S10–6, and put away S1, 5, 4, and the
remaining two.)—Count the dolls that are left.—(He made a mistake
and said 6.)—And how many sticks are left?—(He counted 5 and
added stick 6 to make the number correspond with the presumed
number of dolls.)'

We shall begin by analysing the answers to Question V, which
generally speaking is easier than Question IV for reasons that we
shall see later.

The important new element at this stage is the beginning of
relationship between cardination and ordination. In contrast to
the children at the first stage, each of these children knows
beforehand that the number of sticks that will stay in the cupboard is equal to the number of dolls staying at home and that
the rest of the sticks equal in number the dolls going for a walk.
Tis, for instance, when making the second of these correspondences, finds that one doll is without a stick and immediately
looks for it. When Tal counts five sticks in the cupboard, he at
once says that five dolls stayed at home. Chou, who made the
mistake of thinking that six dolls had stayed at home, concluded
that there should be six sticks in the cupboard and therefore
added one. There is no contradiction between this result and the
fact that at this stage cardinal equivalences are ephemeral (as we

saw in Chapters III and IV and in §3 of the present chapter). Here it is not a matter of comparison between two displaced series, but merely of stating that it is possible for the child to re-make the correspondence once it has been destroyed.

In order to solve problem V, all that is necessary is to divide the dolls into two groups, those 'larger than or equal to n' and 'those smaller than n' (or those 'larger than n' and those 'smaller than or equal to n') and to do the same in the case of the sticks. This does not however imply the existence of the operational system in which each new position represents one more cardinal unit, and vice versa. It merely means that two series or sections of series that are in serial correspondence are also in cardinal correspondence. This distinction is important, for in the second case the only relations of order the child requires are those of the two groups 'greater than or equal to n' and 'smaller than n'. For example, Tis collects the sticks that are longer than S6 and says 'it's all the big ones'; Ora, having seriated sticks S6 to S10 promptly puts the remainder into the cupboard, and Chou does likewise. What the child actually does, therefore, is to estimate by numeration the elements contained in the classes, without proceeding from the ordinal to the cardinal numbers, since at this stage he is incapable of grasping the direct relationship between these two, as we shall see from the difficulties he encounters in tackling Question IV.

The attempts of children at this stage to relate the cardinal and ordinal aspects of correspondence are as yet only intuitive, and take four different forms:

(1) The child either merely makes a guess at the correspondence or orders one of the series and then makes a guess at its correspondence with the other. This is what Tis does, making a mistake with S5 and D6, but getting the right answer in the case of the extreme elements. The child is here making use of implicit co-seriation that is purely qualitative.

(2) The child uses cardination but ignores ordination (cf. the case of Jen, Chapter VI §3). Tal provides a good illustration of this. In order to find the stick corresponding to doll 7, he counts dolls 10, 9, 8, 7, which gives him 4, then looks for four sticks, which he certainly chooses from among the bigger ones, but in arbitrary order (10, 8, 5, 9) and then points to stick 9 as the right one, since it came last and must therefore correspond to D7! Yet Tal was able to solve problem V correctly, which proves that the two questions are not directly related.

(3) The child makes use of ordination, or rather seriation, and ignores cardination, and thus arrives at a correspondence which again is not correct. Cha, for example, in order to find the stick belonging to doll 6 when the sticks are already seriated, seriates

dolls 10, 9, etc., down to 6, but without putting them opposite the sticks, and chooses S4 to correspond with D6 because they happen to be opposite one another.

(4) The child uses ordination and cardination simultaneously, but still does not co-ordinate the position of the element looked for with the cardinal number of the set of elements. Ora, for instance, in the case of doll 6, counts the four preceding dolls starting from D10 (10, 9, 8, 7), then points to S7, i.e. the last of four sticks also counted starting from 10. This is the same type of mistake as we found earlier with regard to Questions II and III at stage two.

These four methods of procedure show clearly that the child is attempting to reconcile order with cardinal value, but is incapable of keeping both in mind at the same time. When he is thinking of the cardinal value, he forgets the position (method 2), when he is thinking of the position he forgets the cardinal number (method 3), and when he is taking both into account he is unable to keep them together when he comes to the detail (method 4). What he has learnt since the first stage is this: if there are ten dolls of different heights, each having a stick of appropriate length, the total number of sticks will also be 10, and if the five tallest dolls go out with their sticks, these sticks will be the five longest of the set. What he has not yet grasped is that the stick corresponding to the nth doll will not only be the nth in the series of sticks, but will also form with the preceding ones a set whose cardinal number is n, or to put it more simply, that the nth element must be the last of a series of n elements. It might seem that the second of these statements is implied in the first, but this is not so. Between the two there are two essential differences, one related to the logical structure of the operations and the other to their psychological mechanism.

From the logical point of view, problem V can be satisfactorily solved by qualitative logic. In the first place, seriation of the dolls or sticks is merely a question of asymmetrical qualitative relationships, each element being seen as different from all the others, and the relationship that distinguishes two elements also being different from all the others. Secondly, the construction of sets 'greater than or equal to n' and 'smaller than n' merely involves defining two classes, in each of which any one element is equivalent to any other (e.g., when Tis says 'it's all the big ones' any one of these big ones is for him equivalent to any other), though obviously each sub-class differs from any other by its peculiar qualities that make seriation possible. Thirdly, the total class of dolls is composed of the class of those 'smaller than n' plus the class of those 'greater than or equal to n'. And lastly, the equivalence between the class of dolls 'smaller than n' and the class of sticks 'smaller than n' can be obtained merely by simple qualitative correspondence between elementary classes, since the two classes have the same extension, or to put it more concretely, each doll has its stick. Problem IV, however, or rather the understanding of the fact that the nth doll must be the last term of a set of n dolls, presupposes disregard of qualities and consideration of each element as being at the same time equivalent to, but different in position from, any other, the difference between any one position and the next also being equivalent to any other. In other words, it presupposes that each element is considered both as an element of a class and of a relationship, not alternatively and separately as in the preceding system, but simultaneously, forming one and the same operational whole, and this, it will be remembered, is our definition of number.

Corresponding to this logical opposition there is the following psychological difference. Problem V, since it depends only on qualitative logic, can be solved intuitively, because (i) qualitative seriation is intuitively achieved at this stage, (ii) the classes in question can easily be defined intuitively, (iii) the division of a class into two sub-classes can easily be made intuitively, and (iv) qualitative correspondence between the classes in question is at this stage frequently made intuitively. In the case of problem IV, however, the numerical operations used by our subjects cannot be carried out intuitively and involve operational co-ordination. That is why children at this stage fail to find a correct solution and it is only when they reach the third stage that they succeed without difficulty. We have here further confirmation of the fact that qualitative serial correspondence can be mastered during the second stage when it can be done intuitively, whereas generalization of qualitative operations and construction of ordinal correspondence, which require a strictly operational mechanism, particularly in the case of co-ordination between cardinal and ordinal numbers, are reserved for the third stage. Our general conclusion, therefore, is that stage two is characterized by the beginnings, but only the beginnings, of co-ordination between ordination and cardination.

During the third stage, however, as we shall now see, not only is problem V solved immediately, but also spontaneously correct results are achieved with problem IV, sometimes after trial and error, because ordinal correspondence is in its final stage, essentially linked with the progress in cardination already analysed in Chapters III and IV. Here are some examples of stage three:

Shen (6;6), Question V: 'The dolls bigger than that one (D5) are going for a walk. Put the sticks that will stay at home into the cupboard.—(Shen looked carefully at the dolls, then took sticks 1, 2, 3, 4, 5 and put them into the cupboard.)—How many dolls are staying at home?—*5.*—How do you know?—*I counted them from 1 to 5.*—This doll (D5) is going for a walk too.—*Then there'll be 4 sticks at home.* (He went to get a stick from the cupboard.)—What are you doing?—*I'm finding the one that must come out* (He seriated the sticks and took out S5).'

Shen had counted the dolls from 1 to 5, and was then asked: 'Which is the biggest?—*The last* (D10).—We could call it the first as well, couldn't we?—*Yes.*—And what about this one (D9)?—*The second.*—And this one (D8)?—*The third* . . . etc.—If we say that a doll is the fourth, how many are there in front of it?—*3.*—And in front of the eighth?—*7.*—How do you know?—*I counted in my head how many were left.*'

Question IV: 'Which doll will this stick (S5) go with?—*That one* (D5).—Why?—*I counted in my head* (pointing at D10–5 and S10–5).'

Vig (6;6), Question IV: 'Which stick will go with this doll (D7)?— (Vig seriated D10, 9, 8, and pointed to S8, but went on with the series and about the middle said: *No, it's that one* (S7) *because they've all got their sticks.*' In other words, he corrected his mistake by co-ordinating position and cardination. 'And with this one (D6)?—*That one* (S6).—How did you find it?—*I looked to see how many there are.*'

Co-ordination between the order and the cardinal number is thus completed. Vig, who begins by giving S8 to D7, thus making the mistake of the second stage, spontaneously corrects himself by using the principle of cardinal correspondence. As for Shen, not only is he prepared to reverse the order of his own numbering (which proves that for him position has become relative), but he also understands that, whatever the order, there are always seven elements before the eighth, etc. Ordinal correspondence is therefore acquired on the operational level, owing to its fusion with cardination.

CHAPTER VI

ORDINATION AND CARDINATION[1]

OUR examination of serial correspondence, or qualitative similarity, and ordinal correspondence, or similarity generalized to any succession of units, has led to the hypothesis that ordination always involves cardination, and vice versa, and this conclusion is in line with the one we reached when analysing the origin of cardinal correspondence.

How indeed, in the case of correspondence with necessary and lasting equivalence between two sets, does the child succeed in attributing a cardinal value to these sets even when he has no clearly defined numbers at his disposal? He does so by arranging the terms in two corresponding rows, i.e. by seriating. And how is he able to distinguish the different units which come 'one after the other'? He can do so because the second makes with the first something more than the first by itself, the third makes with the first two a still larger set, and so on. It is only when each element is combined with the preceding ones that its position can be determined, just as it is only their position that differentiates the units, which in other respects are all equivalent.

Moreover, at the second stage, when one-one correspondence does not yet lead to the notion of necessary equivalence, ordination and cardination are equally interdependent, but as it were negatively so. If indeed the sum of the terms is not seen to be constant it follows, as we saw in the previous chapter, that there cannot be correspondence between the position of the elements of one set and those of the other.

Can we find a psychological proof of this interdependence of ordination and cardination which has already been stressed by Brunschvicg, Arn, Reymond and others from the point of view of mathematical logic? Our analysis of the various types of correspondence seems to show that we can, but it still remains to see the child's reactions when the problem involves counting aloud, with, of course, the aid of concrete material susceptible of being both seriated and evaluated cardinally. We have made three types of experiment in this field. The simplest consists in merely getting the child to seriate sticks representing the steps of a staircase and to

[1] In collaboration with Mlle Zahara Glikin.

estimate the number of steps already climbed and then, after breaking up the series and picking out one of the steps, asking him to estimate how many steps would have been climbed when that one was reached. The second consists in getting the child to seriate cards shaped in such a way that the second is twice as big as the first, the third three times as big as the first, and so on, and then, having disarranged the cards and picked out one at random, asking him into how many units it can be divided. The third consists in getting him to seriate hurdles of varying heights, separated by mats in such a way that there are $n + 1$ mats for n hurdles, and then, having disarranged the material, asking either on how many mats a gymnast vaulting over one of the hurdles would have landed, or to which hurdle a given number of mats corresponds. We shall examine the results of these experiments in this chapter and shall then draw a general conclusion with respect to ordination by comparing them with the results of our analysis of ordinal correspondence in Chapters V and VI.

§1. The experiment with sticks and the problem of seriation

In the previous chapter we touched on the problem of seriation, but the experiment with the sticks, in which the questions put to the child can be to some extent modified, will provide us with a certain amount of additional data. It is therefore useful to take up the problem again as an introduction to that of numerical ordination itself.

The technique used is the following. The child is given a set of ten little sticks of varying lengths and is asked to form the series from the shortest (A) to the longest (K). When this has been done, he is given, one at a time and in any order, nine more sticks (which we shall call a–i). He is told that these had been forgotten and are now to be inserted in their right places.[1]

We then get the series: AaBbCcDdEeFfGgHhIiKk. The child is then asked to count all the elements of the series, including the inserted sticks, and then a number of elements corresponding to a figure with which he is familiar is left in front of him. If, for instance, his counting became hesitant after ten, eight sticks would be left, and so on. Pointing to one of the sticks, we then ask the child how many stairs a doll will have climbed when it reaches that point (the action can either be indicated by a gesture or by making a little doll go from one stick to another as though going upstairs). We also ask how many steps are behind the doll and how

---

[1] The sticks A, B, C, etc., differ in length by about 0·8 cm., and the sticks a, b, c, etc., differ from A, B, C, etc., by about 0·4 cm., the complete set ranging from about 9 to 16 cm.

many it will need to climb to reach the top of the stairs. Finally, the series of sticks is disarranged and the same questions as before are put to the child, who is then obliged to reconstruct the series before replying.

There are three distinct stages in the seriation of the sticks (Questions I and II). First comes a period during which the child always fails to make the complete series, even for A–K, succeeding only in making several short series which he puts side by side without regard to the order of the whole series. Or else he succeeds in building the staircase, but only considers the top of each stick, and disregards the base, and thus the total length of each element, so that his staircase is only regular at the top, and as the sticks are not placed in a horizontal line they are not in the correct order of size. In the second stage, the child succeeds, by trial and error, in making a correct staircase, but has not acquired a system of relationships by means of which error is eliminated and extra sticks can be inserted at once in their right place. In the third stage, each element is without hesitation placed in a position in which it is at the same time bigger than the preceding elements and smaller than those which follow.

With regard to the relations between ordination and cardination (Questions III and IV) we again find three stages, corresponding broadly to those we have just seen. In the first the child does not understand that in order to estimate how many stairs the doll has climbed, starting from the smallest A, he must calculate the position of the stick N in question, and his estimate is purely arbitrary. In the second stage, he gradually understands that he needs to reconstruct the staircase but thinks he must include the whole series, from A to stick N and from N to K, as if the elements above N were as useful in determining the position of N as those below. The distinctive characteristic of children at this stage is their difficulty in dissociating a section of a series from the whole, or they frequently confuse elements A to N (the stairs already climbed) with elements N to K (those still to be climbed). In the third stage the child understands that he only needs to consider the section A to N in order to determine the position of N and that this position corresponds to the number of stairs already climbed.

Here we have two examples of the first stage, showing failure to seriate and consequently complete lack of understanding of the relations between ordination and cardination:

Lil (4;0) I: 'Show me the smallest step.—(She pointed to the right one.)—Now find one that's a tiny bit bigger than that one. (She picked out a big one and put it next to A.)—Show me the biggest.—(She pointed at random to a big one without attempting to compare it with the others.)—Now try to put first the smallest, then one a little bit bigger, then another a little bit bigger, and so on.—(Lil took I and put it next to A, then E, then H, etc., regardless of order.)—We put them like this, look (A, B, C). They make a kind of staircase. Now you go on.—(Lil continued with K, F, D, I, G, disregarding the order.) *Like that?*' Having reached this point Lil discovered a procedure, characteristic of this stage, for making a staircase. She took stick B, then stick H, but made the top of B project slightly beyond that of H without paying any attention to the base. She then added K, F, D, I, G, etc., making a series only with the tops.—She was then asked to begin again, but with a ruler as base to ensure that the sticks were placed horizontally. She made the series A, C, H, G, E. This was disarranged and the whole staircase constructed and then broken up, and Lil was asked to remake it. She placed the sticks in the order A, B, C, D, H, F, E, G.

III: No estimate was possible.

Eli (4;0) I: 'Show me the smallest step.—(He pointed to the right one.)—And the biggest?—(He pointed to one of the big ones.)—Now arrange them (giving him indications that they should make a kind of staircase.)—He put A, B, G, K, H, etc., and then arranged A, B, K, etc., so that the tops made a staircase but the bases were ignored. After various attempts of this kind, he was shown how to make a staircase with a horizontal base. This was then disarranged and Eli tried to reconstruct it, the result being A, I, H, F, D. When asked to count the sticks, he counted 1, 2, 3, 5, 10, 3, 14, etc.

The reactions of these children clearly indicate that they had not yet reached the stage of even intuitive seriation. It is true that very early on, even just after the appearance of sensory-motor intelligence at about ten to twelve months, the child is capable of arranging three objects, e.g. three bricks, in order of size, just as he is capable of distinguishing that these three objects constitute 'more' than two objects, and this is a beginning of cardination. But just as, from the cardinal point of view, the child of 3 or 4 is still unable to decide whether there are more beans in a set of twenty or in a set of twenty-five because he cannot yet make a one-one correspondence between the elements of these sets and cannot make a global estimate of their respective contents, so, from the ordinal point of view, the same child will be incapable of seriating cubes or sticks when their number exceeds a certain limit or when the difference in size or length is so slight as to make systematic comparison impossible in view of the number of elements. We therefore make no claim that children such as Lil or Eli are entirely incapable of any seriation or that they are at a pre-serial stage in the absolute sense of the term. We merely assert that as far as the problem in question is concerned, that of the ten original sticks and the nine to be inserted, these children failed to make any regular seriation without help, and were thus at a pre-serial level as regards this particular problem. As for cardination, it follows that they could not estimate the number of elements in sets of more than two or three objects, since numeration implies ordination. Eli, for example, repeated the number three twice in his attempts at counting. There was therefore no possible relation between ordination and cardination.

It is however of interest to enquire what prevents such children from making a staircase series, the most intuitive of all, since such difficulties, which to some extent persist, can throw light on the later stages, the beginnings of the ordinal period proper.

The first point to be noted is that while these children can at once point out the smallest stick, they choose any big stick when asked which is the biggest, as if the biggest was a stick big in itself, independently of its relationship to the other sticks. This first reaction provides us with useful evidence. When the child at this level is attempting to find the position of one of the sticks, he apparently does not compare it with the whole set or with the remaining elements, but seems merely to look for one that is 'big' in relation to the first one or to one of the 'small' ones. In the second place, a series implies a stable direction in the relationship between the elements and this also appears to be lacking.

At a given moment, however, the child discovers how to build a staircase by taking into account only the tops of the sticks and ignoring the base. In this way the two preceding conditions are partially fulfilled, but since the total length of the sticks is left out of consideration, there is no need to compare each one to those still to be arranged or to the one before it, according to a constant progression. Thus a configuration which is purely intuitive takes the place of the system of relationships. In such a case it is therefore not possible to speak of ordination in the true sense, just as a heap as such in no way involves true colligation, but may be merely a global, unanalysed evaluation. A staircase in which only the tops of the sticks are correctly placed thus merely represents a transition stage between pre-ordinal confusion and ordination, and it is achieved by means of a perceptual structure. Similarly, in the case of cardination, the child makes the transition from global evaluation to one-one correspondence by a comparison of figures which he has only more or less analysed.

We come now to some examples of the second stage, the first being an interesting case intermediary between the first and second stages, and showing the transition from pre-relative judgement to empirical seriation:

Cla (4;6) I. He began by pointing out the smallest and the biggest of the sticks, then, without arranging the others on the same horizontal base, made two series, related to A and K. On the left he put the small ones A, C, F, D, E, G, B, H, and on the right, after removing G from the other set, he put the big ones, G. I, K. He then corrected himself, putting A, C, H, F, then A, B, C, H, E, F, D, then A, B, C, D, E, F, H, and added the elements G, I, K, after H. He then brought the bases into line, corrected the end to F, G, I, K, H, changed the three last into D, H, G, then into F, H, K and finally discovered the correct arrangement. We intervened in no way, except to ask after each arrangement: 'Is that right?'

II. In inserting the extra sticks, he put *d* between C and D, then after E, before B and finally in its correct place before E. He placed *a* correctly, then put *f* between B and C, etc.

III. After this, he was asked to count the sticks and all were taken away except A*a* B*b*C*c*D*d*. Cla understood Question IV. The 8 sticks were then disarranged and he was asked: 'If the doll is here (*b*), how many steps are there behind it?—*2, because that one (a) is behind it.* —How many steps has it climbed.—*2, no 3* (he put A, B and *a* in front of *b*).—How many steps has it still to climb?—(He counted the empty space after *b*) *8.*—Why 8?—*Because there are 8 altogether.*—(The sticks were again disarranged.)—Look, it's there (C). How many steps has it climbed?—(He built up the whole staircase and counted) *4.*—How many has it still to climb?—*10, no 3.*'

Vot (4;10) I. He at once indicated the smallest stick, but picked out H at random as being the biggest, then arranged his series without taking into account the need for a common base: A, H then A, B, H then A, B, C, D, E, F, G, H, I, K.

II. He put *g* before K. He put *c* in place of A, then inserted it correctly. He put *g* between C and D then *i* between H and I, etc.

III. When the whole series had been correctly arranged, 8 elements were kept and Vot understood Question IV. But when the sticks were disarranged, he thought that the doll on *b* had climbed steps *a*, *d*, and D, etc. 'How many has it still to climb?—(He counted 8.)'

San (5;0) I. He chose correctly the smallest and biggest sticks then arranged A, B, C. When he came to D, he compared it with each of the others in turn, even the biggest, and put it after C. Sticks E–K were then seriated with some trial and error, the corrections being made in the series itself.

II. He correctly inserted *i* before K, then compared *e* to E, F, D, E, then to all the others in the row before putting it in position. He did the same with *g*. When he had put *h* before G he cried: '*No, that's not right, it's too difficult.*'

III. He counted correctly up to 9. Eight elements were left and he counted them correctly.

IV. The sticks were disarranged and San pointed to steps A, *b* and B as having been climbed when the doll had got to C (forgetting *a*). For the steps preceding D he reconstructed the whole staircase, and for the steps still to be climbed he pointed to the whole series.

Bru (5;6) I. After some trial and error he arranged the correct series from A to K.

II. In order to insert *h* he moved K, I, H then put it in the right place. For *g* he removed G, put *g* before H, removed E, put G after F, etc. Similarly, he began by putting *e* before E, then after F.

III. Correct replies up to 8.

IV. Sticks disarranged. Bru was at a loss to discover how many steps there were before C: he took *d* and put it first before and then after C, put A before C, then made the whole series. 'How many has it already climbed?—*5* (correct)—And how many has it still to climb?—*8*.'

Dit (5;6). I. He began by making a series of unrelated pairs AB, HG, EF, IC, DK and finally made the correct series except for H, which he added afterwards.

II. Great difficulty: he put *h* after K, *g* after H, *d* between C and D, etc. Finally he put A, *a*, B, *b*, C, *c*, *d*, D, E, *e*, F, *f*, H, *g*, G, I, *h*, K, *i*. 'Is your staircase a good one?—*No, not very*.' He gradually corrected it. Suddenly he saw that *d* was too small for the position he had given it and merely moved it along a few millimetres.

III. Correct up to 8.

IV. Sticks disarranged. Step B was indicated and Dit replied correctly without making the series that 2 steps had already been climbed. 'How many still remain to be climbed?—(He made the series.)—Can you tell without arranging them?—*11 perhaps* (showing that he had not counted the 5 remaining sticks).—And if there were 11 altogether and the doll was on the third, this one (B), how many would it have to climb before getting to the top?—*It would have to climb 11 more*.'

Finally we have two examples of children who succeeded in giving the correct answer when asked how many steps remained to be climbed, but did so by using the empirical method characteristic of this stage:

Mic (5;8). I. Successful, with some corrections.

II. He put *e* between D and E, then corrected himself. He put *i* after H, etc., but corrected himself each time before going on.

III. Correct up to 8.

IV. With the 8 steps disarranged, in order to find out how many there were before D he counted the empty spaces previously occupied on the table, decided that there were 7, then looked for the sticks smaller than D and finally made the whole series and gave the correct answer 6. When the doll was on C, Mic counted correctly 5 preceding steps, but for those still to be climbed he thought he needed to seriate them instead of merely counting how many were left.

Chal (5;10). I and II as in the earlier cases.

III. Correct up to 10.

IV. (Sticks disarranged.) To count the steps before D, he seriated A*a*B*b*C*c*, and then put *d*, E. 'How many has it climbed then?—*6* (correct).—And how many steps have to be climbed from this one (G)?—(He made the whole series and counted correctly.)'

These few examples indicate the general trend of the evolution that takes place during the second stage, i.e. between the level at which the child is incapable of seriating sticks A–K (stage I) and that at which he can make the series without hesitating, including the insertion of the extra elements (stage III). From the point of view of seriation, this second stage is still very homogeneous. Each of the children succeeded, after trial and error, but without help, in constructing the series A–K. Moreover, once the first series had been made, none of the children was able to insert the extra sticks without mistakes and continual trial and error. The present level appears to be characterized by this opposition between success with the first series and failure to insert new elements, and we shall see its consequences in the relationship between ordination and cardination.

First of all, how do these children succeed in seriating the ten sticks supplied simultaneously at the beginning of the experiment, whereas children at the first stage fail to do so? As we saw in Chapter V (§2), for seriation to be possible it is logically necessary that each element should be chosen as being at the same time the smallest of those that are left and bigger than those that have gone before. It involves therefore on the one hand relating each term to the rest, and on the other, following a constant direction in this co-ordination. For instance, Cla and Vot, who begin like children at the first stage, the one by dividing the sticks into 'big' and 'small' as if the series were not continuous, and the other by picking out one of the big ones (H) at random as being the biggest, succeed eventually in forming the series by means of a number of rearrangements and corrections which seem to imply these relations. Similarly San provides the clearest evidence of this dawning of relativity when, after seriating A, B, C, he compares D with all the other elements, measuring it against each one, even the biggest. On the other hand, the fact that the construction of a series requires not only that each element shall be related to the others but also that the directions in which the comparisons are made shall be constant, is clearly shown in the case of Dit, who proceeds by heterogeneous pairs and has to adjust them later on to form a single series.

This twofold progress is, however, limited, in comparison with the method characteristic of the third stage. When San, for instance, conscientiously compares element D with each of the others, though he is certainly more advanced than children at the first stage, it is clear that each of his measurements involves a series of others. It is even clearer in the case of Dit, when he makes his pairs, and generally speaking the trial and error of these various children gives the impression that what is lacking at this level is simultaneous co-ordination of the whole. The series is constructed step by step, not grasped as a logical act 'grouping' all the relations. The reason for this is obvious: these children merely use intuition instead of logical order, i.e. perceptual comparison instead of operation. All that is in fact necessary, if one is incapable of making an additive or multiplicative connection between each detail and all the others, is to construct a configuration through trial and error. This is exactly what was done by the more advanced children at the first stage when they constructed the staircase taking into account only the tops of the sticks. The children at the second stage do the same thing, but take into consideration the length of each stick, and the figure thus becomes analytic and precise, but it is still no more than the intuitive equivalent of an operational series.

The best proof that it is no more than this can be seen in the difficulty experienced by the child in inserting the extra elements *a–i* in the initial series. It is a remarkable phenomenon, which appears to be constant, that the construction of a series is easier than the insertion of new elements. The children who have the least difficulty in solving the first problem (Mic and Chal for instance), make several mistakes in inserting *a–i*, and those who like Cla, Vot and Dit have greater difficulty with the first series make bad mistakes when it comes to the insertion. San, who as we have seen made a systematic comparison for the series A–K, put *h* before G (an error of four places) and finally cried 'No, that's not right, it's too difficult'. The fact is that the insertion of a new element presupposes operations of relationship much less susceptible of being replaced by intuition than those involved in the construction of the straightforward initial series. There is first of all a perceptual problem: a completed figure constitutes a closed configuration and it is therefore more difficult to compare a new element with those already forming part of this global structure than to measure it against isolated elements. But this perceptual difference shows that while the construction of a series can be merely intuitive, insertion cannot be so. In order to form the series without logical co-ordination properly so called, all that is needed is to place *successively*: the smallest of all + the smallest of those that are left + . . . etc., whereas in order to place X in the series $A < B < C$ . . . it must be inserted between X and Y in such a way that *at the same time* (and the expression 'at the same time' must here be taken as having its true meaning of psychological simultaneity) $x > X$ and $x < Y$. This co-ordination of two relations cannot be a matter of mere perception, since X and Y are not given (as is the case when the child has already placed A B C and looks for D only in relation to the remaining elements) but must be determined at the same time and in relation to one another. It should be added that the best proof that this problem is not exclusively perceptual is that the child not only makes mistakes in inserting *a–i* (which is in no way surprising) but is also satisfied with his incorrect results. Vot, for instance, made no attempt to correct his insertions without suggestion. Similarly, as long as there was no adult intervention Dit was satisfied with the series C*ed*D and H*g*GI*hki*, and Mic with the series D*e*E. It is no longer a question of perception, since it would be easy to rearrange the incorrect series. The fact that the child does not do so means that he feels that he is confronted by a new and baffling problem.

If we now look at the relations between ordination and cardination we find an exactly parallel situation. It is only in so far as seriation becomes operational, i.e. in so far as it is based on simultaneous co-ordination of all the relationships, or more precisely on their 'grouping', that the child can combine cardination and ordination. Until this is so, position is merely qualitative for the child, and does not involve a definite number of elements. Thus, between the cases of Cla and Vot on the one hand and Mic and Cha on the other, we can see a continuous evolution taking place, from almost complete lack of understanding to the ability to find empirically the correct solution (after considerable trial and error).

It must be remembered that at this stage all children can indicate correctly how many steps have been climbed, how many are below the doll, and how many it still has to climb, provided that the series is not disarranged (Question III). This proves nothing as far as the relations between ordination and cardination are concerned: it is merely perceptual reading of a situation by means of counting aloud and does not involve operations proper. It is when the series is disarranged that the extent of the child's understanding becomes clear. What is extraordinary is that, although he recognizes the questions he has just been asked for test III, he now fails to give the correct answers.

Yet Cla, Vot and San were able to reconstruct short series of two or three sticks as early as the lowest level of this stage, which proves that they understood the sense of the questions. Cla knew, for instance, that when the doll was at B it had climbed steps A, *a* and B, and San said that when it was at C, steps A, B and *b* were behind it (forgetting *a*). But although they could grasp this intuitively in the case of short series, they were apparently unable to divide the whole series into two sections separated by the step reached by the doll. Cla and Vot, for instance, who knew that at *b* the doll had climbed three steps, counted the eight terms of the series to discover how many steps remained to be climbed. Bru and Dit, who were at the medium level, understood without difficulty that the number of steps already climbed depended on the present position of the doll, but although Bru counted correctly that it had climbed five steps when it was at C, he could not say how many remained to be climbed and counted the whole series. We must again insist, to avoid any misunderstanding, that these children gave correct answers to the same questions when the series was undisturbed, and that it was only when it was disarranged that they were baffled. As for Mic and Cha, who were on the border-line between stages II and III, they succeeded in solving the problem only by constructing the whole series of steps, including those that had already been climbed.

The explanation of these difficulties becomes clear when we look at the way the child constructs his series. In so far as the seriation is truly operational, i.e. with simultaneous co-ordination of all the relations, it is clear that each element arranged according to its height is conceived as being at the same time longer than those that precede it and shorter than those that follow. Hence, when this qualitative seriation, which has become operational, has to be translated into terms of ordination and cardination, that is to say, when the position of a given term has to correspond to the sum of the preceding terms, the relations involved in the construction of the series will ensure that the series can always be seen to be divisible into two sections, the one beginning at A and ending with the given element N, the other extending from the element N to the final element T. Two facts are then evident: the ordinal number N can be translated into a cardinal number N representing the sum of the elements A to N, and the second section is equal to the cardinal number T (corresponding to position T) less terms A to N, i.e. T–N. When however the series has not been constructed through operational co-ordination of relations, but simply by means of a succession of perceptual connections, this intuitive seriation is untranslatable in terms of numerical ordination and cardination, the one depending on the other, because the series cannot be divided.

By concentrating on this contrast between intuitive, qualitative series and qualitative or numerical operational series, it is quite easy to understand why the child has more difficulty in counting the steps still to be climbed than in counting those already climbed. Since an intuitive series is merely a juxtaposition of perceptual relationships, the child finds it relatively easy, when he sees the doll on step N, to reconstruct the series A . . . N, i.e. to seriate qualitatively the steps already climbed, and then count them. The steps still to be climbed, however, involve the complex relation A . . . $<$N$<$ . . . T, i.e. the co-ordination (both additive and subtractive) of the two inverse relations N$>$ . . . A and N $<$ . . . T, which in terms of cardination becomes the subtraction T − N and no longer the simple additive series A . . . N. This fact explains the difficulty experienced by Dit in understanding the relation $8 - 5 = 3$ and in counting the remaining sticks without reconstructing the whole staircase. Generally speaking, this is the explanation of why the child succeeds in translating his qualitative seriation into ordinal and cardinal numbers as long as the series is intact and visible, but is baffled as soon as it is disarranged, every intuitive series varying between rigidity and chaos.

The child's difficulty in translating a position into a number once the series is broken up is thus comparable to the difficulty he finds in inserting new elements into a completed series, and the ease with which he counts the terms of the visible series is comparable to the ease with which he makes an intuitive series of sticks. In both cases there is the same opposition between semi-operational intuition and operations proper which give to the number a reality based on rational relations. To conclude, then, we find that these results confirm and complete the interpretations at which we arrived after our analysis of ordinal correspondence.

Finally, we have two examples of the third and last stage, which is characterized by grasp of the operations involving both the logic of number and that of seriation of asymmetric relations:

Sin (6;0). I. He at once arranged the series A, B, C, D, F, then replaced F by E and continued with F, G, H, I, K.

II. He was asked to put c in position. He measured it against C and placed it correctly on the right of C. He then measured d against D and put it also in the correct position. He placed i correctly between K and I, and so on, making 9 successive insertions without a mistake.

III. Correct.

IV (with the 19 sticks disarranged): 'If the doll is there (c), how many steps has it climbed?—(Sin began by assessing with his finger on stick c the presumed heights of the preceding sticks, then tried to count the presumed positions in the space A–c, but without putting A in position, and finally said) *I'll have to put the staircase back*. (He arranged the sticks before c.)—Well now, how many has it climbed?—*6*.—Which one is it on?—*The sixth*.—How many steps are behind it?—*5* (without counting).—How many has it still to climb?—(He counted the remaining sticks without attempting to arrange them and gave the correct answer) *13*.—And when it's on this one (F) which one is it on? —(He arranged the staircase as far as F.) *The eleventh* (correct).'

Ald (6;6). I–III. He constructed the series A–K immediately, inserted the extra elements almost without hesitation and clearly understood the questions related to the number of steps when the series was unbroken. IV. The 19 sticks were disarranged: 'Look, the doll is here (f). How many steps has it climbed?—(Ald began like Sin in the case of (c), and then said *I'll have to arrange them as far as that* (he did so). *That makes 12*.—How many steps are behind it?—(Without counting.) *11*—And how many has it still to climb?—(He counted the scattered sticks without arranging them and gave the correct answer,) 7.'

The contrast between these reactions and those of the second stage is obvious. Although from the point of view of the initial seriation A–K all the gradations between the two stages are to be found (cf. the misplacement of one element by Sin) the difference in behaviour with regard to the extra elements to be inserted is characteristic. Whereas children at the second stage consider these elements almost as foreign bodies, Sin and Ald react to them as to the others, compare them, measure them if necessary, and place them in position keeping in mind simultaneously the relationships > and <. Let us note that such progress cannot take place unless the child has penetrated deeply into the relationship between ordination and cardination.

It is in fact quite clear that these children know immediately, without testing it, that the number of steps climbed or still to be climbed is determined by the position of the stick on which the doll is placed. Whether they try to count the number of preceding sticks by studying the height of the stick in question, or by calculating the empty places or by actually reseriating the sticks, the principle is the same. But the best evidence of their understanding of the relation between the ordinal and the cardinal number is to be found in the fact that once the steps already climbed have been reseriated and counted, the children feel no need to reseriate the remainder in order to discover how many steps remain to be climbed. They grasp perfectly that the number of steps to be climbed is represented by the number of sticks left scattered on the table. In other words, having reconstructed the series A . . . N, the child understands that the steps N . . . T are represented by the subtraction T – N or (A . . . T) – (A . . . N). That is why Sin and Ald merely count the remaining sticks: thirteen and seven. This apparently simple reaction is in reality quite new and is an indication that the child has reached a level where both logical and numerical operations are possible. It should be noted, in support of what we have just seen, that these children know at once, without counting, that the number of steps behind the doll is equal to (N – 1), thus showing that they understand that the Nth position corresponds to a cardinal value N which is at the same time greater than that of the elements A . . . (N – 1) and less than that of the elements (N + 1 . . . T) and that it therefore lies between these two sections.

§2. The experiment with cards forming a staircase

We have as material a square of cardboard A, representing one unit, a rectangle B the same width but twice as high (thus representing two units), a rectangle C representing three units (same width as A but three times as high), etc. Thus A = 1; B = 2A; C = 3A; D = 4A; E = 5A; F = 6A; G = 7A; H = 8A; J = 9A; and K = 10A. The cards therefore form a staircase, but one which is based on a construction of units and not on arbitrary relations like the staircase in §1.

We begin by asking the child to make the series himself so that he may grasp the principle of this ordination, and then get him to count the cards as far as he can without hesitating. He is then asked: 'How many cards like A could we make with (B) or (C), etc.', until he understands that the second card can be cut up into 2A, the third into 3A, and so on. Once this is grasped, a card is picked out at random ((F) for instance), the staircase remaining in position, and the child is asked how many units this card represents. It is the child's solution to this third type of question that interests us here. If he can at once make F's cardinal value six correspond with its position (sixth), it is clear that he has grasped the relation between ordination and cardination. If, however, he needs to measure each time how many times A goes into E, F, etc., we shall be justified in stating that this correspondence has not yet been grasped. We find three stages, corresponding to those of §1. In the first, seriation is still global and the relation between order and cardination is not understood beyond three or four, even when the order A→K is followed. In the second stage, intuitive seriation gives a correct result after trial and error, and the relation between ordination and cardinal value is understood provided that the order is followed, but not when the cards are mixed. In the third stage, the last question also is successfully solved. Here are some examples of the first stage:

Tes (4;6) seriated the cards correctly as far as D, then made the mistakes typical of this level. He could count up to 15. 'How many cards like that one (A) could we make with this one (B)?—*Two.*—And with that one (C)?—*Four . . . No, it's the same as those* (B + A). (Counting.) *One, two, three, three, it makes three.*—And with that one (D)?— (He counted with his finger.) *Four.*—etc.—And with that one (J = 9)?— (He counted again, following with his finger imaginary sections of the card.) *1, 2 . . . 8.*—And with that one (C)?—*1, 2 . . . 5.*—And with that one (C again)?—*That makes 4 cards.*'

Fiv (5;0) also merely made a global seriation, which we then corrected with him. He counted them correctly. 'How many cards like this one (A) could we make with that one (B)?—*Two.*—And with that one (C)?—*Three.*—And with that one (D)?—*Five.*—Why?— . . . — How can we see that that one (D) is bigger than this one (C)?—*By that* (pointing to the difference in height).—How many more are there each time?—*One.*—Then how many cards like this one (A) can we make with that one (D)?—*Five, no two.*—How many?—(He counted the whole series from A to K.) *1, 2 . . . 10.*—Then how many cards can we make with this one (A)?—*One.*—And with this one (B)?—*Two*—And with this one (C)?—*Three.*—And with this one (D)?—*Five.*'

These children show that they can count the terms of the series without hesitation, and that they can even understand, when two successive terms are compared, that the difference is A or 1. Tes, for instance, sees that C is identical with B + A, and Fiv states that there is 'one more each time'. And yet, when asked to say how many times unit A goes into N, they are unable to find the solution merely by reference to the position of N, and to say, for instance, that since the card is the fourth it contains four units. More important still, they do not even grasp this correspondence between position and cardinal value when the various cards are taken in order. They can see it by direct perception up to three, but after that they either count the possible divisions each time, like Tes, or else they judge by appearances, like Fiv. In a word, they are in possession of all the empirical elements necessary for understanding the law, but they do not understand it.

The paradoxical situation characteristic of the second stage illustrates even better what happens since the children we shall now quote as examples appear to discover the law when the progressive order is followed, but are baffled when the order is reversed, when cards are picked out at random, and even more when the visual seriation is destroyed.

Bet (5;0) first made the series as follows: A, B, C, D, F, G, then inserted E, etc., thus arriving unaided at the correct result, though after some trial and error. 'If we cut up this one (B), how many little ones like that (A) can we make?—*3.*—(We put B and A side by side.)—*No, 2.*—And out of (C)?—*3.*—And out of (D)?—*4*, etc., correct up to 10.—And out of this one (pointing to J again)?—*9.*—And out of (H)?—*10.*—And out of (G)?—*11.*—And out of (F)?—*12.*' Thus when the series was reversed, Bet began correctly by going down to 9, but went on with 10, 11, 12 . . . and only saw the absurdity of it when he came to B. When the cards were disarranged, Bet said 4 for D (judging by its appearance), but 5 for G, then again 4 for D, then 6 for G, and 6 also for H (tracing with his finger the possible divisions on the card itself).

Mic (5;0) successfully seriated and counted the ten cards. 'How many of those (A) can we make out of that one (B)?—*2.*—And out of that one (C)?—*4, no 3.*—And out of (D)?—*5*, etc.' But when, with the series still in place, F was indicated, he did not think of using the system he had discovered and said that F was 4A (counting on the card itself), G was 6A (same method), E was 5 and F '*8, no 12*' (same method).

Bru (5;0): 'Which is the first one?—(He pointed to A.)—And the second?—(B).—If we cut up that one (B), how many little cards like this one (A) can we make?—*2*.—And out of this one (C)?—*3*.—And out of this one (D)?—*4;* etc., up to 10.' But when, without disturbing the series, we pointed to cards at random, he thought there were 4 in E, 6 in H, 3 in D, 7 in E, and so on.

Dit (5;0) succeeded after trial and error in arranging the 10 cards as a staircase and at once understood the law: ' *That one* (A) *is 1, that one* (B) *makes 2; that one* (C) *makes 3; that one* (D) *is 4; that* (E) *makes 5; that* (F) *6 . . . and that* (K) *makes 10 little cards.*' The row was then disarranged and F(6) was indicated. 'How many does this one make?—*4 little ones.*—Are you sure?—*No, but I think so.*—What could we do to make sure?—*Make a staircase .*(He remade it and counted.) *6 little ones.*' But in the case of D(4), Dit failed because he reversed the order. He began by seriating the first 6 cards: 'Can we tell from those how many it makes?—*No, we must put the others as well.*' He made the complete row of 10, then counted from the 10th to the 4th and said: ' *That one* (D) *makes 7, we can make 7 little ones.*—Why?—*Because there are 7 places.*—How's that?—(He put card A seven times on card D and said): *That's 7, that's how it is.*'

The significance of these examples is clear, and they throw considerable light on what occurred at the first stage. There is no doubt that at this stage the child understands the law of the series and adds one to the cardinal number for each new ordinal when the order A→K is followed. And yet, even with the staircase still in place, when a card larger than three or four is picked out at random he can no longer estimate the cardinal value of its units by reference to its position, and at first tries only direct evaluation, tracing with his finger the hypothetical divisions on the card itself, as did Bet, Mic and Bru. Dit, who was more advanced, having reached the upper limit of stage II, understood that once the cards were disarranged he had to reconstruct the series and find the position of each element in order to determine its value. And yet, on the one hand, he thought he had to reconstruct the whole series from A to K and could not tell from the first four cards that the fourth represented four units, and on the other, when he had reconstructed the whole series he calculated the position of D from the wrong end and thus made it seven instead of four.

These strange behaviours make it reasonable to suppose that children at this level have systematic difficulty in grasping the relations between ordination and cardination. What is the explanation, since in this experiment with cards arranged as a staircase the material represents with the maximum of intuitive clarity the law governing the formation of the first ten finite numbers, each ordinal corresponding to each cardinal and vice versa? Obviously the most natural hypothesis is to relate this difficulty to the lack of understanding we found in our analysis of cardination. It will be remembered that at a certain stage of development, in which the average age corresponds to that of the present stage, the child who is successful in making a one-one correspondence between two sets of six objects no longer grasps their cardinal correspondence once the elements of one set are displaced. What appeared to be a one-one correspondence leading to stable colligation thus proves to be only a system without conservation and therefore without true cardination. In this system the colligation is still only intuitive, i.e. dependent on perception of the figure or of the space occupied by the sets in question, and although the child can use numbers to enumerate the elements, this enumeration does not as yet involve true cardinal numbers. Similarly, in the present case it may well be that what appears to be ordinal understanding of the series is dependent on the intuitive act of passing term by term from the beginning to the end, and ceases to exist when this is replaced by consideration of any given term.

This comparison between the difficulties of cardination and ordination is justified by the fact that once the two ideas are grasped they appear to be essentially linked one with the other. If the child fails to grasp the notion of the constant value of a set regardless of the arrangement of its elements, it is because at this level he has not yet acquired the notion of stable ordination. To put it more simply, this hypothesis amounts to a statement that intuitive seriation becomes true seriation only when it becomes operational, and that it becomes operational precisely when there is co-ordination with cardination. Conversely, colligation and intuitive correspondence become true cardination only when they become operational, and this occurs only when there is co-ordination with ordination. Viewed thus, the child's seriation at this stage merely produces as it were 'rigid series' such that the positions of the elements depend on the whole set of seriating, and cannot serve for detailed operations once they are separated from the whole. Just as (until he has acquired the notion of lasting equivalence) the child can only evaluate corresponding sets by a kind of rigid colligation, i.e. without reconciling the conservation of the whole with the mobility of the elements, so, during this stage, he can only base cardinal value on position as long as the positions are linked one with another in a whole, continuous series. Once the series is broken up and it becomes a matter of considering the relationship between a given element and the others, without following the progressive order step by step, 'before' and 'after' lose their cardinal significance, or the cardinal values cease to represent 'before' and 'after'.

As a final test of our thesis let us consider some examples of the third stage, characterized by complete understanding of the problem, i.e. by operational ordination and cardination.

Let (6;0): 'How many cards are there?—*10.*—How many like this one (A) can we make with that one (B)?—*2.*—And with (C)?—*3.* (he counted on the card).—And with that one (D)?—(He began by counting on the card and then cried: *We can make 4.*—And that (E)?— *5, because I know how the figures go!*—(I passed over the next element.) And that one (G)?—*7,*' etc. The cards were then disarranged and G was indicated: 'How many with that one?—(He counted and then at once began to seriate from A to G and said): ' *Yes, it's 7.*'

Ald (6;6) made the series without hesitating and was first asked 'How many like that one (A) can we make out of (C). He replied: *3, I knew I had to count that one (A) as well.*' He had therefore at once counted the positions. 'And with that one (F)?—*6, because there are 3 there* (pointing to K, J, H), *that makes 10, 9, 8,* then that one (G) *7.*' When the series was disarranged, he reconstructed the staircase as far as the element in question and thus found: 5 for E, etc.

These children were immediately able to find the value of one of the cards, whether it was pointed out at random in the staircase or when the series was disarranged. In other words, the series had ceased to be rigid and had become mobile or operational, each term being susceptible of consideration in itself and in its relation to the others, whatever the order, Thus Ald reconstructed the cardinal value of F by determining its position in the decreasing order and Let found the question so easy in the increasing order that he said, 'I know how the figures go'.

In conclusion, we find that the gradual co-ordination of cardination and ordination confirms, on this essentially numerical plane, our earlier findings as to qualitative seriation and serial correspondence.

§3. *The experiment with mats and hurdles*

In view of the difficulty of dissociating the ordinal from the cardinal in ordinary numeration, we devised a further experiment, involving a lag between cardinals and ordinals. When we say that a person is in his twentieth year, we mean that he has completed only nineteen years of life. In a case such as this, it is easier to distinguish the ordinal aspect, that of the current year, from the cardinal, that of the completed years, than in cases where the two notions coincide. As however the notion of time is extremely difficult for the child, we tried to find a spatial equivalent for this situation, and suggested a boy practising jumping who has to clear a succession of seven hurdles of increasing height. To take off and to land he has a series of mats, eight in number, one of which is placed before and after each hurdle. The material given to the child to represent this situation consists of a doll, seven little hurdles of varying heights and eight little mats. When the doll has reached mat three it will have jumped two hurdles, and when it has jumped the fifth hurdle it will have touched six mats, and so on.

The questioning then proceeds as follows. The first two mats are placed in position, one before and one after the first hurdle, and the child is asked how many mats are needed for the hurdles. Once the series of mats and hurdles has been constructed, we make the doll jump and bring it to a stop after one of the hurdles, say the third, i.e. on the fourth mat. The second question is then put: 'How many hurdles have been jumped and how many mats touched?' The question is repeated with the doll in various positions. The third question, asked when the eight mats and some of the hurdles have been removed, requires the child to say how many mats are needed for the remaining hurdles. The fourth question is put when the hurdles have been mixed and one, say the fourth, is selected. The child is asked how many hurdles were jumped before the one indicated. For question five the hurdles are mixed and some of the mats, say five, are placed in a row and the child is asked how many hurdles have been jumped, and which they are. For the sixth and last question some of the mats are again put down and the child is asked which was the last hurdle jumped.

The problems involved are: (1) seriation; (2) the relation between $n + 1$ mats and n hurdles; (3) the cardinal number of a group of hurdles determined by the position of a given hurdle; (4) the ordinal and cardinal numbers of a group of hurdles determined by the cardinal number of the mats. We shall deal rapidly with problems (1) and (3), since they have been studied earlier on in different forms. Problems (2) and (4), however, present the question of the relationship between ordination and cardination in a new light.

The problem of seriation provides evidence of the same stages as before: (1) global seriation, (2) intuitive seriation, the success of which depends on actual perception of the series, and (3) systematic seriation, resulting from the grouping of relationships.

The problem of the relation between the number of mats and hurdles also shows three stages corresponding to those above. In the first, the child does not understand the law; either he is convinced that the number of mats is equal to the number of hurdles, or, having been undeceived, he counts unsystematically each time. In the second stage, he discovers the law empirically through trial and error, and in the third he sees it at once, no matter how many hurdles are involved.

The problem of the number of hurdles corresponding to a given position also shows the three stages with which we are familiar: failure in the first, success in the second, only on condition that the whole series is reconstructed, and complete understanding in the third.

In the case of the fourth problem, again there is no understanding at the first stage. At the second, although the child recognizes that there must be one more mat than the number of hurdles, he meets various difficulties of an ordinal character. At the third stage he is completely successful, notably in solving the question as to the position of the last hurdle jumped, given a certain number of mats (whereas at the second stage this position is considered to be equal to the number of mats).

We give here some examples of the first stage, in which there is neither correct seriation nor understanding of the relationship between the ordinals and cardinals involved in this problem:

Lic (4;0) could only count up to 6. He was given 5 hurdles and only succeeded in seriating them with suggestions from us. 'Now we're going to put the mats one on each side of the hurdles so that the doll won't hurt itself. (The first two mats were placed in position.) How many mats will there be altogether?—(Guessing) *4.*—How many hurdles are there?—*I don't know* (he recounted), *5.*' He then put down the 6 mats himself. 'How many mats are there?—(He counted.) *6.*— And how many hurdles?—(He reflected and looked at them.) *6.*— Count the hurdles.—*1, 2, 5, 6.*—Try again (pointing to each one).—*5.* —And how many mats?—*5.*—Count them.—*6.*—And how many hurdles?—*6.*'

Lic was then given the doll, and he himself made it jump, starting by running across the first mat. It jumped the first and second hurdles and stopped on the 3rd mat. 'How many hurdles has it jumped?—*3.* —Watch carefully (repeating the demonstration).—*2 hurdles.*—And how many mats did it touch?—*2.*—Show me them.—*1, 2, 3.*—And how many hurdles?—(Without counting them.) *1, 2, 3.*—(The doll was then made to jump 3 hurdles and was put down on the 4th mat): How many hurdles has it jumped?—*3.*—And how many mats has it touched?—*3.*—Count them.—*1, 2, 3, 4.*—That's right, and how many hurdles?—*3.*—And how many mats?—*3.*'

All the material was removed and the first 3 hurdles were then placed in order in front of the child: 'How many hurdles are there?— *3.*—How many mats must we put down so that the doll won't hurt itself?—(He put 1 before and 1 after the first hurdle and then of his own accord added 2.) *It's 4.*—And how many hurdles are there?— (Counting) *1, 2, 3.*—Why are there more mats?— . . .'

Ray (4;6) did not succeed in seriating the 7 hurdles without suggestions from us (he put them in unco-ordinated pairs). We then got him to put down 6 mats for the first 5 hurdles (having removed the other 2). 'How many mats are there?—6.—Watch (making the doll jump the first 2 hurdles and leaving it on the 3rd mat). How many mats has it touched?—3.—And how many hurdles did it jump?—3.—Count them.—1, 2.—And how many mats did it touch?—2.—(We then made the doll jump the first 3 hurdles and stop on the 4th mat.)—How many mats did it touch?—4.—That's right. (We made the doll jump 4 hurdles and stop on the 5th mat.) How many mats did it touch?—5.—And how many hurdles did it jump?—5.

The mats were removed and only the first 3 hurdles left: 'How many hurdles is it going to jump?—3.—And how many mats shall we put down so that it can run without hurting itself?—3 (putting them down), Oh! 4.—And how many hurdles are there now (adding the 4th)?—4.—And how many mats shall we have to put down?—4,' etc.

We then mixed the hurdles, pointed to the 3rd and asked Ray how many the doll had jumped. He pointed to the 2nd. 'And any others?—He pointed to the 1st.—How many did it jump altogether?—3.' He was unsuccessful however with four.

Finally the 7 hurdles and the 8 mats were mixed together, and then 3 mats were put in front of the child: 'Look, the doll touched these mats. How many hurdles did it jump?—3.—Show me them.—(He put hurdle 1 opposite mat 1, hurdle 4 with mat 2, and hurdle 5 with mat 3).'

These then are the reactions of the first stage. It is obvious that these children can neither seriate the hurdles without help, nor discover the cardinal number of those already jumped from one selected at random. This we already knew, and it need not delay us here.

As for the relationship between n hurdles and $n + 1$ mats, there is complete lack of understanding. Admittedly there is an artificial convention in the data, but it is explained to the child and he himself places the mats in position. In spite of the fact that he has the whole series of hurdles and mats arranged in front of him, he continues to make the same mistake, perpetually making a one-one correspondence between hurdles and mats. Lic, for instance, after counting five hurdles put down six mats, counted them and decided that there were six hurdles. Finding that there were only five, he then refused to believe that there were six mats and said there were five. Having counted them again he once more concluded that there were six hurdles! In the same way Ray, after saying that five mats were needed for five hurdles, himself put down six, yet he constantly wavered between the idea that there must be n mats because there were n hurdles, and that there must be $n + 1$ hurdles since there were $n + 1$ mats.

Although at first sight this confusion appears to affect only car-dinal correspondence, it is of interest also in the study of ordination. It is not a question of an isolated phenomenon; the same thing occurs, for example, in the case of the child who, trying to cut a strip of paper into three, makes three cuts and fails to see that he is dividing it into four. In both cases the mistake is due to lack of co-ordination between cardination and position. To understand that if each hurdle is between two mats there will be $n + 1$ mats for n hurdles, requires the capacity to view the position simultaneously from the two sides, whereas the child has an irresistible tendency to place himself at one point of view only, either 'before' or 'after' and thus forgets either the first or the last mat. Hence, although in practice he is perfectly capable of constructing a sequence of $n + 1$ mats for n hurdles, he gives a simple one-one correspondence as its cardinal description, merely identifying the number of mats with that of hurdles.

We now come to the reactions of the second stage: intuitive seriation and empirical discovery of the relationship between the number of mats and hurdles, but without understanding of that relationship.

Ris (5;0) succeeded in seriating the 7 hurdles, but only after some mistakes. A mat was put down on each side of the first hurdle: 'How many mats will there be if we put one each side of all the hurdles?— (He put down the other mats without replying, and then said): *They're all the same size.*—How many mats?—(He counted) *8.*—How many hurdles are there?—(He counted them again) *7.*'

The doll was made to jump 4 successive hurdles and was left on the 5th mat: 'How many hurdles has it jumped?—(He counted) *4.*—And how many mats did it touch?—(He counted) *5.*—And how many hurdles does that make?—(He counted again) *4.*—And how many mats does that make for 4 hurdles?—(Once again he counted) *5.*' Ris's lack of confidence in deducing the law is obvious: at each question he recounted the set.

Four hurdles were left in front of the child, in order, but without the mats: 'How many hurdles are there?—*4.*—And how many mats must we put so that the doll won't touch the ground?—(He counted the spaces before the 1st, between the hurdles and after the 4th) *5.*—And how many hurdles will it jump?—(He recounted) *4.*'

The hurdles were mixed together on the table and the 5th was selected. After some trial and error Ris succeeded in arranging the 4 preceding hurdles, but only by forming the whole series: 'How many hurdles has it jumped?—*5.*—And how many mats must we put down? —(He recounted the spaces) *6.*'

The hurdles were mixed and 4 mats, end to end, were put before the child: 'I'm going to ask you a riddle. Which hurdles has the doll crossed?—(Ris inserted H2 between M1 and M2, H3 between M2 and M3, and H4 between M3 and M4. He knew quite well which was the smallest hurdle, H1, but had put it aside and began with H2, ending with H4.)—Does the doll begin by jumping this one (H2)?—*No.* (He put H_1 before M_1.)—Is that right?—(He removed H_1.)—But which hurdle does it jump first?—*The 1st.*—Well then?—(He put H_1 in front of M_1 again.)—How many mats are there?—*4.*—How many hurdles must there be then?—*4.*'

Finally 5 mats were placed end to end and the child was asked: 'Which was the last hurdle jumped if the doll only touched these mats?' (The doll was placed on mat 5.) Ris was sure that H_7 was the last and seriated the hurdles from H_7 (between M_4 and M_5) to H_5.

Jen (6;0) seriated the 7 hurdles, making some corrections, then placed the 8 mats in position and counted mats and hurdles. Afterwards, however, he thought that when 4 hurdles had been jumped there were 4 mats, and then for a series of 5 hurdles he was intending to put 5 mats, and only made the correction when he counted the spaces to be filled.

Four mats were placed end to end: 'How many hurdles has the doll jumped when it gets to this point (the doll was on mat 4)?—(He took hurdles 1 to 4 and put H_1 before M_1, H_2 before M_2, etc. He then added H_5 and promptly removed it). We began again with 4 mats: 'How many hurdles has it jumped?—*4.*—Which ones?—(He then inserted H_1 between M_1 and M_2, etc.) *Ah! it's 3!*' But he put H_4 between M_3 and M_4 so that H_4 should correspond to M_4!

Five mats were then placed close together, and with the doll on the 5th Jen was asked which hurdle had been jumped last. He pointed to H_7 and made various other attempts before finally saying: '*Ah, the 4th!*'

The continuity between these reactions and those of the previous stage is of considerable importance to our analysis. In the first place, it is obvious that these children learn to seriate like all children at this level, intuitively and empirically. Secondly, they need to remake the whole series before they can discover how many hurdles have been jumped before a hurdle in a given position. Thus the reactions at this stage to the new questions involved in the problem of hurdles and mats are in full agreement with those we found in the earlier experiments.

At this stage, instead of systematically making a one-one correspondence between the number of hurdles and mats, as he did earlier, the child uses a purely empirical method. Ris, for instance, counts mats and hurdles every time, correctly, but without drawing any conclusion. Jen, on the other hand, like the more advanced children of this stage, acquires an elementary grasp of the law, but it is merely a generalization of his own experience and does not involve real understanding.

The questions relating to the number of hurdles corresponding to a given number of mats, to the order of these hurdles and to the position of the last, produce reactions which are still uncertain but which show certain striking features. The child is almost compelled to insert the right number of hurdles, since their position is determined between one mat and the next (cf. Ris). Yet he falls into the same mistake as at the first stage if, instead of inserting the hurdles one at a time, he tries to express the relationship or to select all the required hurdles. Both Ris and Jen, for instance, think they will need four hurdles for four mats, thus showing that the law is not really grasped.

From the ordinal point of view, two features are worth noting. It sometimes happens that the child's tendency towards one-one correspondence makes him put hurdle *n* immediately in front of mat *n*, but on the other hand he sometimes puts the last hurdle, the seventh, in front of mat *n* and then makes the correspondence backwards. Ris, for instance, inserts hurdles 2, 3, and 4 when there are four mats, and fails to replace hurdle two by hurdle one, and both Ris and Jen put hurdles four, five, six and seven when there are five mats, so that hurdle seven shall be the last.

In conclusion, these reactions show once again the child's incapacity at this level to co-ordinate seriation and cardination. When he is concerned with the cardinal number of the hurdles he either forgets the ordinal aspect or seriates in relation to the last mat only, and when he is concerned with seriating in relation to the last hurdle, he forgets the number of mats and forms series such as $4 \rightarrow 7$.

We now come to the reactions of the third stage, in which all the questions produce correct solutions. The first example illustrates the transition from stage II to stage III:

Bru (5;0) seriated the hurdles correctly. 'How many hurdles are there?—*7.*—How many mats (putting down the first 2)?—*7.*—Put them down.—*8.*—Why are there more mats than hurdles?—*Because there are two more mats* (pointing to the two ends).'
The doll was made to jump to the 4th mat: 'How many hurdles has it crossed?—*4.*—And how many mats does that make?—*3, no 4.*—And how many hurdles?—*3.*'
The first 4 hurdles were left on the table, without mats: 'How many hurdles?—*4.*—And how many mats shall we need?—*5.*'
Four mats were put end to end: 'How many hurdles will the doll cross?—*3.*' Then with 5 mats: 'How many hurdles?—*4.*—Which will be the last one?—(He at once seriated $1 \rightarrow 4$ and pointed to the 4th.)'
Shen (6;6) seriated the 7 hurdles correctly. 'We're going to put the mats one on each side of the hurdles. How many will there be?—*6, because there are 7 hurdles* (He put them between the hurdles.)—No, watch (putting down M1 and M2).—*8 then* (He put them down.).'
The doll was made to jump as far as the 4th mat: 'How many hurdles has it crossed?—*3.*—And how many mats has it touched?—*4.* —Why?—*Because there are 3 hurdles.*'
A series of 6 hurdles was left, without mats. 'How many mats has

the doll touched?—*8, because there are 7 hurdles.*—Look at them.—*Oh yes, 7, because there are 6 hurdles.*'

He was shown the 4th hurdle, by itself: 'How many mats?—(He put up hurdles 1 to 3 and answered): *5 mats because there are 4 hurdles.*'

Six mats were put end to end: 'How many hurdles will the doll jump?—*5, because there are 6 mats. If there were 6 hurdles we'd have to put one on the last mat.*' (He made the series H1 > 5 and put them in between the mats.).

Aug (6;0) seriated the 7 hurdles and when mats 1 and 2 had been put down he was asked: 'How many mats will that be?—*7.*—Why?—*I counted the hurdles. Oh, no, 8 mats because there are 7 hurdles and we must put one mat in front.*'

The doll was then put on the 4th mat and Aug decided that it had jumped 3 hurdles. When shown the 5th hurdle by itself, he seriated the 4 preceding hurdles and decided that there would be 6 mats. When there were 4 mats, he knew that the last hurdle was H3; etc.

These examples show that all these children could make the series without hesitation, i.e. they could at once co-ordinate the relations 'greater' and 'smaller'. They show, moreover, that in the case of an isolated element, the child is capable at this level of discovering and seriating the preceding elements without needing to form the whole series.

As for the relationship between the number of hurdles and mats, the examples given show that complete understanding of the question is possible at the age of 7. It is true that only Shen is at once aware, on hearing the question, that n hurdles require $n + 1$ mats, but although Bru and Aug expect to have to put down as many mats as hurdles, they immediately understand the relationship once the series is formed. This constitutes the new development of this stage. The reasons the children give are very instructive. For Bru, there are $n + 1$ mats 'because there are two extra mats', i.e. one at each end. For Shen, if there were n mats for n hurdles, 'we'd have to put a hurdle on the last mat', i.e. the last hurdle would not be followed by a mat. For Aug, 'we must put a mat in front'. It is obvious that all these explanations imply that if our point of view is that of 'after', we must put a mat before, and that if our point of view is that of 'before', we must put a mat after.

Once this relationship is understood, the question of discovering the number of mats needed for a series of n hurdles is obviously immediately solved. As for the problem of making a given series of hurdles, beginning with the first, correspond to n mats, it is, interestingly enough, solved at the same time. By the very fact of always relating n objects X to $(n + 1)$ objects Y, the X being inserted between the Y, and of doing so consciously and systematically, the child becomes capable—and it is this that is new at this stage—of ordering the hurdles, beginning with the smallest without thinking that the biggest must necessarily be the last, whatever the number of mats involved.

In short, the solution of this problem, like those of the cards and sticks, shows that operational ordination and cardination are essentially interdependent. Understanding of the cardinal relation between n objects X and $(n+1)$ objects Y presupposes, in fact, operational ordination of the relations 'before' and 'after', and this ordination presupposes a cardinal relationship of the same nature.

§4. Conclusions: Ordination and Cardination

We have now reached the point at which the results we have reached in this and the preceding chapter with regard to the ordinal number must be compared with the data obtained concerning cardinal correspondence.

The law of succession that we found in the experiment with the sticks (i.e. global seriation, intuitive seriation, and operational seriation) was found in all the various tests in which seriation intervened. Even in the case of the cards, where seriation was particularly easy since the elements differed considerably from one another and formed a regular scale, the same three stages occurred.

The results obtained in our examination of serial and ordinal correspondence are in full agreement with this first finding, but the results of the experiment with the dolls, with their sticks and balls, provide a valuable complement, viz.: there is no more difficulty for the child in making a one-one correspondence between two series that he has to construct simultaneously, than in ordering a single series. We find, in fact, the same three stages in the development of serial correspondence as in simple seriation: (1) failure to make the correspondence, (2) intuitive correspondence, and (3) systematic correspondence. We find also that at the second stage there begins to be dissociation between qualitative seriation and serial correspondence on the one hand, and between purely numerical ordination and ordinal correspondence on the other, a dissociation which becomes complete at the third stage, so that at the operational level both qualitative operations and numerical operations come into their own.

Before going further we shall indicate how these three stages of seriation and ordinal correspondence are related to the levels of colligation and cardinal correspondence.

(1) Corresponding to the first stage of seriation, both as regards the structure itself and the average age of the children, there is the first stage of cardination. In both, the various reactions have at least two characteristics in common: their global nature, and the

fact that immediate perceptional experience prevails over operational, logical composition. When the child makes an arbitrary row of sticks and dolls, merely distinguishing the big elements from the small, or when he imitates only the general line of a staircase, focusing on one end of the elements and forgetting the other, his reactions are exactly those of the child who, in trying to find a quantity equivalent to a row of six counters, pushes 7–9 counters closer together and thinks that the quantities are equivalent because the rows are the same length. In both cases, it is the global aspect that predominates. A further proof is to be found in the fact that when sections of the corresponding series are to be reconstructed (e.g. in order to discover which stick belongs to the nth doll), the child disregards the number of the elements he himself has arranged. The explanation of the common global character of these elementary reactions lies in the fact that in both cases the criterion of truth is perception, and not a system of operations that can be composed. Proof of this is to be found in the breakdown of the child's belief in the correspondence once the shape of one of the series is altered.

(2) The second stages in ordination and cardination also correspond, viewed not only from the point of view of results but of similarity of mechanisms. The child no longer reacts globally: he is capable of correct analysis, but this analysis is limited to perceptual data and has not as yet reached the level of operational composition. The child who is capable of constructing a cardinal correspondence but who ceases to believe in that correspondence when one of the series is expanded or contracted, is certainly capable of analysis, but only believes in the relationship as long as it is actually perceived. Now it was precisely these characteristics that made us distinguish a second stage in ordination, intermediary between the global and operational levels. It is clear that in seriation the child has not thoroughly mastered all the relations involved and has to proceed by trial and error. Moreover, once the series is completed, he experiences certain systematic difficulties in inserting new elements, as if the series constituted a rigid, closed set. When it is a case of two corresponding series, the position is the same: the child at this level is as incapable of grasping the one-one correspondence when one of the series is contracted, expanded or reversed as he is of assuming cardinal equivalence. Admittedly the child makes an attempt to discover the ordinal correspondence, but only because he is asked to do so, and thinks that there is a possibility of a return to the original situation. When it is a matter of disarranged series, however, the child is no longer sure that each element has its virtual corresponding element (cf. Cha, Chapter V, §2, Lie and Pel, ibid., §3, etc.). While it is possible that

there may be a lag between the two discoveries of cardinal equivalence and permanence of position, the fact remains that we find the same attitudes in both fields in the second stage, as in the first.

(3) In the third stages, we find the same homology between the structures and the results shown in the tests for ordination and cardination. Both are characterized by the victory of operation over intuition: in both cases the child co-ordinates beforehand all the relations involved, because operational composition triumphs over perception, or rather, because the latter is from now on controlled by the former.

Clearly then, the same processes and the same levels are to be found in the development of both ordination and cardination. But obviously any attempt to express the situation in statistical form and to apply correlation formulae to these tests would involve us in questions for which we must confess we have little interest. Is, for instance, this or that problem of ordination of which we have made use, of exactly the same difficulty as this or that other problem, either of ordination or cardination, independently of ordination and cardination in general? It is obvious that in each test a considerable number of heterogeneous factors intervene, e.g. the words used, the length of the instructions given, their more or less concrete character, the relationship between the instructions and the individual experience of the child, the number of elements involved, the intervention of numbers the child knows, etc., etc. We noticed wide differences in the results of the various tests of cardinal correspondence, showing that we never succeed in measuring understanding of this correspondence in its pure state and that the understanding is always with respect to a given problem and given material. The calculation of the correlation between the levels of cardination and ordination, without the accompaniment of an extremely thorough qualitative analysis, could therefore give only misleading results, unless our experiments were transformed into 'tests' in which statistical precision could no doubt easily be obtained, but at the cost of no longer knowing exactly what was being measured. We shall now consider how far our various analyses of the progressive co-ordination between the cardinal and the ordinal number converge, and shall attempt to explain this convergence.

During the first stage there is as yet no co-ordination between processes of a cardinal nature and those of an ordinal nature. Two different kinds of experiment are to be distinguished here, those in which the child has to determine a class by means of a position in a series (i.e. to discover a cardinal value by reference to an ordinal), and those in which he has to determine a position in a series by means of a class (i.e. to discover an ordinal value by reference to a cardinal). The experiment with the sticks, for instance, belongs to the first of these groups. The child has to discover which steps (class) and how many (number) have been climbed when a given step is selected (qualitative position or ordinal number). What happens is that the child who understands the question when the staircase has been constructed (all he has to do is to count the steps as far as the point indicated), proves to be incapable, during the first stage, of grasping that he only needs to count the sticks below the one selected. The card experiment also belongs to the first group, the only difference being that it involves a process of composition by units, thus enabling the child to obtain a visual intuition of the series (1), (1 + 1), (1 + 1 + 1), etc. And yet, even when he has the whole series of cards before him and the order one to ten is followed, the child at the first stage fails to find the cardinal value (the number of units) of a card by reference to its position, if it is higher than two or three. In the experiment with hurdles and mats, both of the groups we have just distinguished are exemplified. For instance, when the child is asked to determine, by reference to a given hurdle, which and how many hurdles have been jumped, or which set of mats and how many have been touched, we are still dealing with the first type of test, and during the first stage the child is unable to discover the right solution.

The tests of the second type produce an exactly complementary result. The child at the first stage fails entirely when asked to discover the position of the last hurdle jumped, given a certain number of mats. The same thing occurs when, in questions II to V relating to the dolls and sticks, he has to discover which stick belongs to a given doll by reconstructing the earlier part of the series. This requires the use of the set, i.e. the cardinal value of the set of preceding elements, either by making the correspondence or by counting. If one of the series is displaced, or merely reversed, the child at the first stage thinks he can discover the corresponding elements without reference to the number of preceding terms, and if one of the series is disarranged, he again fails for the same reason. When he is merely asked to put together the sticks and dolls bigger or smaller than a given element, he so thoroughly confuses ordinal and cardinal values that even the number of dolls and sticks is not equal! This last reaction, characteristic of the first stage, is the most striking of all those we have quoted, and in itself synthesizes the results of the two types of experiment.

On the whole, then, we can conclude that at the level of the first stage the child is not capable of deducing from a given position the corresponding cardinal value when this value is not actually perceptible, and conversely, that he cannot deduce a position by reference to a given cardinal value if he himself has to reconstruct it, even by manipulation.

The reactions of the second stage are much more complex, since they represent a beginning of co-ordination between cardinal and ordinal structures. It is therefore essential to examine carefully how far the results of our various experiments converge. As for those of the first type, it can be said that, generally speaking, the child is beginning to understand the relationship between order and quantity, but only when the whole series is involved, and without grasping that a given position necessarily corresponds to an exact cardinal value. In the card experiment, for instance, the child at the second stage succeeds in giving the value of each card when the sequence 1–10 is followed, but if one is picked out at random, even with the complete series before him he cannot find its cardinal value by merely counting from 1 to its position. Towards the end of this stage, he does succeed in doing so, but fails if the sequence is destroyed, in spite of the fact that he can of course reconstruct the series if he wishes. In the experiment with sticks, the child succeeds in discovering, in the case of each stick, how many steps the doll has climbed and how many remain to be climbed, as long as the staircase is complete. He can still do so even when the increasing order is no longer followed and a stick is picked out at random, because here the question does not involve a law of composition, as was the case with the cards, but merely the counting of one or two visible sets. But once the staircase is broken up, when a given stick n is selected the child finds systematic difficulty in answering the same questions, i.e. in remaking the series 1 to n, and more particularly n to the last element t. Even if he succeeds, after considerable trial and error, in discovering that 1 to n steps have been climbed, he needs to remake the whole series in order to find out how many remain to be climbed, not realizing that he need only count the remainder. Even then, he confuses the whole with the part $n \ldots t$.

These two reactions seem to be typical of the second stage: understanding of the relationship between an intuitive series seen as a whole and a cardinal value also seen as a whole, but lack of understanding of the necessary bond between a given position and the corresponding cardinal number. This is fully confirmed by the experiment with the hurdles. On the one hand the child discovers by experience that $n + 1$ mats correspond to n hurdles, but fails when the series is destroyed and he is asked how many mats will be needed for, say, three or five hurdles. On the other hand, if one of the hurdles is selected, after the series has been destroyed, he has to remake the whole series (as in the case of the sticks) in order to discover how many hurdles have been jumped.

L

The same difficulties are found by children of this level in tests of the second type, i.e. in determining a particular position by reference to a number or a qualitatively defined set. When for instance the child is asked which was the last hurdle jumped if n mats have been touched, he fails to give the right answer, usually confusing the last (seventh) hurdle with the one before the nth mat. Similarly, when it is a question of correspondence between dolls and sticks (Questions II, III and IV), we find that the various mistakes made are all due to the fact that when the child is thinking of position he forgets the cardinal number, and conversely. In particular, when the series are destroyed, the child at the second stage is incapable of finding the stick that corresponds to a given doll, and conversely, (Question IV), through failure to co-ordinate their positions and cardinal values. Only Question V (relating to the walk) is solved correctly, showing that the child is capable of collecting all the dolls bigger than or equal to n, and those smaller than n, and of finding the corresponding sticks, particularly the nth. This is apparently at variance with the results of the experiment with the sticks, in which the child fails to discover how many stairs have been climbed and how many remain to be climbed, unless he can see the whole staircase. But as we said earlier, this problem only requires the construction of the two classes, 'this doll and all those bigger than it' and 'all those smaller than it', and a construction of this kind can be achieved by a purely intuitive method. Question IV, on the contrary, presupposes understanding of the fact that the nth doll is the last term of a cardinal number of n dolls, and this relationship, which involves abstraction, is psychologically operational, and no longer intuitive. We have the same situation in the problem of the sticks. To discover how many steps have been climbed when the nth step is reached, the child must understand that the nth is the last term of n steps, and to discover how many steps remain to be climbed he must grasp the relationship $t - n = \{ n + 1, \ldots t \}$. If therefore the child at the second stage only succeeds after considerable trial and error in forming the series $1 \ldots n$ by an intuitive method, he naturally fails to discover the number $t - n$, which involves an operational relation between the whole and its parts. This contrast between the results of Question V with the dolls and those of Question IV, and of the problem with sticks, is a further indication of the characteristic feature of this stage: co-ordination between position and cardinal value as long as the series remain whole or the classes are complete, but lack of co-ordination in the case of particular elements. In other words, intuitive co-ordination and operational inco-ordination.

Finally, in the third stage, the position is very simple in comparison with the previous stages. The child successfully solves all the problems, whether he is asked to determine the cardinal value, given a particular position, or the converse. He has therefore grasped the close correspondence between ordination and cardination, and co-ordination in the case of particular elements is the sign that this level is operational.

Now that we have made clear these general characteristics, we shall try to explain them. It will not be difficult, since the three stages in co-ordination of cardinal and ordinal numbers correspond to the three stages in seriation, which in their turn correspond to the three stages in cardination and cardinal correspondence, as we saw earlier.

The impossibility, during the first stage, of relations between ordination and cardination is due entirely to the fact that at that level cardination and ordination properly so called do not yet exist. Cardinal evaluation is merely global judgement, without conservation or even one-one correspondence, depending on the configuration of the set, the space it occupies and the spread of the elements. As for seriation, it is merely the juxtaposition of one term to another, in a sequence in which there is no law governing all the terms, and in which the 'big' elements are merely contrasted with the 'small' elements, either in pairs or in disconnected elementary series. Between these two processes there can be no connection: they are even to some extent antagonistic, for the following reasons. There is no dissociation in this case between ordination and qualitative seriation, or between cardination and the construction of totalities or sets of the nature of classes. But seriation requires that each element shall be distinguished as different from the others, whereas classification consists in putting together a certain number of elements seen as equivalent. Experiment has shown that at this level the child, in his efforts to seriate, disregards sets (which he is capable of forming), and in his attempts to evaluate totalities, disregards order.

In the second stage, things are different. There is a beginning of systematization of qualitative operations within the field of perception. Although the class and the asymmetric relation cannot be composed one with the other on the qualitative plane, since for the former the elements are seen as equivalent and for the latter as non-equivalent, it is not difficult to express seriation in terms of classes, and vice versa, and this constitutes a first connection between the two systems. In the problem of dolls and sticks, for instance, the child at this stage can divide the series into two classes, 'those bigger than or equal to n' and 'those smaller than n' for the various values of n, and conversely he can make the serial correspondence between the sets thus defined. Such constructions are still, however, only semi-operational, being limited to the field of intuition and thus failing to achieve their full logical result.

Moreover, the fact that there are the beginnings of operations means that there is a beginning of differentiation between the qualitative mechanisms and the numerical mechanisms which depend on the notion of homogeneous units susceptible both of seriation and colligation. But apart from the numbers 1 to 3, at about the age of 3, 1 to 4 at about the age of 4, and 1 to 5 at about the age of 5, the construction of number cannot remain within the field of perceptual intuition and can therefore be completed only on the operational plane, whereas qualitative operations, by virtue of their simplicity, are susceptible of greater development on the intuitive plane. It follows that at this level the intermingling of the cardinal and ordinal processes that constitutes number is only in its early stage, and there is not as yet true co-ordination.

Thus, in the field of perception, the cardinal evaluation of the second stage is achieved by means of the one-one correspondence which involves a kind of ordination. Conversely, in every intuitive series the child understands that each term can be counted, and forms with the preceding terms a set susceptible of being counted. There is therefore elementary co-ordination between the two processes. But the cardinal correspondence is not lasting, and does not as yet entail permanent and necessary equivalence, firstly because it is not sufficiently dissociated from qualitative correspondence, and secondly, because it is still dependent on perception. The same is true of ordination, which is not sufficiently differentiated from qualitative seriation, which is also still intuitive, i.e. the order is understood only in so far as the total series is actually perceived. These two limitations (incomplete differentiation between quality and number, and semi-operational processes confined to the perceptual plane) are a sufficient explanation of the fact that during the second stage there is no systematization and generalization of the co-ordination between ordinal and cardinal.

If indeed the position of an element is to be expressed univocally as a definite cardinal value, the set formed by this and the preceding elements must have sufficient cohesion to allow of its being decomposed into parts whose sum equals the whole. In the experiment with the sticks, for instance, if the doll is on the third step of a staircase of eight steps, the child must be able to grasp that even if the staircase is broken up the whole is still $8 = 3 + 5$ steps and the steps that remain to be climbed are $8 - 3 = 5$. But at this level a cardinal whole exists only so long as it is perceived as such; if it is decomposed, the whole is destroyed, which means that the position of each element in the series cannot yet be translated immediately into a cardinal value. Conversely, for a cardinal value to correspond exactly to a given position, it is necessary that the nth position shall be seen to be permanently after the $(n-1)$th and before the $(n+1)$th, and this presupposes the invariance of the sets $\{n-1\}$, $\{n\}$, $\{n+1\}$, etc. In a word, the intuitive, semi-operational character of the cardinal wholes and the series explains the non-conservation of the sets and positions.

During the third stage, however, co-ordination is achieved, as a result of the triumph of operation over perceptual intuition, i.e. of reversible grouping over static recognition. Hence we find (1) generalization of qualitative operations; (2) differentiation between these and numerical operations, and (3) necessary inter-action of cardinal and ordinal.

(1) What constitutes the operational character of the reactions of the third stage is that, as in the case of conservation of quan-tities and lasting cardinal equivalence, the relations involved have become reversible. There was no reversibility in the arbitrary seriation of the first stage, and intuitive seriation vanishes with the disappearance of the configuration. Only operational seriation is independent of changes in the field of perception, being based on relations that can be composed because they are susceptible of rigorous inversion. As we have seen, to seriate operationally is to co-ordinate the two inverse relations $s > r$ and $s < t$, and this implies the possibility of setting out the series in either direction.

Once reversibility is achieved in seriation and classification, 'groupings' of operations become possible, and define the field of the child's qualitative logic (obviously on the concrete plane appropriate to the mental level at the age of 7 to 11, and not on the formal plane, for which several more years will be needed).

Let us consider any set of elements shown to the child, the dolls in Chapter V, for instance. On the one hand, he may conceive of them as similar, i.e. disregard their differences and only consider their common properties. This first point of view, that of *equi-valence* of the elements, leads to the construction of the concept of logical *classes*. For example, any two dolls may differ in size, but both belong equally to the class of the dolls on the table. If P is this set of dolls, the child will form the class by putting together the dolls $A + A' + B' + \ldots = P$, where the sign $+$ means putting together, and each of the elements is the singular class formed by each individual doll. But on the other hand, by the very fact that the child distinguishes the elements one from another, he con-ceives of them as different by other qualities than their common quality of 'doll'. This second point of view, that of *non-equivalence*, is that of asymmetrical *relations*. Every asymmetrical relation is an inequality, either because $A' > A$ and $B' > A'$, or (when A, A', B' ... are indistinguishable) because of their positions. We shall say, then, that there is construction of relationships when A, A', B' ... are distinguished, and of relations when the relationships that represent any criterion by which the elements are distinguished are composed.

Classes and asymmetrical relations are *complementary*, i.e. it is impossible to construct classes without relations which distinguish the elements, and to construct relations without classes which define the linked elements. But they are no more than complementary, i.e. there are no qualitative relationships that are at the same time classes and relations, since the class disregards differences and the asymmetrical relation disregards equivalences. Thus the very fact of combining A and A' into the class B $(A + A' = B)$ makes them equivalent in that they are of the class B, whereas the combination of the two relations into a single relation leads to a seriation of the terms of the relationships, not to their equivalence. It follows that classes give rise to *hierarchical wholes* $(A + A' = B; B + B' = C; ...$ etc., up to P), and transitive asymmetrical relations to *seriations*. But until number is introduced, we cannot infer any true cardination from these hierarchical wholes, nor any true ordination from these series. The concept is merely a synthesis of qualities, and the class merely a combination of elements that are qualified but not counted. The asymmetrical relation, on the other hand, being a relationship between qualities, is essentially quantifying, and in so far as it distinguishes the elements instead of combining them, it prepares the way for number. When however number does not intervene, the asymmetrical relation leads only, through its compositions, to those quantities which Kant called 'intensive' because they are not reducible to a system of units.

Such are the main additive compositions of which the child at stage III becomes capable, through generalization of qualitative operations.

(2) As soon as the child is capable of these logical compositions, he also becomes capable of deducing from them the corresponding numerical compositions and of distinguishing the two. *Number* is indeed possible to the extent that the elements A, A', B' ... are viewed no longer as being either equivalent or non-equivalent, but as being *at the same time* equivalent and non-equivalent. To use a formula that seems less contradictory, number is neither merely a uniting class nor merely a seriating relation, but both a hierarchical class and a series. But we have just seen that on the qualitative plane a logical relationship that is at the same time a class and a relation is impossible. The only possibility therefore, is to eliminate

the qualities and to consider each element as a unit equivalent to the others. We then have, simultaneously, $A = A' = B' \ldots$ etc., which expresses the equivalence characteristic of classes, and $A \rightarrow A' \rightarrow B' \ldots$ in accordance with the non-equivalence inherent in any system of asymmetrical relations. In other words $(A + A' = B)$ becomes $(A + A = 2A)$, and $(B + B = C)$ becomes $(2A + A = 3A)$, etc., which defines the iteration of the unit in the system of integers.

Obviously we are not suggesting that number is reduced to classes and relations; we are merely indicating their mutual relationship. It is essential that there shall be no misunderstanding as to this point, for as we shall see in the next chapter, the concept of class does not precede that of number, but is acquired simultaneously, the two concepts being interdependent. Without the notion of the cardinal number that is implicit in the words 'a', 'none', 'some' and 'all', it is impossible to conceive of classes included one in the other. Classes are therefore, in a sense, non-seriated numbers, just as numbers are seriated classes, and the psychological, as well as the logical, constitution of classes, relations and numbers is a single development, whose respective changes are synchronic and interdependent.

(3) There is then no doubt as to the explanation of the co-ordination between ordinal and cardinal numbers during the third stage. A cardinal number is a class whose elements are conceived as 'units' that are equivalent, and yet distinct in that they can be seriated, and therefore ordered. Conversely, each ordinal number is a series whose terms, though following one another according to the relations of order that determine their respective positions, are also units that are equivalent and can therefore be grouped in a class. Finite numbers are therefore necessarily at the same time cardinal and ordinal, since it is of the nature of number to be both a system of classes and of asymmetrical relations blended into one operational whole.

PART THREE

ADDITIVE AND MULTIPLICATIVE COMPOSITIONS

CHAPTER VII

ADDITIVE COMPOSITION OF CLASSES
RELATIONS BETWEEN CLASS AND NUMBER

THE purpose of the last chapters of this book is twofold. On the one hand, we have to examine how the construction of the positive integers is completed by the discovery of additive and multiplicative operations. We shall not here be concerned with investigating how the child learns addition and subtraction tables, etc., at school, learning which is frequently merely verbal. Additive and multiplicative operations are already implied in number as such, since a number is an additive union of units, and one-one correspondence between two sets entails multiplication. The real problem, if we wish to reach the roots of these operations, is to discover how the child becomes aware, when he discovers that they exist within numerical compositions, that they are necessary. On the other hand, we shall develop rather further than we have hitherto done the analysis of the relationships between number, class and relation, through the use made by the child of numerical operations. In Chapters VII and VIII we shall examine simultaneously the relationship between class and number, and the additive compositions of one and the other. Chapters IX and X will be devoted to the beginnings of multiplication as the result of the development of correspondence between several sets given simultaneously, and between their relations.

Hitherto, we have considered number as a seriated class, i.e., as the product of class and asymmetrical relation. But this in no way implies that class and asymmetrical relation come before number. On the contrary, number can be regarded as being necessary for the completion of truly logical structures, as we shall attempt to show in this chapter. Instead of deriving number from class, or the converse, or considering the two as radically independent, we can regard them as complementary, and as developing side by side, although directed towards different ends.

If we regard the extension of concepts as being inseparable from their comprehension, every notion thus corresponding to a class,[1]

---

[1] It is as false psychologically to suppose that we always think in terms of comprehension as to affirm that reasoning only proceeds by means of classes. The mind constantly oscillates between these two aspects of the concept.

161

it becomes obvious that concepts and numbers have an important common basis, namely the additive operation, which brings together the scattered elements into a whole, or divides these wholes into parts. In the words of Leibnitz, the logic of classes or propositions consists in an algorithm of the whole and the part. The difference between number and class, on the other hand, lies in the fact that in number the parts are homogeneous units, while the parts of a class are still only qualified classes, and are united only by virtue of their common qualities (e.g., the class of Animals can be subdivided into Vertebrates and Invertebrates). In every additive composition, however, 'intensive' quantification necessarily intervenes in the relationships of inclusion: there must be 'more' elements in the whole than in one of its parts, and therefore the four essential determinants for any combination of classes, 'one', 'none', 'some' and 'all', clearly have a quantitative significance.

The first problem to be considered is therefore the following. Can the quantitative relationships inherent in the inclusion of the part in the whole, which are intuitively grasped at the second stage described above, be manipulated operationally before the third stage, i.e. before the constitution of number? In other words, is not the additive composition of classes the psychological counterpart of the additive composition of numbers, or, to put it more shortly, is number not essential for the completion of the notion of class? It may in fact be, that it is not until the notions of invariance and conservation of numerical wholes are acquired, that the child is capable of regarding as permanent the relations of the part to the whole in the realm of classes, and consequently of constructing coherent relationships of inclusion. If such is the case, it is obviously of vital importance for us to understand how these notions are constituted, and how both class and number result from the same operational mechanism of grouping.

§1. Technique and results

In order to study additive composition of classes, i.e. the inclusion of partial classes in a wider class, in as close connection as possible with the problem of conservation of quantities, it was necessary to examine the logical relationship between the terms 'some' and 'all', in order to bring out the element of quantifica-

---

according to the needs of the moment. In the proposition 'birds are vertebrated', or even 'birds are vertebrates', for most people comprehension only comes into play, but in 'Birds constitute only a part of the Vertebrates' the stress is clearly on the extension of the concept.

tion inherent in any addition, either of classes or numbers. For this purpose, we planned a series of experiments of the following type. B was a set of objects forming a logical class definable in purely qualitative terms, and A a part of that set forming a sub-class also definable in qualitative terms. The problem put to the child was then merely that of discovering whether there were more elements in B than in A, or in other words, whether class B was wider than its sub-class A.

We began by using the same material as for the problems of correspondence and conservation of quantities. We took, for instance, a box containing only wooden beads (class B), most of them brown (class A), but two of them white (class A'). The child was then asked whether the box contained more wooden beads or more brown beads. This question involves the most elementary form of additive composition of classes: $A + A' = B$, therefore $A = B - A'$ and $A < B$. As this problem proved to be very difficult for children of from 4 to 6, we expressed it in more intuitive terms. On the one hand we asked the child which of two necklaces would be longer, one made with the brown beads or one made with the wooden beads. In order to ensure that he grasped the difference between A and B, before putting the question we placed two empty boxes by the box of beads, and asked: 'If we take out the brown beads and put them here (first empty box), will there be any beads left in this one (the full box)?' and: 'If we take out the wooden beads and put them there (second empty box), will there be any left in this one (the full box)?' Understanding of these two questions in no way implies a correct solution to the problem of the necklaces. On the other hand, we varied the data of the problem in several ways: e.g., by using for class B a set of blue beads, most of them square (A) but two or three round (A'), or by making class B a collection of flowers containing twenty poppies (A) and two or three bluebells (A'), the question then being 'which will be the bigger bunch, one made with all the flowers, or one made with all the poppies?' etc.

The various types of material produced similar results, which indicate three stages, corresponding to the three stages found earlier. At the first stage, the child is not yet capable of under-standing that the B classes will always contain more elements than the A classes, the reason being that he cannot think simultaneously of the whole B and of the parts A and A', which means, logically, that he does not yet regard class B as resulting from the addition of A and A', and class A as resulting from the subtraction of A' from B. During the second stage, the child gradually comes to under-stand that the B classes contain more elements than the A classes, but he makes this discovery intuitively. It is only when he is compelled to visualize the necklaces or the sets that he finds that B is larger than A; he does not assume this fact because of the inclusions resulting from additive composition. In particular, the child frequently discovers that B is larger than A precisely at the moment when he is thinking of the exact number of elements in class A' or in class A. Finally, during a third stage, the child grasps immediately that class B is larger than class A, because he approaches the problem from the point of view of additive composition.

§2. *Stage I: Absence of additive composition*

First we have some examples of reactions to the problem of the brown beads and the wooden beads:

Stro (6;0): 'Are there more wooden beads or more brown beads in this box?—*More brown ones.*—Why?—*Because there are only two wooden ones.*—But aren't the brown ones made of wood?—*Oh yes!*—Well then, are there more brown ones or more wooden ones?—*More brown ones.*'

As most of the answers given were of this type, we gradually made the problem more concrete, beginning by getting the child to imagine the necklaces that could be made with the brown beads and the wooden beads:

Bis (6;8): 'Are there more wooden beads or more brown beads?—*More brown ones, because there are two white ones.*—Are the white ones made of wood?—*Yes.*—And the brown ones?—*Yes.*—Then are there more brown ones or more wooden ones?—*More brown ones.*—What colour would a necklace made of the wooden beads be?—*Brown and white* (thus showing that Bis clearly understood the problem). —And what colour would a necklace made with the brown beads be?—*Brown.*—Then which would be longer, the one made with the wooden beads or the one made with the brown beads?—*The one with the brown beads.*—Draw the necklaces for me. (Bis drew a series of black rings for the necklace of brown beads, and a series of black rings plus two white rings for the necklace of wooden beads.)—Good. Now which will be longer, the one with the brown beads or the one with the wooden beads?—*The one with the brown beads.*' Thus, in spite of having clearly understood, and having correctly drawn the data of the problem, Bis was unable to solve it by including the class of brown beads in the class of wooden beads!

Fat (7;3): 'Are there more wooden beads or more brown beads?—*More brown ones.*' I then drew the brown beads and two white beads on a large sheet of white paper. 'Put a ring round all the brown ones.—(The child made a ring round the brown ones with a pencil.)—Now make a ring round the wooden ones.—(He drew a circle round the two white ones only.)—But aren't the brown ones made of wood?—*Oh yes!* (he rubbed out the circle round the two white ones and drew one round the whole set of beads.)—Well now, if we made a necklace with the wooden beads, and a necklace with the brown beads, which would be longer?—*The one with the brown beads.*'

As there was still the same difficulty for the child, we tried to simplify the problem further by putting near the box containing the beads two empty boxes, in one of which he was to imagine the brown beads, and in the other the wooden beads. The problem still remained insoluble for the younger children:

Bes (6;2): 'Are all these beads made of wood, or not?—*They're all made of wood.*—Are there more wooden ones or more brown ones?—*More brown ones.*—If I put the brown beads in that box, will there be any beads left in this one?—*Yes, the white ones.*—And if I put the wooden beads in that other empty box, will there be any left?—*No.*—Well then, if we made a necklace with all the wooden beads that would be in that box, and if we made another necklace with the brown beads that would be in the other box, which would be longer?—*The brown one.*'

Eug (5;6): 'What are these beads made of?—*Wood.*—What colour? —*Brown.*—And those?—*White.*—And what are they made of?— *They're made of wood too.*—If I put all the wooden beads into this empty box, will there be any left?—*No.*—And if I put all the brown beads into that other box, will there be any left?—*Yes, the white ones.*—Then which would be longer, a necklace made with the wooden beads out of that box, or one made with the brown beads out of the other box?—*The one made with the brown beads.*'

Oli (5;2): 'Are all these beads brown?—*No, there are two white ones.*— Are they all made of wood?—*Yes.*—If we poured all the wooden beads into this, would there be any left?—*No.*—If we poured all the brown beads into that, would there be any left?—*Yes, the two white ones.* Then which would be longer, a necklace made with the brown beads out of this box, or one made with the wooden beads out of that box?— *The one with the brown beads.*'

Our final attempt to simplify the problem apparently made it more complicated for the child, but it has the advantage of bringing out one of the main difficulties in the solution:

Laur (5;5): 'If I put the brown beads in this box, will there be any left?—*Yes, the two white ones.*—And if I put the wooden beads in that other box, will there be any left?—*No.*—Why?—*Because they're all made of wood.*—Well now, two little girls want to make necklaces with these beads. One of them wants a necklace made of the brown beads, and the other wants one made of the wooden beads. Do you understand?—*Yes, but will the one who's making the wooden necklace only take the white beads?*— No.—*She'll have the brown ones as well?* (N.B. the spontaneous character of these two questions.)—What do you think?—*Yes.*—Why?—*Because they're made of wood as well.*—Which necklace will be longer then, the one made of the brown beads or the one with the wooden beads?—*The one with the brown beads.*—Why?—*Because there are more of them.*— Show me the beads that the girl will take to make the necklace of brown beads.— (He pointed correctly.)—Now show me the ones that the other girl will take to make the necklace of wooden beads.—*Those* (pointing to the two white ones).—Only those?—*There aren't any others!*'

Sout (6;10): 'If I put the brown beads into this box, will there be any left?—*Yes, the white ones.*—And if I put the wooden beads in that other box, will there be any left?—*No.*—Now listen. Two little girls want to make necklaces with these beads. One of them wants to make hers with the brown beads, and the other wants to make hers with the wooden beads. Which will be longer?—*The necklace of brown beads will be longer, because there are more.*—Which beads will the girl take to make the brown necklace?—*Those* (the brown ones).—And which will the other girl take to make the necklace of wooden beads?—*The white ones.*—Why?—*Because the other girl will have taken the brown ones.*'

We have here clear evidence of the systematic difficulty experienced by children under 7 or 8 in including one class in another, and in understanding that a total class is wider than one that is included in it. Two objections might however be made to the preceding experiments, one concerning the part played by language, and the other the part played by perception.

With regard to the first, a logical class is defined and determined only when it is named by a word or a combination of words. Through the language he learns from the adult, the child finds himself, relatively early, in possession of a system of classes already forming a hierarchy as a result of inclusions. Thus when he learns to use words such as 'sparrow', 'duck', 'hen' as well as the word 'bird', he is compelled to include the classes corresponding to the first three in the general class of 'birds'. Observation and experiment show clearly that this is not immediately grasped by the child, as can be seen from the difficulties he systematically experiences with regard to inclusion. But sooner or later he comes to understand it, with the aid of language itself. In the case of the beads, the difficulty seems to be increased by the fact that there is no single word to indicate the general class and the particular classes, but only combinations of words, 'wooden beads', 'brown beads', 'white beads', in each of which 'beads' occurs. What would be the result if the experiment was repeated with classes each having a specific name, e.g., 'poppies' and 'bluebells', both belonging to the class 'flowers'?

As for the second objection, it might be argued that the fact of putting some forty brown beads with only two white ones creates a systematic illusion in the child's mind. A situation of this kind would seem to be indispensable in order to compel the child to reason, or in other words, to ensure that reflection and not mere perceptual judgment determines the solution. It is however possible that the data prevent reflection by the fact of being so much polarized in one direction. What would be the result if the proportions or the perceived qualities were varied?

In order to answer the first objection, we put the same questions to the child, but using logical classes each designated by a specific word. Here we have some examples of reactions in the case of flowers:

Arl (5;0): 'Look, are there a lot of flowers or a few in this field (a drawing representing 20 poppies and 3 bluebells)?—*A lot.*—What colour are they?—*They're red and blue.*—The red ones are poppies and the blue ones are bluebells.—*Yes.*—I want to make a very big bunch. Must I pick the flowers or the poppies?—*The poppies.*—Show me the poppies. (She pointed correctly.)—Show me the flowers.—(She made a circular movement to indicate the whole of the drawing.)—Then will the bunch be bigger if I pick the flowers or the poppies?—*If you pick the poppies.*—If I pick the poppies, what will be left?—*The bluebells.* —And if I pick the bluebells, what will be left?—*The poppies.*—And if I pick the flowers, what will be left?—(Reflection.) *Nothing at all.*— Then which will be bigger, the bunch of flowers or the bunch of poppies?—*I've told you already.*—Think (repeating the question).—*The bunch of poppies will be bigger.*—And what about the bunch of flowers?— *It won't be the same.*—Will it be bigger or smaller?—*Smaller.*—Why?— *Because you've made a big bunch of poppies.*'

Ric (5;11): 'Look at these poppies and these two bluebells. If I take all the flowers, or if I take the poppies, which will be the biggest bunch?—*The bunch of poppies because there are more.*—Show me the poppies.—(She pointed correctly.)—Show me the flowers.—(She pointed to the whole picture.)—Then which bunch will be bigger, the one with all the flowers, or the one with the poppies?—*The one with the poppies.*'

Stro (6;0) was watching me drawing 15 buttercups and 2 bluebells: 'What are those?—*Buttercups.*—And those?—*Bluebells.*—Are they all flowers?—*Yes.*—Are there more flowers or more buttercups?—*More buttercups.*—Why?—*There are only two bluebells.*—But aren't the buttercups flowers?—*Yes.*—Then are there more buttercups or more flowers? —*More buttercups.*'

And now two examples of reactions to questions about girls and children:

Juil (5;6) watched me drawing 12 girls and 2 boys: 'Are there more girls or more children in this class?—*More girls.*—But aren't the girls children?—*Yes.*—Then are there more children or more girls?—*More girls.*'

Bes (6;2): 'Are there more girls or more children?—*More girls.*— Why?—*There are only two boys.*—But are the girls children?—*Yes.*— Then are there more girls or more children?—*More girls.*'

These two questions thus give rise to the same kind of answer as was given in the case of the beads. And yet the question referring

M

to girls and children is clearly easier than the question about the beads, and we found that half the children of 6 that we questioned, and even some who were only 5, were able to answer it. The difficulty of the problem of the flowers seems to be intermediary between the other two. The interest of these results lies in the fact that they indicate clearly that the use of classes which have specific names is an aid to differentiating between them and forming the hierarchy. At the same time, the fact that in the case of the beads the child has to construct the classes without being influenced by the language, means that this experiment brings out more clearly the difficulties the child experiences.

As an answer to the second objection, we made three series of control experiments to eliminate the disadvantage of the previous technique. In the first place, we used a set of beads defined by their colour and not by the material, so that this quality of the whole should be more obvious, and the partial classes were defined by their shape, round, square, etc. Secondly, we repeated the experiment with the brown and wooden beads, but using about twenty brown beads and fifteen to seventeen white or green ones. Lastly, when the child had to imagine two necklaces, one made with the total class and one made with the partial class, we gave him two sets of beads in two separate boxes as an aid to differentiating between the whole and the parts. These new techniques, although they were of some slight help in reaching the right solution (at least the last two), nevertheless produced the same reactions as the earlier ones, thus proving that the difficulty involved in inclusion is largely independent of factors of perception.

First we have some examples of reactions in the case of a total class defined by colour:

Arl (5;0) was shown ten little blue cones ('roofs') and three blue beads: 'Look. Are there more blue things or more roofs?—*More roofs.*— What colour are the beads?—*Blue.*—And the roofs?—*They're blue too.* —Then are there more roofs or more blue things?—*More roofs.*—Why? —*Because there are a lot.*—And what about the blue things?—*Everything's blue.*—Are there more blue things, then, or more roofs?—*More roofs.*'

Dur (5;6) was shown ten square blue beads and three round blue beads: 'What colour are these beads?—*Blue.*—Are they all square?— *Some are round and some are square.*—What will be left if I take away the square ones?—*The round ones.*—If I take away the blue ones, what will be left?—*None at all.*—(He pointed with his finger at the whole set.)— One little girl wants to make a necklace with the square ones, and another little girl thinks that the necklace should be made with the blue ones.—Which one would be longer, the one with the square beads, or the one with the blue beads?—*The one with the square beads.*'

Jea (6;0). The questioning began in the same way. 'Then which necklace would be longer, the one with the square beads or the one with the blue beads?—*The one with the square beads.*—Why?—*Because there are more of them.*—Why?—*Because there are more square ones.*' Jea then drew the two necklaces, one made only of the square beads, the other of both round and square ones (ten squares for the first and eight square ones plus two round ones for the second).—Good, then which will be longer?—*The one with the square beads.*—Why?—*Because there are more.*'

Hub (5;6). The questioning began in the same way. 'One little girl wants to make a necklace with the square beads. Another girl wants to make one with the blue beads.—(Hub laughed and said spontaneously): *They're all blue!*—Yes. Which necklace will be longer then? —*The one with the square beads, because there are more.*'

These answers are exactly the same as those given in the case of the wooden and brown beads.

We now come to some reactions to questions relating to brown beads and wooden beads when the two sub-classes are approximately equal in number:

Tap (5;6). The questioning was the same to begin with. 'Which necklace will be longer, then, the one made with the brown beads (20) or the one made with the wooden beads (20 brown and 18 green)?— *The one with the brown beads.*—Why?—*Because there are more.*' Tap was then given two sets of beads in two separate boxes, each one containing 20 brown and 18 green, all made of wood. 'The little girl who has this box makes her necklace with the brown beads, and the girl who has the other box makes her necklace with the wooden beads in it. Which necklace will be longer?—*The brown ones, because there are more.*—And what colour will the necklace of wooden beads be?—*Only green.*'

Jea (6;0): Same replies.

Ros (5;6) had not been asked the earlier questions, and was shown a set of 20 brown and 18 green beads. The questions he was then asked followed the same pattern, but the whole set was referred to as 'the round beads': 'What colour are these?—*Brown.*—And those?—*Green.* —And what shape?—*They are all round.*—If I put the brown beads in this lid, will there be any left in the box?—*Yes, the green ones.*—And if I put the round ones in that lid, will there be any left in the box?—*No, they're all round.*—And if I put the brown ones in this lid, will there be any left in the box?—*Yes, the green ones.*—And if I put the round ones in that lid, will there be any left in the box?—*No, they're all round.*—Well, then, if you make a necklace with the brown ones, and then undo it and make a necklace with the green ones, and then undo it and then make a necklace with the round ones, which one will be the longest?— *The one with the brown beads.*—Why?—*Because there are more.*' I then gave Ros two identical sets of green and brown beads in two separate boxes and said to him: 'Have you got two friends at school?—*Yes, André and Oliver.*—Well now, I'm giving one box to André (putting it on the right), and the other to Oliver (putting it on the left). Are they the the same?—*Yes.*—Now André is going to take the brown ones out of his box to make a necklace, and Oliver is going to make a necklace

with the round ones in his box. Which of them will be longer?—
André's, because he'll take more beads; there are more brown ones.'

Finally, we have an example of the reactions obtained when the
same proportions were kept and the total set was defined by its
colour:

Be (5;6) was given a box containing 10 big yellow beads and about
15 small yellow ones. The questioning began as before, and I then
asked: 'Which necklace would be longer, one made with the little
beads or one made with all the yellow ones?—*The one made with the little
ones.—*Why?—*There are more.*—But aren't they yellow as well?—*Yes.*—
Then which necklace will be longer?—*The one made with the little beads.'*

As can be seen, there is little difference between this reaction
and the earlier ones.

When the child is given two identical sets of beads, he arrives
slightly more easily at the correct answer, since he can consider
simultaneously one set from the point of view of the brown beads
and the other from that of the whole set. This fact does not however eliminate all the difficulties of the problem, as we have
already seen in the case of Tap and Ros. Here are some further
examples:

Er (5;6). There were two sets of blue beads, each one containing 10
square beads and 3 round ones. 'Which necklace will be longer?—*The
one with the square beads.—*Why?—*Because there are more.*—Are they blue
or not?—*Yes.*—Then which necklace will be longer, the one that A.
makes with the square beads in this box, or the one that M. makes with
the blue ones in that box?—*The one with the square beads.'*

Suz (6;0). Same questions. '*The necklace of square beads will be longer.*—
How many are there?—*Ten.*—And how many blue ones?—*Three.*—
What colour are the square ones?—*They're blue as well.*—Well then?—
The blue one will be longer. The square ones are blue as well.—So if J. takes
the square ones out of this box to make his necklace, and L. takes the
blue ones out of his box to make his necklace, which one will be longer?
—*The one with the square beads.—*Why?—*Because there are more square
ones.'*

It is useless to quote other examples, since they are all of the
same type, and confirm the results we obtained before the technique was modified. It now remains to interpret these facts.

All the children we have quoted understood the nature of the
sets involved in the problems of inclusion. They grasped the fact
that all the beads were wooden (or blue, etc.) and indicated that
they did so either verbally or graphically, or by imagining the
transfer to another box. Bis, Bes, Eug, etc., stated without hesitation that all the beads were made of wood: Stro, who began by
thinking that there were only two wooden beads (the white ones),

said later that all the brown ones and also the white ones were made of wood. These children were therefore clearly conscious of the general definition of the total set in question. Moreover, they were able to draw the two necklaces, the one made with all the beads (including the two white ones) and the other with the brown beads only. In addition to this, all these children grasped without difficulty that, if all the wooden beads were taken out and put into an empty box, there would be none left, whereas if only the brown ones were taken out, the white ones would remain. It cannot therefore be disputed that all these children possessed the notion of total class required by the questions and were capable of the general statement defining that class: 'All the beads are wooden.'

And yet, as soon as it becomes necessary to think simultaneously of the whole and the part, as our question requires, difficulties arise. The child apparently forgets the whole when he thinks of the part, and forgets the part when he thinks of the whole. Or rather, when he thinks of the whole, he can envisage the parts which have not yet been dissociated, but when he tries to dissociate one of the parts he forgets the whole, or disregards it, and merely compares the part in question with the remaining part. Thus when he is concerned with the brown beads, he compares them with the white ones, and not with the whole set of wooden beads. In other words, the children quoted above cannot establish a permanent inclusion between the whole and the parts: as soon as the whole is divided, even in thought, the parts cease to be included in it and are merely juxtaposed without synthesis.

It thus seems to be the relationship of inclusion that is the stumbling-block for these children. For them, wholes are not logical classes, but elementary schemata of assimilation or syncretic aggregates, in which the relation between the part and the whole is not yet a quantitative relationship, or even 'intensively' quantifiable, i.e. there is neither part nor inclusion, but merely qualitative participation. The child is well aware that the brown beads are made of wood and that they therefore form part of the same whole as the white ones, as he proves by his drawing of the necklace which includes both the white and the brown beads, and by his statement that if all the wooden beads are taken out of the box, none will be left. But when it is a question of envisaging simultaneously the class of wooden beads and the class of brown beads, i.e. of taking the point of view of the inclusion, in their extension, of two classes, difficulties reappear, and the child is incapable of including in the 'wooden' class the elements he has just counted in the 'brown' class. It can therefore be said that qualitatively the child understands that one bead can be at the same time both brown and wooden, but that from the point of view of quantitative classification he cannot place the same beads in two sets simultaneously. If he is merely counting the wooden beads, he includes the brown ones, but if it is a question of counting first the brown ones and then the wooden ones, he puts the brown ones into the first set only, and does not understand that the first set forms part of the second.

To sum up, as soon as the child envisages one part separately, the whole as such is destroyed. If we call the whole B, the part in question A, and the other part A', the difficulty found by children at the first stage in understanding the relationship between the part and the whole is due to the fact that they cannot see the whole as the result of an additive composition of the parts: B = A + A' and A = B − A'. For the child, the whole is merely a set B characterized by two attributes, 'brown' and 'not brown', whereas when A is considered separately from the whole it becomes a new set characterized by the quality 'brown'. But if A is thus dissociated from B, B is regarded as being reduced to the remaining set A' defined by the attribute 'not brown'. If the latter is a small set, the child then says that A is larger than B, which is regarded as identical with A'. Or again, if B is defined by the attribute 'wooden', which is common to all the elements, B = A + A' if A is defined as 'brown and wooden' and A' as 'not brown and wooden'. For the child, however, when A is separated from B, A is characterized only by the attribute 'brown' and the whole B disappears and is replaced by A' defined by the attribute 'wooden'.

It does not, however, always happen that the whole B disappears when one of its parts is separated from it. What sometimes occurs is that the whole seems to be preserved, and even influences any evaluation of the parts resulting from its division. We observed this apparently inverse phenomenon in the case of correspondence:

Gfe (5;0) made a one for one exchange of ten beans for ten that I took from a bag one at a time, and put them in a row in front of him: 'Have you and I both got the same?—*No.*—Where are there more?—*There* (pointing to my 10 beans).—Why?—*Because there were more in the bag.*'

Stro (6;0) had in front of him 10 yellow beads taken from a box in which a number still remained, while the 10 corresponding red beads which he had given me one by one had not been taken out of a box: 'Have we got the same, or has one of us got more?—*I have.*—Why?—*Because there are more in the box.*—But are there more there (the 10 yellow ones) than here (the 10 red ones)?—*Yes, because there are still some in the box.*'

Arl (5;0), Obs. I. We exchanged 10 leaves in a garden for 10 stones, and we had a reserve supply of stones, but not of leaves. 'Are they the same?—*There are more leaves.*—Why?—*Because there are a lot.*—And how many stones?—*Not as many.*—Why?—*Because you haven't taken all the stones.*—Why haven't I taken all the stones?—*There weren't any more leaves to take.*—Then have I got the same number of leaves as you have of stones?—*No, because there are a lot of leaves. There are more leaves.*—Why?—*Because there weren't enough leaves to put a lot of stones.'*

Obs. II. A moment later, Arl had 8 stones and the experimenter had a lot. A one for one exchange was made, the stones being placed in two separate heaps of 8 away from the experimenter's supply: 'Have we got the same?—*No.*—Who has more?—*I have.*—Why?—*Because you gave them to me from that big heap.*—And what did you do?—*I only had a few.*—Well?—*You had more stones* (pointing to the big heap).—Yes, but what about these and those (the two heaps of 8)?—*I've got more.*—Why?—*I've got stones from there* (pointing to the original supply).'

These very interesting reactions, which at first sight appear to be in contradiction to the earlier ones, and even to contradict one another, are in reality a useful control experiment. The two situations are different. In the first, the whole B was compared with its own parts A and A', while in the second, a part is compared either to another whole or to a part of that whole. In the second case, that of correspondence, what usually happens is that when A is separated from the whole B, the whole or the remainder are simply forgotten. This occurred with almost all our subjects in Chapters III and IV, but it sometimes happens, as is shown by the exceptional cases quoted above (Gfe, Stro, Arl and others), that the child's evaluation is influenced by the original sets.

When this is the case, we find two kinds of reactions which seem to be contradictory. Arl, for instance, first thinks (obs. I) that his ten leaves form a larger set than ten stones, because the ten leaves form a whole while the ten stones are only part of a whole. In contrast to this, Arl (obs. II), Stro and Gfe think that if A' is part of a whole B' larger than B, then A' is larger than B even if A' and B are in one-one correspondence.

These curious facts are due to exactly the same cause as the child's incapacity to envisage the part and the whole simultaneously, i.e. to the primacy of global quantification over operational quantification.

It must be remembered that the observations just quoted (Gfe, Stro and Arl) were related to one-one correspondence, and enabled us to prove that for children at this first stage correspondence is not a criterion for quantification. Their criterion is the global evaluation of the sets. Hence, when Arl (obs. I), after exchanging ten leaves for ten stones says 'there are more leaves' or 'there are a lot' because there are none left after the operation, and that there are less stones because they have not all been used, what he means is that the leaves form a closed set, in contrast to the ten stones which are only part of a whole that has not been exhausted. 'All' the leaves are therefore more than 'some' stones, irrespective of any correspondence, because a whole that is intuitively perceived at the same time as a part is greater than that part.

Conversely, when Arl (obs. II), Gfe and Stro concentrate not on the part but on the whole (provided that the remainder is considerably larger than the part in question), the opposite phenomenon occurs, and for the same reason. The part taken from a large whole whose remaining elements are still visible, acquires through this participation the value of the whole and therefore seems to be larger than the other set. Logically, such reasoning is of course in contradiction with the earlier one, but from the intuitive point of view of global perception, it is the result of the same criteria of immediate and non-operational evaluation.

We are now in a position to understand why, in the case of the brown and wooden beads, and in other similar cases, the child thinks that when a part is compared with a whole that contains it, the part is larger than the whole (if the remainder is small). If all the criteria used by the child are intuitive and not operational, it is obvious that a whole divided into two parts, even mentally, ceases to exist, since it is no longer perceptible. The child can perceive either the whole or its parts, but not the whole and one of its parts simultaneously.

In a word, it seems clear that at this stage the child is still incapable of additive composition of classes, i.e. of grasping logical addition or subtraction. This means that he cannot handle successfully the relationship of inclusion, and replaces the nesting of classes by mere intuitive relationships between the sets in question. Precisely because these relationships are intuitive, and dependent on actual perception, they cannot result in any stable composition, and we therefore find on the logical plane the same fundamental phenomenon common to all the reactions of the first stage in relation to numerical problems: non-conservation of wholes.

Our analysis both of the first levels of cardinal correspondence (Chapters III–IV) and of the first stages of conservation (Chapters I–II) has made plain the fact that very young children find systematic difficulty in grasping the permanence of a whole irrespective of its transformations, e.g., difficulty in understanding that beads poured from one container into two others still constitute the same whole. When the beads are no longer in the original container that whole no longer exists for the child. On the numerical plane, therefore, exactly the same phenomenon occurs as on that of conceptual inclusion, with which we are concerned here: once the part is separated from the whole, it is no longer defined or conceived in terms of the initial whole, but only in relation to the present situation and to the remaining parts. Thus both on the numerical and the logical planes we can say that the relationship of part to whole is at first neither a fractional relationship nor a relationship of inclusion, but merely a qualitative participation. The parts placed in the two containers are indeed seen as deriving from the original whole, but they are definitely not considered as essentially belonging to a logically indestructible whole. That is why the whole, whether number or concept, is not regarded as invariable from the start, but as varying in qualitative value according to the displacements of its parts.

It follows that in the realm of concepts, the child under 7 is incapable of the colligation that gives rise to logical classes and ensures their permanence by defining the inclusion of their parts. In other words, in the case both of numerical sets and logical classes, totalities are not preserved because the parts are not united in a whole, this synthesis being the additive composition that is common to numerical sets and classes.

§3. Stages II and III: Progressive reversibility of operations

The second stage is characterized by the intuitive discovery of the correct answer, i.e. by trial and error and not by immediate composition. Here we have three examples:

Gail (6;0): 'If you make a necklace with the brown beads in this box or with the wooden beads, which will be longer?—*The necklace of brown beads will be bigger.*—Why?—*Because there are more brown beads.*—Are there more wooden beads or more brown beads?—*More brown beads. No, more wooden beads. No, they're the same!*' Thus Gail almost succeeded in including one class in the other: the only thing he had not understood was that the class of wooden beads contained two more elements than the class of brown beads.

Tail (7;2): 'Are there more brown beads or more wooden beads in this box?—*More brown ones.*—Are the white ones made of wood?—*Yes.* —And the brown ones?—*Yes.*—Then are there more wooden beads or more brown ones?—*More wooden ones, because there are two white ones as well.*—Which would be longer, a necklace made with the brown beads or one made with the wooden beads?—*They'd be the same.*—Are the white beads made of wood?—*Yes.*—Then which necklace would be longer?—*Oh! the wooden one would be longer because there are the two white ones.*'

Gon (7;2): 'If we made a necklace with all the wooden beads and a necklace with all the brown beads, which would be longer?—*They'd be the same.*—Draw the necklace with the wooden beads.—(Gon drew a row of brown beads close together.)—Are all the wooden beads brown? —*Oh no! There are two white ones* (adding them).—Now draw the neck-

lace of brown beads.—(He drew them close together in a line.)—
Which is longer?—*They're both the same.*—Why?—*They're the same.*—
Are the necklaces the same?—*One of them only has brown beads, and the
other has white ones as well.*—Then which one is longer?—*They're the
same.*—How many brown beads are there?—*About forty.*—And how
many white ones?—*Two.*—Then which is longer?—*Oh, the wooden one!*
—Why didn't you see that before?—*I thought they were the same.*'

These children begin either by thinking, like those of the first
stage, that there are more brown beads than wooden beads (Gail
and Tail), or that the brown beads and the whole set have the
same extension (Gon). Gail and Tail afterwards remember (as
Gon does from the beginning) that the brown beads are also made
of wood, and therefore decide that the class of wooden beads is
identical with that of the brown beads. Gail goes no further than
this, but Tail and Gon then discover that 'there are two white ones
as well'. It should be noted that Gon, in order to conclude that
the total class of wooden beads is wider than that of the brown
beads, is compelled to have recourse to the approximate numbers
of the two parts, while Tail does so implicitly in one case and
explicitly in the other. It is evident, therefore, that it is when these
children are able to think simultaneously of the total class characterized by the attribute 'wooden' and the partial classes defined
by their colour, that they gradually discover correct additive
composition and inclusion.

At the third stage, the discovery is spontaneous and immediate:

Bol (6;6): ' *The wooden necklace will be longer than the brown one.*—Why?
—*Because there are more.*—But why are there more?—*Because there are
the white ones as well.*'

Plat (6;9): 'Are there more wooden beads or more brown ones?—
More brown ones.—If we made a necklace with the wooden beads and a
necklace with the brown ones, which would be longer?—*The one with
the wooden beads* (without hesitating).—Why?—*Because there are the two
extra white ones.*'

Laur (7;2, the same child who was at stage one at 5;5): 'Are there
more brown beads or more round beads in this box?—*More brown ones.
Oh no!* (spontaneously), *more round ones, because there are the two white ones
as well.*—Which would be longer, a necklace made with the brown
ones, or a necklace made with the round ones?—*The one with the round
ones.*'

Nal (8;0): 'Are there more brown beads or more wooden beads?—
More wooden ones.—Why?—*Because the two white ones are made of wood as
well.*—Suppose we made two necklaces, etc.?—*Well, the wooden ones
and the brown ones are the same, and it would be longer with the wooden ones
because there are the two white ones as well.*'

All of these children are capable, at once, or almost at once, of thinking simultaneously of the total class and of one of its parts. They can therefore see that the part and the whole are defined by the same attribute, but that the whole also comprises the remaining part. 'They are the same', says Nal, meaning that the brown beads are also made of wood, and 'There are the two extra white ones', says Plat. All of them therefore understand both that $B = A + A'$ and that $A = B - A'$.

These correct answers appear so simple that we are led to wonder how children at the first stage can fail to solve the problem. How is it that they cannot envisage the whole and the parts simultaneously when the children quoted above understand the same inclusions without any difficulty? Two separate problems are involved here, that of the synthesis of the attributes and that of addition in extension. ·

A logical class is a union of elements possessing a common quality. Thus class A is composed of the beads defined by the colour 'brown', and class A' is composed of those which are 'not brown' (in this case white). Adding these two classes consists in defining the smallest class that will contain them both, the sum being defined by the qualities common to both. Addition of classes therefore always implies logical multiplication, i.e. each element belonging to a system of added classes necessarily belongs to two classes simultaneously, all the elements of either of the parts possessing the attributes of that part and of the whole. Thus one possible explanation of the difficulty experienced by children at the first stage might be that these children are unable to think of the two attributes at the same time, whereas the older children can do so without difficulty. A second possible explanation, however, is that the difficulty lies in the additive composition, and this was our explanation in §2. These two interpretations coincide and neither is sufficient to account for the initial difficulties. Children at the first stage are well aware that the brown beads are made of wood, and say so explicitly, but when part A is separated from the whole B they forget that the brown beads are also wooden. We could therefore equally well say that the additive synthesis fails for lack of logical multiplication, or that the multiplicative synthesis fails for lack of logical addition. For the sake of simplicity, we shall confine ourselves to the additive point of view in order to explain why both of them fail, but the same arguments would hold from the point of view of multiplication.

The real reason for the difficulty of the younger children and the success of the older ones is that the former are still on the plane of perceptual intuition, which is immediate and irreversible, while the latter use an operational mechanism that is reversible. The additive synthesis of the parts into a whole, or the co-ordination of the attributes defining the classes in question, are only possible as the result of reversible intellectual constructions made by the child, and it is in so far as his mental experiences remain irreversible that co-ordination of the attributes, additive inclusion, and arithmetical colligation are impossible.

Let us look first at the very revealing examples of Laur (5;5) and Sout (6;10) in §2. Laur began by stating quite clearly that if the brown beads were removed the two white ones would remain, and that if the wooden beads were removed nothing would remain 'because they're all wooden'. He went even further, and asked spontaneously whether for the wooden necklace he should take 'only the white ones', and when we said no, he added 'the brown ones as well . . . because they're made of wood as well'. There was therefore apparently no doubt in his mind. And yet, when asked which necklace would be longer, he replied 'the one with the brown beads . . . because there are more'. He was asked to point to the beads corresponding to the two possible necklaces, and it was then that his first real difficulty arose. He pointed correctly to the brown beads for the first necklace, but for the wooden necklace he pointed only to the white beads 'because there aren't any others', in other words because the brown beads had already been used up mentally in making the first necklace. In the same way, Sout, who like Laur understood the data, thought that the wooden necklace would contain only the white beads 'because the other girl will have taken the brown ones'. The difficulty is clear. These children could picture taking the brown beads from the set to make a necklace, but when they had to construct mentally another necklace with the set of wooden beads, they regarded the brown beads used for the first necklace as no longer available, and thought that only the two white ones were left. Obviously, for the adult there is no difficulty here, since what characterizes deduction, in contrast to empirical manipulation, is precisely the capacity to construct all the possible combinations by returning every time to the starting point, and then comparing them as if they were present simultaneously in the mind. The fact that I have imagined a necklace made of brown beads in no way prevents me from using the same brown beads when I imagine a necklace made of the set of wooden beads. The child, on the contrary, apparently regards his mental experiences as actual, and therefore, when he has constructed one necklace mentally, he cannot mentally make another with the same material. Whereas the mobility and reversibility of the adult's mental construction enable him to decompose and recompose the sets at will, thus revealing their various implications, inclusions and other relations, the irreversibility of the child's thought and representation prevents him from acquiring the power of decomposition that is necessary for combining analysis and synthesis, and therefore for the understanding of inclusions and relations.

There is no difficulty in explaining the other examples in the same way. The child succeeds in drawing the necklaces correctly because he does not need to think of one while he is drawing the other.[1] The drawing of the necklaces is correct while their mental construction is not, because in the drawing the necklaces are reproduced one after the other and merely juxtaposed, which does not involve any internal reversibility of the operations, whereas reversibility is essential for their simultaneous mental construction.

In the same way, the child can divide the set of beads and can put, in imagination, the brown ones into one empty box, and then the wooden ones into another empty box. When he does so, he thinks first only of the brown beads, and can then think of the set of wooden beads leaving aside the question of colour. In this case there is again no reversibility of thought, but merely the juxtaposition of two successive thoughts without logical connection between them, i.e. without operations. This accounts for the fact that, when these children are again required to construct the two necklaces mentally at the same time, they again fall into the same mistake, in spite of having answered correctly the questions about the two empty boxes. Examples like those of Gail, Gon and Tail, however, whose answers are correct, or almost so, show that at that level they can think simultaneously of the brown necklace and the wooden necklace made with the same beads, since they begin by saying that the two necklaces will be the same length. This means that the construction of one necklace does not prevent their thought from returning to the initial set and making another necklace with it. It is this beginning of reversibility which enables these children eventually to discover the correct inclusion. Gail is not entirely successful, Gon is successful when he uses numbers at the same time as he combines logical classes, and Tail succeeds through direct intuition of the relationships of inclusion.

Before going further, a possible objection must be considered. It might be argued that the child's difficulty in mentally constructing two simultaneous sets is not due to the irreversibility of his thought, as we have just suggested, but merely to lack of understanding of his instructions. Might he not think that two necklaces were actually to be made with the same material? It was precisely with this possibility in mind that we finally used two sets

[1] This is still true, as we have seen, even when the child is given two identical sets of beads, because the mental use of the first prevents the free use of the second.

of beads in two separate boxes, and as we have seen, this technique made little difference to the results. The difficulty is therefore not due to verbal misunderstanding.

On the logical plane, this psychological irreversibility can be expressed in the following way. To conceive the parts in terms of the whole is to compose simultaneously the two equations $A + A' = B$ and $A = B - A'$ i.e., to carry out both the inverse and the direct operation. To think in an irreversible way, on the contrary, is to be unable to proceed from one of these operations to the other, i.e. to be unable to use operations as such. It is to replace a two-way mobile operational mechanism by successive static perceptions which it is impossible to synchronize and therefore to reconcile.

Children at the third stage have reached the point at which they are capable of psychological reversibility and logical composition of inverse and direct operations. From the additive point of view, Nal's statements ('the wooden ones and the brown ones are the same' but the necklace 'would be longer with the wooden ones because there are the two white ones as well'), are equivalent to saying that $B = A + A'$ and $A = B - A'$. It is equally obvious that from the multiplicative point of view the child at the third stage regards the elements in the part as being at the same time in the part and in the whole.

In conclusion, we should have a quite false picture of true, live, logical thought if we regarded it as being merely the static schemata of syllogistic inclusions. Every reasoning is a reversible construction, and there are as many different reasonings as there are types of construction. Even when, as here, the reasoning is related explicitly only to a set of classifications, thought never appears as a static nesting of elements, but as a system of active operations of groupings and dissociations, in a word, as a true, continuous construction. Just as arithmetical, algebraic or geometrical reasoning consists in combining objects (numbers, signs or figures) by means of the operations of arithmetic, algebra or spatial construction, so in the case of classification, reasoning consists in combining objects by means of operations on classes (logical addition and multiplication, etc.), and in thus grouping objects and classes in hierarchical systems, or separating them one from another. Thus in our problem, when the child has to think simultaneously of the brown beads and the wooden beads, he has to unite objects and then separate them again in order to construct another union, each element being at the same time in both constructions. Similarly, co-ordinating the various lengths consists in constructing a real series, and then unmaking it and reconstructing another one containing more elements.

If then thought, when classifying, has this active, operational character, it is obvious that, when we attribute the difficulties of inclusion merely to the fact that the child cannot think simultaneously of two or more data, we are only describing the surface of things, i.e., merely observing in the field of consciousness the outcropping of the underlying operations. The real truth is that what is lacking is the mobility necessary for carrying out the operations, for combining and separating them, for constructing and reconstructing simultaneously. It is therefore in terms of reversibility that the difficulties of synthesis must be described, or in other words, dynamism must be introduced into the static terms of the description.

§4. Number, and additive composition of classes

The lesson to be learnt from the preceding facts is that class and number have a common mechanism, that of their additive and multiplicative operations. Let us now consider how classes must be grouped in order to function normally, how the 'grouping' of classes differs from 'groups' of numbers, and what are the relationships between these two kinds of systems.

The two equations which determine the solution of the problem of the beads examined in this chapter, i.e., $A + A' = B$ and $A = B - A'$, constitute the elements of any additive 'grouping' of classes. Once these elements are acquired, the following sequence can be composed: if B is included in C, and C in D, then $B + B' = C$; $C + C' = D$; etc., and the inverse operations will be $D - C' = C$ or $D - C = C'$; $C - B' = B$ or $C - B = B'$, etc. These equations are associative with respect to addition and subtraction, i.e., $B + B' + C' = C + C'$, etc., and $D - C' = B + B' = A + A' + B'$, etc. But with respect to itself, each term is an 'identical operation', since $A + A = A$, and in the case of classes containing others $A + B = B$, if A is included in B.[1]

This peculiar relationship which distinguishes logical 'groupings' from 'groups' of integers, $1 + 1 = 2$, $1 + 2 = 3$, etc., indicates the fundamental differences between classes, in which iteration is disregarded, and numbers, of which iteration is characteristic.

In what does this difference consist from the psychological point of view? If we again take the example of the beads, class A is defined by the union of the elements having the common quality 'brown', but obviously the number of these elements, like those of class A', is not fixed, unless by a convention which has

[1] Cf. 'Le groupement additif des classes', *Compte rendu des séances del a Société de Physique et d'Histoire naturelle de Genève*, vol. lviii (1941), pp. 107-112.

nothing to do with the logic of classes. If $B = A + A'$, and if A and A' contain at least one element, all that we know is that class B will contain more elements than A or A', and that the attribute characterizing B is common to all the elements of A and A', while no element in A has the attribute of A' and conversely. Apart from the intensive quantifications $A < B$ or $B > A'$, $A + A' = B$, and the terms 'one', 'none', 'some' and 'all', class in extension ignores quantity and has nothing of the extensive quantification characteristic of number. Obviously, in order to be able to state that $A + A = 2A$ the two classes A and A' must be quantitatively comparable, but we do not know whether there are more, less or the same number of elements in A and A'. When $A + A$ represents the logical addition of two classes defined by the same attribute, they form a single class, and therefore $A + A = A$.

How then are classes to be transformed into numbers? In order to simplify the problem, let us suppose the various classes A, A', B', C', . . . etc., to be singular, i.e. each containing a single element while B, C, D, etc., will contain several elements. Let us suppose, for instance, that A is a round, brown, wooden bead; A' is a round wooden bead, but is not brown; B' is a round bead, but is not wooden; C' is a square bead, D' is a counter; E' is a bean and so on. Then $A + A' = B$ will be the round, wooden beads; $B + B' = C$ will be the round beads; $C + C' = D$ will be the beads; $D + D' = E$ will be the beads and the counter; $E + E' = F$ will be the things on the table, and so on. The question then is: what operations are necessary to obtain the numbers 1, 2, 3 . . . 6 from this classification?

As we saw in Chapters III–VI, Russell's solution to this problem is too simple. For him and his followers, two classes have the same number when there is a one-one correspondence between their elements. Let us suppose we have another table on which there is an identical set of objects, A, A', B', C' . . . etc., being defined in the same way. There will be an exact one-one correspondence between the two sets F and F_1, but what do we mean here by the term correspondence? If we confine ourselves to the logic of classes, by which elements are united according to their attributes, it is obvious that A will correspond to A_1, A' to A'_1, B' to B'_1, C' to C'_1, etc., but it would be false to say that the square bead C' will correspond to the counter D'_1, or that the round glass bead B' will correspond to the bean E'_1. The qualitative correspondence between the two classes F and F_1 merely means that these two classes have the same hierarchical structure, the same classification, but not the same number. As we saw in Chapters III–IV, there are various kinds of qualitative correspondence, which depend on the spatial position of the elements and have no numerical significance. When an anatomist compares the bones in the skeleton of mammals with those of other classes of vertebrates, the correspondence he makes is qualitative, and not mathematical, whereas in our case, if we assert that any element in F can correspond to any element in F_1, we have the right to conclude that F and F_1 correspond numerically term for term, and that this correspondence defines the number six. This number is not a 'class of classes', but the result of a new operation brought in from outside, which is not contained in the logic of classes as such. In fact, this 'quantifying' correspondence is only achieved by disregarding all the attributes in question, i.e. by disregarding the classes.

In order to transform classes F and F_1 into numbers, the first essential condition is that their terms shall be regarded as equivalent from all points of view simultaneously. This is however contrary to our earlier statement with respect to classes. If we assume that we disregard the differences between A and A', then class B will not be equivalent to the number 2 but only to the union of 'round, wooden beads' irrespective of their colour. If we then again take into account the difference between A and A', A and A' will no longer be equivalent to one another except with respect to B. In order that B shall be equivalent to the number 2, B must be the union of any pair of elements, A and A', or A and E', or B' and C', etc. In that case, $A = A' = B' = C' = D'$, etc., and these objects, having lost their differences, will constitute a homogeneous class, 'the things on the table'. In a word, if we say that $A + A'$ = two objects, $A + A' + B'$ = three objects, etc., we are regarding these elements as being so many units equivalent to one another and yet distinct, and this twofold prerequisite cannot be reduced to the schema of additive composition of classes without some further operation.

This brings us to the second condition: the equivalent terms must remain distinct. In saying that $A + A'$ = two beads, we are stating that A is any bead, and A' any other bead, but essentially different. In what does this difference consist? We can no longer have recourse to the difference in colour, or to any other qualitative difference, for in so doing we should merely have the schema of classification described earlier, that of addition of classes and not of numbers. By 'any other bead', we shall therefore simply mean a bead 'placed next to', 'coming after', 'selected after' the first one. That is to say that in addition to the inclusion $A + A' = B$, characteristic of classes, a principle of seriation is involved, and as we saw in Chapters V–VI seriation is merely an addition of differences, as distinct from addition of classes which is an addition of elements that are equivalent from one given point of view.

These two conditions are necessary and sufficient to give rise to number. Number is at the same time a class and an asymmetrical relation, the units of which it is composed being simultaneously added because they are equivalent, and seriated because they are different one from another. In qualitative logic, the operational fusion of these two characteristics is impossible, since addition of classes is commutative because the addenda are equivalent, while seriation is not commutative because the terms are not equivalent. Number, on the contrary, is the outcome of generalization of equivalence and generalization of seriation. For instance, the first unit in two is equivalent to the second, and if their order of enumeration is changed, the second becomes the first and vice versa.[1]

To sum up, we can now see why the additive hierarchy of classes, seriation of relationships, and operational generalization of number (i.e. the construction of the numbers above 1, 2 . . . 5, which are intuitive) appear at approximately the same time, about the age of 6 or 7, when the child's reasoning is beginning to go beyond the initial prelogical level. The reason is that class, asymmetrical relation, and number are three complementary manifestations of the same operational construction applied either to equivalences, differences or to both together. It is, in fact, when the child's intuitive evaluations have become mobile and he has therefore reached the level of the reversible operation, that he becomes capable of inclusions, seriation and counting.

It is obvious that if number is the fusion of class and asymmetrical relation into a single operational whole, this synchronism has its logical explanation, but it can also be explained psychologically. Since each number is a whole, born of the union of equivalent and distinct terms, it cannot be constituted without inclusion and seriation. Moreover, although intensive quantification does not presuppose individual numbers, it does require that the child shall be capable of constructing these numbers, otherwise the relationships which determine the extension of classes would lose all meaning. It is because this is so that all the facts contained in this chapter show that class and number are mutually dependent, in that while number involves class, class in its turn relies implicitly on number.[2]

[1] Cf. in *Compte rendu des séances de la Société de Physique et d'Histoire naturelle de Genève*, vol. lviii (April 18, 1941), our article on the relationship between logical class and number.

[2] Madame Refis Mehmed Semin, who repeated the same experiments with Turkish children, principally in Istamboul, obtained results very similar to ours.

CHAPTER VIII

ADDITIVE COMPOSITION OF NUMBERS AND ARITHMETICAL RELATIONS OF PART TO WHOLE[1]

IN the previous chapter, we saw that during the first two stages of the construction of number, logical inclusion of one class in another involves systematic difficulty for the child because he is incapable of considering the parts and the whole simultaneously. This problem naturally has its counterpart in the numerical field, in which the arithmetical union of parts into a single whole constitutes one of the fundamental operations that give rise to number, i.e. addition. Unlike addition of classes, in which iteration has no place, the addition of a number to itself produces a new number. It is therefore of vital importance to prove whether, as we assumed in the previous chapter, additive composition of parts into a whole gives rise, in the case of number, to difficulties comparable to those of inclusion of classes in a total class, or whether the difficulties of inclusion are exclusively logical. In so doing, we shall be able to continue our analysis of the construction of number and study the role of the additive operational mechanism.

§1. *Techniques and results*

We shall use successively three parallel methods. The aim of the first is to discover whether the child is capable of understanding that a whole remains constant irrespective of the various additive compositions of its parts, e.g., $4 + 4 = 1 + 7 = 2 + 6 = 3 + 5$. The child is told that he is to have four sweets for 'elevenses' and four for tea-time. The next day he is to have the same number, but as he will be less hungry then at eleven o'clock than at tea-time, he will only eat one sweet in the morning and all the others in the afternoon. Beans are put before the child to illustrate each statement, three beans being removed from one set of four and added to the other to represent the position on the second day. The child

---

[1] With the collaboration of Mme Tatiana-Katzaroff-Eynard and Mlle Zoé Trampidis.

is then asked to compare the two lots, 4 + 4 and 1 + 7 and to say whether he will eat the same number of sweets on both days.

Three successive types of answer can be observed. At the first stage, the two sets are not regarded as equivalent, while in the third stage they are, and between the two we find intermediary reactions (stage II) in which the equivalence is not constructed by additive composition, but results from verification either through correspondence or numeration. This first technique thus enables us to show that for the younger children a numerical whole having the cardinal value eight is not the result of additive composition, but consists in an intuitive whole or as many global sets as there are parts perceived as smaller wholes, the sum of these parts then having no meaning.

This being so, the question then arises as to what will happen if the child himself is asked to make the transfer from one set to another in order to establish the equivalence between them. For this purpose, the child is given two unequal sets of counters, e.g., eight and fourteen, and he is asked to make them equal (the language used being borrowed from the vocabulary of the child himself). If he does not at once show interest in the problem, a story is made up to stimulate him. When he ceases to attempt to equate the sets, first of all he is asked if there is now the same number in both, and then, if he continues to be unsuccessful, the numbers are reduced and the question of division made easier. The operations of equalization are indeed by themselves insufficient for a complete analysis of additive composition, and they must be compared with the complementary operation of subdivision.

The results obtained can be classified as follows. During the first stage, the child does not understand that in adding counters to the smaller set he takes them from the larger set. He cannot therefore see the two sets in relation to one another, and evaluates them only globally. During the second stage, he does relate the two sets, but only intuitively, and by means of the configurations, which he equates by empirical trial and error. Lastly, during the third stage, he proceeds by way of operational correspondence and composition.

The third technique, which is complementary to the other two, tests the child's reactions in the case of division of a whole into two equal parts: 'There are some counters here. Divide them into two parts, one for you and one for me, so that we both have the same amount'. We again find the same three stages as before.

§2. *Relations between parts and whole, and changes in composition*
of parts

In Chapters III and IV we investigated how the child gradually replaces elementary methods of evaluation based on spatial perception, first by qualitative correspondence, and then by correspondence with quantifying equivalence. The results obtained in that analysis must be borne in mind in order to understand what follows, since the two sets $4+4$ and $1+7$ can only be compared if the child uses the same quantifying methods.

The first stage, which corresponds to the other first stages found earlier, and in particular to the stage at which two partial classes cannot be included permanently in an invariant whole, is characterized by the fact that the children grasp neither the equality of the two sets in question, I $(4+4)$ and II $(7+1)$, nor the permanence of the second whole in spite of changes in the distribution of its elements. Here are two examples:

Gin (5;9): 'Is there the same amount to eat on both days, there (I) and there (II)?—*No, there's more there* (II).—Why?—*There's a big lot* (7), *and a little lot* (1). *There* (I) *there are 4 and 4.*—But are those (7) and that (1) together the same as those (I)?—*No, because there are more there* (7).'
An (6;11): 'Is there the same amount there (I) and there (II)?—*No. There's 1 there* (II) *and there are 4 there* (I).—How many were there before here (II)? (The two sets of 4 were arranged again, then, before the child's eyes, 3 were taken from the first set and added to the 4 of the second.) Aren't they the same, these (II) and those (I)?—*No. Now there's only 1 here* (II) *and there are 4 there* (I).—Could we make them into 4 and 4 again here (II)?—*Yes* (doing so).—Will you have the same amount to eat on both days $(4+4$ and $4+4)$?—*Yes.*—And now (changing again to $7+1$)?—*No, because there are less here* (II).'

There is no difficulty in interpreting these reactions. On the one hand, the child does not regard the whole II as permanent, in spite of having himself removed three sweets and changed the structure $4+4$ into the structure $7+1$. On the other hand, his comparison of the structure $7+1$ with $4+4$ does not help him to discover this permanence of the whole. We have here, therefore, merely a repetition of the phenomena found in so many forms in Chapters I–IV, the only difference being that in this case the child is asked to solve the problem of conservation by simple addition of the elements. The reason why he fails is that, once again, he is guided by the perceptual relationships, which he does not correct by means of operations, and therefore, according as he concentrates on the seven or the one in set II, thinks that there are more or less in II than in I. And yet he is perfectly aware that he has to compare the set $7+1$ with the set $4+4$. Gin, for instance, says:

'There's a big lot (seven) and a little lot (one). There (I) there are four and four.' In spite of this, the only criterion for these children is perception, and they do not attempt to construct the sum 7 + 1 = 8 and compare it with the sum of 4 + 4.

At the second stage, the child who begins by showing the same reactions gradually comes to see (or can be made to see) that although we have 7 > 4, we have also 1 < 4 and that these two inequalities may compensate each other:

Dini (6;6): 'Will you have the same amount of sweets to eat on both days?—(After considerable thought.) *No. There are less here* (I) *because there are more there* (II).—But here (1) there are less. What do you think?—(much astonished) *Then there are more here* (II).—Why?—*Because those* (7) *are more.*—What did the mother do? (II was rearranged as 4 + 4, and the child removed 3 sweets and made it into 7 + 1 again). Well then, will you have the same amount to eat on both days?—*No, because here* (7) *there are more, and there* (4) *there are less, and here* (4) *and there* (1) *there are less.*—Well then?—(show of surprise by the child, who had just discovered that there were more or less in II according as he looked at II from the point of view of the 7 or the 1.) *I think there are more here* (I).—Why?— . . . —But at first you say there are more here (II), and then you say there are more there (I).—(He looked for a long time at the two sets, and then, with a kind of emotion he said): *They're both the same!*—How did you find out?—*I had a good look, and I saw that you could put 3 of those* (7) *here* (1).'

Riq (7;0): 'Is there the same amount in these (II) and those (I)?—*No.*—Where are there more?—*There* (II).—Why?—*There are 4 and 4 there* (I), *and here* (II) *there are those* (7) *and that* (1).' But almost immediately Riq seemed to hesitate. He looked carefully at II and then slowly took 3 of the 7, one at a time, and put them with the 1: '*They're both the same. That makes 4 and 4 as well.*'

These children begin by reacting like those of the first stage. There is at first neither addition of the elements 7 + 1 nor subordination of the parts to the whole. But at a given moment, these children discover spontaneously, or when the idea is suggested, that the set 1 + 7 seems to be both larger and smaller than the set 4 + 4 according as he concentrates on the seven, which is larger than four, or the one, which is smaller than four. In the case of Dini, this double simultaneous comparison is explicit, and though in the case of Riq it is tacit, it is equally clear. The child is then compelled, by this interference of the relationships, to co-ordinate the parts into a whole. Here again we find, as we found in Chapter IV with respect to length and density, that by comparing the initial form of a set with its subsequent transformations, the child discovers that the increase in the elements of one of the sub-sets is compensated by the decrease in the elements of the other. It is the co-ordination of these relationships which makes possible the elaboration of a permanent totality, and therefore the subordination of the parts to a real whole, as is illustrated by the case of Riq, who verifies his discovery by taking three of the seven elements in II and adding them to the one, so as to reconstruct the set $4 + 4$.

This transition from intuitive non-conservation to operational conservation enables us to see the first appearance of addition and also to understand the difference between this arithmetical addition and the logical addition of classes dealt with in the previous chapter.

Addition is a reversible operation. There is therefore no more than a suggestion of it when, at the first stage, the child does not understand that a whole B divided into two parts A and A' is still the same whole. The operation of addition comes into being when, on the one hand, the addenda are united in a whole, and on the other, this whole is regarded as invariant irrespective of the distribution of its parts.

With regard to the last point, we shall see that the hypotheses we made at the end of the previous chapter are justified. At the first stage, when the child compares the two sets, he is not capable of co-ordinating all the relations that exist between the various sub-sets, and draws his conclusion from one of his observations only. For instance, when he sees that seven is larger than four, he concludes that II is larger than I, and when he compares one and four, he reaches the opposite conclusion. At the second stage he grasps that there are complementary relations, and this co-ordination leads him to discover that when one sub-set is reduced by the removal of elements which are added to the other, these transformations compensate each other.

But this co-ordination is still only intensive quantification, and is not yet numerical, since these transformations do not require that the elements shall be counted. Riq, for instance, although he counted four and four, did not count the elements of the sub-set of seven. The transition from addition of classes to addition of numbers occurs when the sub-sets are no longer regarded as groups of elements which have some qualitative individuality, but as units which can be equated without being identified. All the elements in the various sets and sub-sets become units which are equivalent and distinct and are involved in operations, which at the third stage function automatically and immediately, without the need for preliminary intuitive co-ordination.

Laur (7;3): 'Will there be the same amount on both days?—*Wait. There* $(7 + 1)$ *they're not arranged the same as here* $(4 + 4)$, *but they're the same, because here* (7) *there are the 3 from there* (1).—How many will you eat?— *There* (I) *4 and 4, and here, 1 at first and then the 5 others.*—Why 5?— *Because there are 3 more. Oh no! there are 7 there. There are 8 on both days.*'

The fact that Laur made a mistake of arithmetic shows that he was reasoning and not merely counting empirically. His reasoning is perfectly sound.

Ter (7;6): 'Will you eat the same amount on both days?—*Yes.*— Why?—*Because they're the same.*—How many each day?—*8.*—But there are 4 here (I) and there's only 1 there (II).—*Yes, but we've put the 3 here* (II).'

These reactions show that at this level the child understands at once that the differences between the corresponding sub-sets are the same: Ter says, 'we've put the three here', and Laur, 'here there are the three from there'. Moreover, these children immediately express the transfer in numerical terms, without feeling the need for qualitative reasoning. In other words, each sub-set is seen in relation to the other, and both are seen in relation to their sum. Hence all the relations in question form an operational system such that the whole, which has become invariant, is the result of composition through addition of the parts, and that the relationships between the parts are univocally determined by combined additions and subtractions.

It is clear, moreover, that understanding of arithmetical addition and subtraction presupposes all these conditions. It is true that even children who are still at the earlier stages can be taught to repeat formulae such as $2+2=4$; $2+3=5$; $2+4=6$, etc., but there is no true assimilation until the child is capable of seeing that six is a totality, containing two and four as parts, and of grouping the various possible combinations in additive compositions. When these conditions do not obtain, addition as an operation is not understood. The child at the first stage preceives that when $4+4$ becomes $7+1$, one of the sub-sets increases, but this intuition becomes addition only when this increase is compensated by a decrease $(4+3)+(4-3)=8$. It is this interdependence of direct and inverse operations that we shall now examine in relation to a single, typical example.

§3. *Equating of quantities*

The problem dealt with above showed that a system of additions and subtractions combined is essential to the invariance of a whole formed by additive composition. We shall now study the child's reactions to an analogous problem, but one which requires him to equalise unequal parts, and not the converse. No reference will be made to the whole as such, the child being free to construct it or not in making his additive composition. This problem produced results complementary to those found earlier. In order to classify them, we must distinguish between the method used by the child

to estimate the equality obtained or to be obtained, and his understanding of the mechanism of additions and subtractions.

With regard to the first of these, the stages correspond to those
found in Chapter IV, §1. During the first stage, when the child is
asked to equalise two sets of counters, one of eight and one of
fourteen, he merely takes a few counters from the larger set and
adds them to the other and makes only a global comparison of the
results obtained by this empirical transfer. At the second stage, he
spontaneously constructs configurations, so as to compare and
equate the two sets. It was these spontaneous figures which led us
to investigate the mechanism of reproduction and qualitative
correspondence at the same age. At the third stage, the child
proceeds by way of one-one correspondence, with or without
verbal enumeration. It is of course to be expected that since this
problem is more difficult, there will be a lag in the average age
here as compared with that of the stages of reproduction, but the
order and the evolution are the same.

As for the mechanism, the child does not understand at the first
stage that the additions and subtractions necessarily compensate
each other, i.e. when he adds a number of elements to one set, he
does not expect the set from which they were taken to decrease by
the same amount. During the second stage, he is aware that this
is what occurs, but only on the intuitive plane, and therefore,
apart from the figures, he is incapable of judging the equality and
of foreseeing the result of the additions and subtractions. During
the third stage, he can handle the transfers operationally, and
there is therefore well-regulated reversibility. Here we have
some examples:

Jac (5;0). $A = 8$; $A' = 14$. 'Where are there more?—*There* (A').—
Make them the same.—(He removed a few elements at random from
A' and added them to A, making $A = 13$ and $A' = 9$.)—Are they the
same?—*No*.' He then removed counters from one set to the other
several times, looking only at the smaller set as he did so, as though the
larger one was inexhaustible, the results obtained being: $A = 6$ and
$A' = 16$; $A = 15$ and $A' = 7$; $A = 6$ and $A' = 16$, and finally $A = 17$ and
$A' = 5$. After that he gave it up.

No (5;6). $A = 8$; $A' = 14$. 'Have we both got the same?—*No*.—
Arrange them so that they are the same.—(It so happened that he
removed 3 counters from A', leaving $A = A'$, but the space occupied by
the two sets was not the same.) Are they the same now?—*No*.' He took
2 more from A' and added them to A, then put back 4 in A' so that
$A' = 13$ and $A' = 9$.

Gil (5;5). $A = 10$ and $A' = 16$. He moved some counters from A' to
A, arranging the sets with no special configuration, but so that the
surfaces covered were approximately the same, A being 15 and A' 11.
'Are they the same?—*Yes*.—Show me why.—(He pointed to the two

heaps) *Here and here.*—How do you know?—*Daddy taught me to count on my fingers.*

Ha (4;5). A = 8 and A′ = 14. He took 2, and then 2 more, which he added to A, so that A = 14 and A′ = 8. 'Are they the same now?—*No.* (He took 4 from A, leaving A = 10 and A′ = 12.)—Is that right?—*No.* (He took 1 more from A′ and thus had A = A′ = 11).'

Li (4;9) had reached the next stage when it was a case of small quantities, but was still at the first stage when dealing with the same numbers as the other children. With A = 8 and A′ = 14, he took 1, then another 1, then 2, from A′, leaving A′ = 10 and A = 12. 'Are they the same?—*Yes.*' With A = 4 and A′ = 6, he took 1 counter from A′ and then made two figures of 5 consisting of squares with a counter in the middle.

These reactions provide valuable evidence for the understanding of the mechanism of additive composition. They show that at first, when the child is trying to equate the two sets, he is quite unaware that in increasing one he decreases the other. Whether the addition 8 + 14 = 22 is actually made or not, it is obvious that the solution of the problem requires the implicit or explicit assumption of the existence of an invariant whole, irrespective of the modifications. The problem is therefore exactly the same as that of the previous section, but the operation required is the inverse. The child at this level appears to be unaware that the total number of counters is constant, and that therefore the counters added to one set are necessarily subtracted from the other. It might be argued that the child does in fact know that he is subtracting, since he takes the counters from one set and puts them in the other. But our contention is precisely that in this case there is no true addition or subtraction, but merely empirical action, the results of which are quite fortuitous as far as the child is concerned. These operations only become operations as a function of regulated composition of the whole and the parts, i.e. as a function of a logical 'grouping' or of an arithmetical 'group'. At the beginning of this stage, the child does not regard the two sets—we might almost say he does not perceive them—in relation one to the other. He does perceive that one is larger than the other, and therefore adds counters to the smaller one, but in so doing, he forgets the larger set and does not even look at it as he removes the counters. Jac, for instance, only looks at the smaller set while making his transfers, and thus constantly reverses the proportions, going from 8 + 14 to 13 + 9, then to 6 + 16, 15 + 7, 6 + 16, and finally 17 + 5. Between the extreme case of Jac and cases like Ha and Li who eventually succeeded in equating the two sets, all the intermediary stages are to be found.

The wholes, as understood and perceived by the child at this stage, are then, as we said earlier, at the same time rigid and unstable. They are rigid because they are perceived globally, but they are also unstable because no principle of conservation ensures their permanence. When the mind is capable of true additive composition, on the contrary, wholes are both mobile and stable.

The tendency, observed in the case of Li, to arrange the counters in comparable figures in order to equate them, appears at a given moment as a reaction to these difficulties. When this procedure is generalized to all the operations of equalization, the child has reached the second stage, of which we now have some examples:

Fel (5;4). A =8 and A′ =14. Fel took 3 elements at random from A′ and added them to A, then arranged each set in a circle, leaving 3 or 4 elements inside. A was then a circle of 7 counters with 4 in the middle, and A′ a circle of 8 with 3 in the middle. 'Are they both the same?—*Yes.*' But it is not certain that Fel saw that the number of elements was the same in both cases, and that he was not merely basing his estimate on the similarity of the figures. He was then given A = 10 and A′ =20. He proceeded in the same way, but this time finally achieved two exactly similar figures: two circles of 11 counters with 4 in the middle. 'Are they exactly the same?—*Yes.*—How do you know? —*Because they're round.*' When, however, the distribution of the elements in A′ was modified, so that there were only 3 in the middle and 12 forming the circle, Fel ceased to think the two sets were equivalent and thought A′> A. As soon as the figure is changed, therefore, from being a factor contributing to qualitative correspondence, it becomes a source of uncertainty.

Fel was then given A composed of 12 counters (9 in a circle and 3 in a horizontal line on the diameter) and A′ composed of 22 counters (16 in a circle and 6 on the diameter). 'Make them the same—(He took 3 of the 6 counters from the middle of A′ and added them to the 3 in A, so that A = 9 + 6 and A′ = 16 + 3.)—Is that right?—*Nearly. No, there are still less there* (A). (He added some more to A, then removed some, leaving A = 18, of which 11 were in a circle, and A′ = 16, 12 forming the circle and 4 in the middle.)—Who will have more to eat?— *Me* (A′) *because the ring's big.*—But who has more in the middle?— *Oh yes!* (removing 1 counter from the circumference of A′ and putting it in the middle).—Are they the same?—(He made as if to remove some elements from the centre of A, but changed his mind) *No, because then there'll be 3!*' He then gave it up, the figure having now become only a source of insuperable difficulties.

Tho (6;2). A =8 and A′ =12. He took 2 elements from A′, then 1, then another 1, leaving A = 12 and A′ =8. He then made the 12 counters of A into a rectangle formed of 4 rows of 3, one above the other, and then arranged A′ as a less regular quadrilateral. 'Are they the same?—(He looked at them, then after some hesitation arranged the 8 elements of A′ in 4 rows of 2, thus having a rectangle comparable to A.) *No, there are more there.*' He arranged A as 6 pairs one above the other, then equalized the lengths of A′ and A, and divided the remainder between them, one by one.

Gin (5;9). A = 10 and A' = 20. He at once arranged two parallel figures, 5 pairs for A and 10 pairs for A'. He then removed half of A' and divided them two at a time between the two sets.

These reactions indicate the beginnings of additive composition, but only on the intuitive plane. The very fact of changing the unequal heaps into figures compels the child to keep on comparing the two sets and to notice that each transfer is at the same time an addition to one set and a subtraction from the other. But, as can be seen in the case of Fel, as soon as the figure is altered, the equivalence vanishes, because there is as yet no operational conservation. Consequently, there can be no invariant whole, but only wholes that are better structured through spatial intuition. Thus, both from the point of view of additive composition and of the method of evaluation, the second stage is midway between the incoherence of the first and the operational coherence of the third. All the intermediary stages between these levels are, of course, to be found. There is, for instance, the case of Gin, who is almost at the stage of finding the equivalence purely through correspondence, but has not yet acquired the notion of the constancy of the sets.

At the third stage, the child's progress in correspondence is such that he can use it as a tool for equalization, and can establish the equivalence independently of the arrangement of the elements, which means that operational additive composition is now possible.

Fa (5;6). A = 8 and A' = 14. He arranged the counters in A as 4 pairs and put opposite them 4 pairs from A'. He then took the remaining 6 in A', put 2 on one side, 2 on the other, then 1 on one side and 1 on the other. He thus used exactly the same method as Gin, but whereas Gin was still hesitant and relied entirely on the figures, only making the correspondence after inspecting them, Fa made the correspondence beforehand and believed in the conservation independently of the distribution (cf. Chap. IV).

An (6;0), with the same sets, at once put the 8 counters of A in a row and then placed the first 8 of A' opposite them. He then took 2 of the remaining 6, then 1 more, and added them to A, so that A and A' = 11.

Laur (7;3) made a row of the 8 counters in A and counted them, then took 8 from A' (14) and put them opposite those of A, but in a more compact row. He then divided the remaining 6, without counting them, putting first 2, then 1, on each side.

What is new at this stage is that the child already knows, when he is equalizing the sets, that if one set is larger than the other, he must divide the difference. Consequently he assumes from the beginning the permanence of the set and forms a system of hierarchical nestings. The case of Laur is particularly clear in this respect. He first takes from A' a set equal to A, and divides the remainder into two halves. Fa does the same thing when he starts with two rows of four pairs each and divides the remainder, and An also, but rather less definitely.

The main difference between these children and those of the second stage is that the latter cannot determine the remainder except by means of the figures, i.e. after the event, and without co-ordinating beforehand the relations involved. For them, therefore, the remainder is not yet the result of a numerical subtraction, but of the empirical transfer of a purely intuitive set of elements, there being no question of additive composition, as is proved by the fact that there is no conservation. Fel, for instance, ceases to believe in the equivalence of the sets when one of the figures is altered in shape, but not in number. Children at the third stage, on the contrary, establish the equivalence by means of an *a priori* decomposition of the sets, and the equality is lasting, because conservation results from composition which is now mobile and reversible.

To sum up, once again we find that numerical addition and subtraction become operations only when they can be composed in the reversible construction which is the additive 'group' of integers, apart from which there can be nothing but unstable intuition. It is easily proved that this 'group' issues from 'grouping' of classes by addition, through the same process of equalization of differences described in §2.

§4. *Division into two equal parts*

It is clear that here we shall find the same stages as in the previous section, the only difference between the two experiments being that, instead of having to make two unequal sets equivalent, the child is now required to divide a given quantity into two parts, and if he does not at once make them equal, can proceed to do so by the same methods as before.

At first sight, this problem might seem to be related to multiplicative, rather than to additive, composition (half being a division), but as any whole is the union by addition of its two halves, it has its additive aspect, more particularly if the child proceeds empirically, first dividing the whole into two parts and then equalizing them. What we are concerned with here, therefore, is the process by which the child transforms the logical operation $B = A + A'$ into a numerical operation $A_1 + A_2 = 2A = B$.

During a first stage, the child cannot grasp the fact that the sum of the parts is equal to the whole, nor does he recognize the lasting equivalence of the two halves, even when he has obtained them by distributing the elements term for term in two corresponding sets. Here are some examples:

Arl (5;0) was asked to divide 18 counters: 'Divide them so that you and I have exactly the same amount.—(Arl put both hands over the pile and made a rough division into two parts. It so happened that the result was 9 and 9, but one half occupied more space than the other.)— Have we both got the same?—No.—Who has more?—You (the less compact heap).—Make them so that we both have the same.—I'll have to change them round.' Arl then merely changed round the two sets, as if that was enough to make them equal. This is therefore a perfect example of the reactions observed at the first stage in §3.

When he was asked to divide 20 counters, with a single movement of the hand he divided the pile into two parts, one containing 9 and the other 11. He then arranged the counters in A in a vaguely rectangular form, and A' in a roughly similar shape. 'Are they the same?—Yes.— (The elements in A' were then closed up.)—And now?—No.'

Co (5;0). Like some of the other children at the first stage, Co took the counters one by one, thus apparently carrying out an operation of correspondence belonging to a higher level, but this was not really so, as we shall see. Having divided the 18 counters, one at a time, into two heaps of 9, he was not certain that the two halves were equal! 'Have I got the same amount as you?—(He looked at the two heaps, which were of slightly different density, then tried to make them the same.)— But how did you divide them?— . . . —Are they the same?—No.— How do you know?—(He arranged the heaps.)'

In view of the method of distribution spontaneously adopted by Co and others, we then applied the technique described in Chapter II, §1:

Mal (5;0). Two dolls were put on the table, and Mal was asked to divide 16 counters between them, putting the counters one at a time into two empty boxes. 'Have they got the same amount?—Yes.—(We emptied the boxes in front of the dolls, one heap of 8 being more compact than the other.)—No, that one has more (the less compact heap).' Same reactions when the child put the elements into the boxes, one with his left hand and one with his right, simultaneously. (cf. Chap. II, §1, Port and Gfe at the end of the experiment).

At the second stage we have the following reactions:

Pi (5;1), with a total set of 18, took one counter after another and put them into two sub-sets, making a mistake of one unit, the result being 10 and 8. He then arranged each sub-set as a row of pairs, and compared the lengths of the two rows. Then he spaced out the pairs of the row of 8 so that it was the same length as the other, but seeing the difference in density, he took 1 counter from the 10 and added it to the 8, so that he had two similar sets of 9. 'Are they the same?—Yes.— (The elements in A_1 were then arranged as two rows, 6 and 3.) Are they still the same?—*No.*—Why?—*I've got more* (=A$_2$ the unchanged figure).'

Char (6;0) began like Pi, making the same mistake of 1 unit, then arranged A$_1$ (10) in two rows of 4 plus 2 isolated counters, leaving A$_2$ (8) scattered. 'Are they the same?—*Yes. Oh no! There are more.*' He then also made A$_2$ into two rows of 4, and added 2 more, thus reversing the inequality. Finally he put 1 element at the top of each figure, and thus had 9 and 9.

Tho (6;0), in order to divide 18 counters, made two squares containing 9, and after comparing the detail of the figures, was satisfied that they were equal. To divide 24, however, he made a square of 9 and a rectangle of 12, then added the remaining 3 to the square of 9, thus obtaining two rectangles of 12. But as he added the 3 to the bottom of the square, while the rectangle of 12 was on its side, he had two similar figures differently placed, and was not at all sure about them. 'Have we both got the same?— . . . —Has one of us got more?— *Yes, there* (the upright rectangle).' He then reconstructed the other rectangle in an upright position!

These reactions are exactly comparable to those of the corresponding stage in the case of equalization of two unequal sets: comparison through the figures without lasting equivalence or conservation of the whole.

At the third stage we have the following reactions:

Dré (6;10) divided 18 counters 1 or 2 at a time into two sets of 9, and was sure that they were equal even when the distribution was changed.

Laur (7;3) divided 18 counters, taking them 2 at a time until he came to the last pair, and then put 1 on each pile. 'Are they the same (spacing out the elements of the second set)?—*Yes.*—Why?—*Because I put the same on both sides.*—And what about all these (making a single heap of all the counters), are they the same as the two heaps?—*Yes, because I divided them and then you put them as they were before.*'

We can see here the completion of additive composition, as a result of the child's understanding that the two parts, considered as units, are equal, and that the sum of the parts is equal to the initial whole. This also explains the transition from additive to multiplicative composition. An arithmetical multiplication is an equi-distribution: $m \times n$ is m sets of n terms or n sets of m terms which correspond one to one. In this sense, the addition A$_1$ + A$_2$ =2A is therefore also a multiplication, in which the set A$_1$ is coupled with another set A$_2$, the two sets being in one-one correspondence. In the same way, addition of classes implies multiplication. In the problem of the beads considered in the previous chapter, for instance, the beads were at the same time 'wooden' and 'brown', or 'wooden' and 'not brown'. In the case of logical classes, the inverse operation is abstraction or dissociation; in arithmetic, it is ordinary division, of which we have just seen an example. Additive and multiplicative compositions, whether numerical or qualitative, are therefore correlative, and the mastery of the one implies that of the other, as we shall see in the following chapter.

§5. Conclusion

As we have seen, there is a great measure of agreement between the results of these various tests with respect to additive composition. In each case, there is an initial stage of non-composition, an intermediary stage of intuitive composition, and a final stage of composition proper, this being defined by the invariance of the whole and the reversibility of the operations involved. These three stages correspond, moreover, to those described in the earlier chapters.

Additive composition comes late on the scene, in spite of appearances. A consideration of the facts usually observed in connection with the beginnings of counting might suggest, at first sight, that addition is understood as soon as the first sets of two, three or four objects to which a numeral is assigned are formed. We shall show briefly that this is not so, that addition presupposes the conditions analysed above, and that, particularly in the child's spontaneous behaviour, the synthesis of colligation and enumeration is necessary before the operational level which defines number proper can be reached.

Let us begin with enumeration, which in the opinion of many writers on the subject implies addition, even in its most primitive forms. Preyer, for instance, regards as a beginning of addition the behaviour of a child who picked up all the ninepins in a set one after the other, each time saying 'one, one, one', then 'one, another, another'. To this, K. Buhler[1] rightly objected that true addition cannot occur without a clear awareness of the sum. Decroly[2] notes in the case of S. at 1;7, the term 'again' in the sense of an 'invitation to repeat an action'. At 1;8, however, S. said 'another' as she picked up the cards from a pack she had thrown on the floor, to indicate two cards she had not yet picked up. At 1;11, S. again said 'another' to indicate a second cat after she had already seen one. In these examples, Decroly sees a 'suggestion of addition', but obviously it cannot be addition in the sense of construction of an invariant whole. There is merely awareness of a succession of events, and a more or less vague feel-

[1] K. Buhler, *Die geistige Entwicklung des Kindes*, p. 104.
[2] O. Decroly, *Essais de psychogenèse*, pp. 53–4.

ing that the sets in question are exhausted or increased. Naturally, although this enumeration is qualitative, the idea of quantity is present in it, since it is linked with the notion of 'more' (another) and 'less' (no more), but this quantification is not yet numerical, since 'one' and 'another' are neither units of number nor elements of classes. It would be quantification of classes in extension if the child at this level were capable of invariant inclusions, and the quantification of seriation if he could co-ordinate asymmetrical relations. But as both these operations are beyond him, even on the intuitive plane, it is merely a matter of 'gross quantities' in the sense used in Chapters I and II. There can therefore be no question, in these examples, of addition proper.

Can we, on the other hand, find the beginnings of addition in 'colligation' as defined by Husserl? In his *Logische Untersuchungen*, in which he made a thorough analysis of the notion of colligation, Husserl makes a fundamental opposition between colligation, which gives rise to sets that are categories, and global qualities that are merely perceptual, which he calls 'quasi qualitative Momente' or 'figurale Momente'. It is obvious that the figures used by the child at the third stage for the evaluation of quantities (Chapters I–IV) reveal precisely these perceptual global qualities, and not the colligation which Husserl calls 'categorial', and which for the psychologist is operational. At the level of elementary enumerations, there is no operation by which the child can colligate the units into a real and stable whole.

Elementary enumeration and addition are mutually dependent. The reason why the primitive enumeration 'another, another' is not additive is that it does not lead to a stable totality, and the reason why primitive addition does not reach the level of colligation, and remains global and intuitive, is that additive enumeration is lacking. There is indeed a regular rhythm of interactions between the two complementary movements, the analysis of the elements which is enumeration, and their synthesis which is addition. As early as the first stage, there is consciousness of wholes and of elements, but they are two successive types of perception, and are not combined, which explains the global syncretism of the former and the non-additive juxtaposition of the latter. At a further stage, however, the colligation of the whole gradually merges more and more with the seriation of the elements, finally leading to the construction of number and of additive and multiplicative operations.

It is true that in the case of small sets—two, three or four—there is already simultaneous perception of the whole and of the elements. There is therefore a beginning of union, or as Husserl says, of fusion, but without the elements being previously isolated.

o

But this union can constitute either a class or a number, according as the mind is directed towards conceptual classification, or towards addition of units. Apart from these privileged examples, which give rise to what might be called the intuitive numbers 1 to 5, numbers that still adhere to the objects numbered and are perceptual rather than operational, children at the first stage cannot perform enumeration and addition one as a function of the other. Hence their failure to grasp one-one correspondence, which involves the union of these two processes in a single whole.

While it is clear that neither process is sufficient by itself to ensure the appearance of correspondence, a first synthesis between enumeration and addition becomes possible when, in comparing configurations, the child succeeds in establishing the resemblance between the elements in detail at the same time as between the figures as a whole. It is precisely this synthesis which produces one-one correspondence, but only on the intuitive level. On the one hand, examination of the configuration provides a kind of intuitive colligation, and on the other, enumeration of the elements takes the form of seriations based on their position, or on some other directly perceived quality. It is this intuitive synthesis of enumeration that has become seriation, and of addition that has become intuitive composition, which characterizes the second stage, and which was already foreshadowed in the first stage in the case of small sets of one to five objects.

This intuitive synthesis indicates definite progress towards additive composition. In the first place, every enumeration that becomes a seriation can be translated into an addition, the increases and decreases being from now on restricted by the intuitive colligation of the figure. In the second place, every evaluation based on the figure leads to an additive union of the sets structured by the figure. It must be understood, however, that serial addition, which is not commutative, and addition of classes which is, can only merge into arithmetical addition so long as they are temporarily united through perceptual intuition. Experiment shows that, during this second stage, the synthesis breaks down as soon as the figure is altered. There is then no longer conservation of the whole, and the serial addition loses its numerical significance. At this level, therefore, operational addition does not yet exist.

At the third stage, however, the synthesis between enumeration and colligation is lasting: both have become operational and independent of the perceived figures. When the child counts the elements of a set, he is now capable of understanding that the position of each term in the series is defined in relation to the set of seriated elements, the set constituting, moreover, an invariant whole. He is thus capable of serial addition or addition of classes when qualities intervene, and of numerical addition when qualities are disregarded.

This progressive co-ordination of colligation and enumeration can be explained by the fact that the child's thought is gradually becoming reversible, while the initial lack of co-ordination is due to its irreversibility. Addition and enumeration are at first unco-ordinated because, for the child, the perception of a figure and the perception of its elements, seen one after the other, have nothing in common. The two succeed one another, and the child may even agree that a return from one to the other is possible, but he does not regard one as necessarily leading to the other. With intuitive correspondence, there is progress in co-ordination, in that the child can count the elements of one set by using those of another, though he still considers the first set as a closed whole. Colligation and enumeration thus become as it were co-reversible, one appearing as the inverse operation of the other within the same field of perception. But when the configuration of one of the sets is changed, there are again perceptions irreducible one to the other, and though a return to the initial situation is seen to be possible, the reversibility is not regarded as necessary. With the operational correspondence of the third stage, however, when co-ordination between enumeration and colligation is complete, any configuration of a given set can become any other of the same set, since on this point the child's thought is now completely reversible.

What then is the difference between necessary reversibility and empirical return to the initial situation? What difference is there between two successive unrelated perceptions and two figures that are necessarily related? Is it not merely that the former are not yet identified one with the other, whereas the latter are regarded as identical through a mental act? There certainly is an activity of the mind: a physical or mental movement is never wholly reversible, since it occurs in time, and time is not reversible. And this act of the mind is already present at the moment of perception, since perception is a structuration, although it is static. From this point of view, the difference between perception and thought is therefore one of degree. It is the difference between 'less' and 'more' reversible, with the reservation that when reversibility reaches a certain point, it is complete, as in the case of mathematics. Perception is, in fact, only an instant in the reversible movement of thought. There certainly is also identity, and the colligated set is of necessity identical with its enumerated elements, but this identity is the result and not the origin of the reversibility, since the essence of thought is irreducible to identity.

It is operations that are the essence of thought, and it is of the nature of operations continually to construct something new. Thus if $1 + 1 + 1 = 3$, the three units that are added are identical with three in the sense that the total three can again give, by enumeration, three units identical with the original three, but the additive operation has created a new entity, the totality three, which as such is not identical with the juxtaposed units. Conversely, the enumeration of three terms is not identical with the initial totality three. If we agree with E. Meyerson that the new construction comes from reality, whereas the mind confines itself to identification, we are in fact saying that reason is irrational, as Meyerson himself eventually admitted. It seems to us preferable to accept the existence of operations and to distinguish them from empirical constructions precisely by their reversibility, identity then being only the product of inverse operations.

Two perceptions that do not necessarily lead one to the other are merely two perceptions such that their constituent operations form a closed system internal to each of them, whereas two figures necessarily leading one to the other correspond to perceptions such that their constituent operations are sufficiently extended to be co-ordinated with others, so that either figure can be composed by means of the other. At the first stage, the child's thought is still irreversible, in that each perception is a particular moment in the stream of his experience, without stable means of return, since there are no operations by which one perception can be composed with another. The two processes, intuitive colligation and enumeration, therefore take place in turn, the one replacing the other. This fact explains the initial primacy of perception, since a single operation cannot dominate the perception to which it gives rise. During the second stage, there is co-ordination, but only within the field of the perceptions, which thus expand in the direction of thought. The one-one correspondence then forms the link between enumeration and colligation, except when the configuration is destroyed. Finally, during the third stage, the operations go beyond the field of perception, and in so doing, attain complete reversibility. These then are the three aspects of a single process that defines the evolution of reason: transition from perception to primacy of deduction, progressive co-ordination of operations, and gradual development of reversibility.

CHAPTER IX

CO-ORDINATION OF RELATIONS OF
EQUIVALENCE AND MULTIPLICATIVE
COMPOSITION OF NUMBERS[1]

In Chapter III we examined the question of one-one correspondence using flowers and vases, eggs and egg-cups, etc.
These experiments can be taken further in two ways. On the
one hand, when the child has established the equivalence between
a set of flowers F_1 and a set of vases V_1, the experiment can easily
be repeated with the same set of vases V_1 and a new set of flowers
F_2, the question put then being: If F_1 is equivalent to V_1, and
V_1 to F_2, will F_1 be equivalent to F_2? On the other hand, a new
type of question might be put: If all the flowers in sets F_1 and F_2
are put into the vases V, so that there is an equal number in each
vase, how many flowers will there be in each vase? Once this
second problem is solved, a further question can be put: If
instead of putting two flowers in each vase we want to put them
in narrow tubes that will only hold a single flower, how many such
tubes will be needed to take all the flowers? For this problem, the
flowers will be removed from the table and only the original
vases V_1 will be left.

In this chapter, our purpose is to study: (1) some examples of
one-one correspondence between several sets, and not merely
between two sets as before; (2) the transition from this composition of relations of equivalence to arithmetical multiplication.
Composition of relations of equivalence is the same thing as
composition of classes, since a class is a collection of elements
that are equivalent from some particular point of view.[2] Moreover, since arithmetical multiplication is an equi-distribution,
equivalence through one-one correspondence between two or n
sets A is a multiplicative equivalence, indicating that one of the
sets A is multiplied by two or by n. From the psychological point
of view this simply means that a one-one correspondence is an

[1] With the collaboration of Mlle Edith Vauthier.
[2] Symmetrical relations are the relations that link the elements of a class, and
can therefore be called class relations. Cf. *Compte rendu des séances de la Société
de physique de Genève*, 15 mai, 1941.

implicit multiplication, so that when the child has established the correspondence between several sets, he will sooner or later become aware of this multiplication and use it as an explicit operation.

§*1*. *Constitution of one-one correspondence and composition of relations of equivalence*

Relations of equivalence based on one-one correspondence are particular relations, the discovery and use of which presupposes the acquisition of a set of mathematical notions such as invariance of sets, seriation, etc. Composition of relations of equivalence, on the other hand, constitutes so general a mechanism that it seems to require only logic. For example, if $X = Y$ and $Y = Z$, then $X = Z$ whatever the value of X, Y and Z. This expression of the transitivity characteristic of any relation of equivalence is at the same time the expression of a reasoning that involves the whole structure of thought. It expresses both the equivalence of three classes and the co-ordination of two relations, and applies both to mathematical and qualitative realities. Whether this reasoning concerns numbers, areas, weights, classes or relationships, the difficulty, or lack of difficulty, involved seems to be independent of the content of the thought and to derive from the form alone. If logic were innate, the child ought therefore to be able to use such structures long before he discovers the mathematical notions, or at least the two questions ought to be independent for him.

In our view, however, logic is a construct, and it remains to be proved that a formal mechanism such as the composition of two relations can be constructed independently of the content involved in the co-ordination. Moreover, we have continually found, in the course of our investigation, that logic of classes and logic of relations intervene in the construction of mathematical notions, and conversely. We may therefore expect that the formal structure $X = Y$; $Y = Z$, therefore $X = Z$ will not be acquired all at once, irrespective of its content, but will need to be reacquired as many times as there are different contents to which it is applied. In other words, a formal structure is merely a co-ordination at a given level, which can take place only in so far as the terms or relations to be co-ordinated are understood, and must therefore be reconstructed as a new co-ordination each time a new class of notions is involved.[1]

Broadly speaking, it can be said that children who fail to understand composition of relations of equivalence also fail to

[1] Cf. J. Piaget and B. Inhelder, *Le développement des quantités chez l'enfant*, in which the structure in question is applied to volume, weight, etc.

grasp one-one correspondence, whereas those who understand one-one correspondence are at once able to compose several relations. This is not as natural as it might appear. Success in the tests of correspondence requires that the corresponding sets be regarded as equivalent whatever the distribution of the elements, provided that they were once in correspondence. The composition X equivalent to Y and Y equivalent to Z therefore X equivalent to Z, involves difficulties of a different kind, since the elements of the sets X and Z are never opposite one another. This composition is impossible for children who cannot spontaneously make the correspondence between two sets, or who do not regard their equivalence as lasting, only if we assume that formal structures are merely a co-ordination of their contents. The composition then presupposes that understanding of the equivalence has already been achieved. What is more striking is that children who succeed in the tests of equivalence can at once compose the relations thus discovered, which proves that once they are constituted, the multiplicative operations inherent in correspondence are made explicit in the form of multiplications proper.

Here we have two examples of failure, the children in this case (and throughout §1) being the same as those quoted in Chapter III:

Fum (4;4), who was at the stage of global comparison, failed (we as saw in Chap. III, §2) to understand that the blue flowers he himself had put into the vases still corresponded to them after they had been removed and spaced out. He was then told to put the same number of pink flowers in the same vases, and when asked: 'Are there as many pink flowers as blue ones?' he replied first '*I think so*', and then '*There are more blue ones*'.

Even when he counted verbally, he found composition no easier: 'I want to put a pink flower and a blue flower in each vase. Will you count the vases?—*Ten.*—And the blue flowers?—*Ten.*—And the pink flowers?—*Ten.*—Well now, if you put a blue flower and a pink flower in each vase, will there be enough flowers?—*I don't know.*—Can you tell before you do it (he was beginning to put them in)?—*No. I don't know.*'

Til (4;11) was at the second stage as far as exchange of 10 pennies for 10 flowers was concerned (Chap. III, §4), i.e. he could make the one-one correspondence, but did not regard the equivalence as lasting. He first bought 6 blue flowers for 6 pennies. 'Now, I'm a kind shop-keeper, and I'm giving you back your money. You can buy some of these pink flowers with the same pennies. You must give me one penny for each flower, as before.—(We began the exchange.)—Will you have the same number of pink flowers and blue flowers?—*No, there'll be more pink ones.*—Why?—*You've taken more* (looking at the reserve supply).—(The exchange was completed and the pink flowers were put opposite the pennies.) *Oh! It's the same number.*—Now we're going to put the pennies opposite the blue flowers.—(He did so.) *It's the same number.*—

Well then, watch (taking the 6 pink flowers and beginning the exchange again). Can we buy the same number of pink flowers as blue ones with the pennies?—*No, more.*'

These children obviously cannot co-ordinate the equivalences, and do not regard each of them separately as lasting. We come now to two examples of a second group of children who succeed with some of the tests and fail with others. In the first case they can formally co-ordinate the equivalences, but fail to do so in the second:

Fet (5;5), as we have already seen (Chap. III, §2) was at the third stage in the case of the flowers and vases: whatever the arrangement of the flowers after being taken out of the vases, he was sure that they were equivalent 'because they were in there'. The ten blue flowers were then removed and he was asked to put the pink flowers into the vases. They were taken out again, and he was asked: 'Is there the same number of pink and blue flowers, or not?—*Yes, because they were in there, and the others too.*'

In spite of this, he was not sure, after exchanging 8 flowers for 8 pennies, one at a time, that the two sets were equivalent. When the flowers were spaced out, he thought there were more of them. Once he had counted them, however, he seemed to be certain of the equivalence: 'Is there the same number?—*Here there are 8 and there there are 8.*—Now I'm going to buy you some pink flowers, watch (exchanging 8 pennies, one at a time, for 8 pink flowers, which were left on the table, while Fet had the blue ones in his hand). Is there the same number of pink ones and blue ones?—*No. There are more pink ones.*—Why?—*Because.*'

Bet (5;8) also thought the blue flowers were equivalent to the vases '*because they go in*'. Afterwards, he put in the pink ones, which were taken out and bunched together: 'Are there as many pink as blue?—*Yes.*—Why?—*Because . . . there, look* (putting them in correspondence to prove it.)'

He did not however think there was lasting equivalence between the blue flowers and the pennies after the one for one exchange. Having been convinced by actually seeing the correspondence, he exchanged the same pennies, one by one, for the blue flowers: 'Is there the same number of pink and blue?—*No, there are more blue ones.*'

In such cases, there is perfect correlation between the understanding of lasting equivalence and composition of equivalences. We now have some examples of a third group of children who are not entirely successful in the tests of equivalence, but who later make a correct composition:

Os (5;10), already quoted in Chap. III, §2, was somewhere between the second and third stages as far as the flowers and vases were concerned. He thought they were equivalent when they were near one another, but not when they were some distance away. But though his reaction was the same in the case of the pink flowers, he asserted that the pink and blue flowers were equivalent: '*They're the same, because there are 10 here* (the blue ones, which he had counted) *and 10 there* (the pink ones, which he had not counted).'

Pit (6;11) also was intermediary between the second and third stages. He presumed that the pennies exchanged for the blue flowers continued to be equivalent to them (except when they were very widely spaced out), but needed to keep on verifying the equivalence to be sure. We then exchanged the same pennies for the pink flowers: 'Are there as many pink flowers as blue ones, or not?—*Yes* (but he at once verified it by actually making the correspondence).'

Lastly, we have some examples of children who are successful both with the equivalence and the composition (we did not find any examples of success in the first without success in the second).

Rum (4;11) was clearly at the third stage with respect to the eggs and egg-cups, flowers and vases, and the exchange of flowers for pennies (Chap. III, §2–4). For the first of these tests, after the 8 eggs had been taken out of the egg-cups and placed in front of them, he put in 8 others, which were then taken out and placed behind the egg-cups: 'Are there as many eggs here as there?—*Yes, there are 8 here and 8 there* (without counting the latter).' When the blue flowers and the pink ones had been put successively in the same vases, he also said: '*They're the same, because there are 10 there* (the blue ones, counted) *and there are 10 here* (the pink ones, not counted).' When first the pink flowers and then the blue had been exchanged for the same pennies, we put the following question, which was deliberately suggestive, so as to test the strength of his conviction: 'You can see that I haven't any more blue flowers (they were in a bunch near him). I want to buy the pink flowers with the money you gave me (exchanging them one by one, and putting the flowers widely apart). Where are there more?—*They're the same.*'

Ul (5;3), in the case of this last test: '*They're the same, because there are 10 vases, and there are 10 pink flowers and 10 blue ones.*'

Ay (5;2) also: *There are 10, 10 and 10* (having counted only the blue ones).'

As soon as the child has grasped the relation of equivalence, therefore, he is capable of composing two of these relations. As can be seen from the reactions of Os and Pit, he may even grasp the composition rather more quickly than he does the equivalence if the configuration of the sets is misleading. The fact that composition is not possible without real understanding of the equivalences to be composed is not as natural as it might appear when expressed in this way. Both the adult and the child after the age of 11 or 12 are capable of reasoning formally with rigour about propositions that are obviously false or are not understood, and moreover the child is able to adapt himself to the words and collective notions of his linguistic environment. Thus many of the children who are incapable of understanding that ten flowers taken out of ten vases will still be equivalent to the ten vases whether they are bunched together or spaced out, are able to count up to ten. There might therefore be in the case of these children a formal or verbal use of multiplication of these equivalences before they were really understood. The fact that this is not so proves that the composition required of them is a true co-ordination.

In the second place—and this is what we expected to find when we began our investigation—composition of the relations of equivalence might not have occurred until much later than the understanding of the relations of equivalence between two sets. It frequently happens that children find much more difficulty in handling the relationships between three terms than between two terms. Sharing among three, for instance, is a much more delicate operation than sharing between two. How then are we to explain the fact that the equivalence of three sets is not more difficult to grasp than the equivalence between two, or in other words, that composition of two relations is as easy as the construction of one of them? The explanation is simple: the composition of two equivalences is already implied in the construction of a single lasting equivalence between two sets, since the different successive forms of the two sets seem to the child to be different sets. It follows that the understanding of lasting equivalence between what for us is only two sets, in fact requires a complex composition of the relations of equivalence that link six sets three by three. For example, when the set of vases V and the set of blue flowers F are put in one-one correspondence, they become optically several sets V_1, V_2, etc., F_1, F_2, etc., when their configuration changes. There will be lasting equivalence between the two sets when composition of the various relations of equivalence three by three takes place. The introduction of a new set F' (pink flowers) does not increase the difficulty, since the relations are of the same type, the only difference being that in one case it is the position of the elements and in the other the colour that is different. The introduction of a set containing new elements thus does not change the formal mechanism of the child's thought, which had to be constructed while he was constructing the relations of equivalence themselves.

It can therefore be said that the capacity to compose two relations of equivalence, i.e. to unite in a single whole three sets containing different elements, merely indicates that the formal mechanism, hitherto immanent in the very construction of these relations, is freed, and can henceforth be applied to any new combination of relations between sets with different terms. This liberation, or external co-ordination, takes place as soon as the construction of the equivalences, or internal co-ordination, has been completed.

§2. *Stages of composition of relations of equivalence*

We have seen, in the case of the same children as in Chapter III, the close correlation between the reactions to tests of correspondence and those of composition of relations of equivalence. In this section we shall briefly examine the stages of this composition with a different group of children, and in §3 we shall study their reactions to multiple correspondence and numerical multiplication.

We shall pass rapidly over the first stage, at which there is failure in both construction of correspondence and composition of equivalences. We give a single example, similar to those of Fum and Til in §1, but where the technique of questioning was more precise:

Com (4;10) himself put, one by one, 10 flowers (X) into 10 vases (Y). They were then removed and placed in a bowl. The same was done with 10 other flowers (Z), which were placed in another bowl, rather further apart. 'Are there as many flowers here (X) as there (Z)?—*There are more here* (Z). *There* (X) *there are less.*—(X were then spaced out and Z closed up.)—*There are more in this pile* (X) *and less in that* (Z).—Where were the flowers before?—*There* (pointing to the vases Y), *in all those little glasses.*—Were they exactly right?—*Yes, these were* (X).—And what about those (Z)?—*Yes.* . . . (he had put them in himself). *Now they'll come to here* (pointing to the 9th vase) *because there are less.*"

During the second stage, that of one-one correspondence but without lasting equivalence (Chapters III–IV), there is gradual development of composition, but it is intuitive, depending on perceptual contact, and not yet operational. Here we have some examples, arranged in order of achievement:

Rys (4;9) was capable of one-one correspondence. He took 10 flowers, put them into the vases, from which they were taken out and put close together in a bowl (X). The same procedure was followed with 10 other flowers, which were spaced further apart (Z). 'Are there as many here and there?—*Here* (X) *it's smaller and there* (Z) *it's bigger.*—And now (closing up Z and spacing out X)?—*Ah! now there are more here* (X), *they've all been moved. There* (Z), *there are less, they've all been moved as well.*—Why are there less?—*Because there are a lot of flowers over there* (X).—Where were these flowers before?—*We put them into the vases* (Y) *and then we took them out and put them there.*—(The situation was again reversed.)—*There are more there* (Z).—Why?—*I can't tell.*—(They were then bunched together.) And now?—*Oh! they're the same!*'

Rol (5;4). Same experiment. The flowers (Z) were close together: 'Are they the same (X and Z)?—*There are a lot there* (X) *because we put them in as well, but here there are less, because you've put them closer together.*— And are there as many vases (Y) as flowers?—*There's the same number as those* (Z, close together).—And what about those (X, spaced out)?— *Yes, the same number as well: they were put in twice* (i.e. X and Z).—Well then, are there more, less or the same number in this bunch and that (X and Z)?—*There are more here* (X).' But as soon as the 3 sets were put in parallel rows he accepted the equivalence X = Y = Z.

Bal (5;6) put 10 eggs (X) into 10 egg-cups (Y). The eggs were then spaced out in a pan. He put 10 other eggs (Z) in the same egg-cups, and these were then put close together in another pan. 'Are there as many eggs in this pan as in that one?—*There are more in that one* (X).—Why?— *Because we put them in all the egg-cups* (Y).—And what about those (Z)?— *We put them in less egg-cups* (and yet he himself had put them in).— Watch (beginning the experiment again with only 7 elements of each set). Now is there the same number there and there (X and Z, the egg-cups being arranged in horse-shoe shape)?—*They're the same.*—Why?— *Because you put them just like those* (the egg-cups).—(The experiment was begun again with 10 elements, the egg-cups being in a row.)—And now (X and Z)?—*They're the same.*—Why?—*Because they all went into the egg-cups.*'

Uld (5;8). With 10 flowers (X) close together in one bowl and the other 10 (Z) spaced out in another bowl: '*There are less there* (X) *and more here* (Z).—Why?—*There are exactly 1, 2, 3 . . . 10* (counting flowers X).—And what about those (Z)?—(He counted.) *Oh, there's the same number!*—Why?—*Because it's the same size* (pointing to the length of the row of vases Y). *So there's the same number.*' In the case of the eggs, Uld at once said that X = Z: '*They're the same.*—Why?—*Because there's the same number of little wooden cups.*'

Hoeg (5;11). With flowers X spaced out and flowers Z close together: '*There are more here* (X). *They're more like that.*—(The densities were reversed.)—*Oh! there are more here* (again indicating X!)—But don't they take up less room?—*I must be wrong then* (confused), *but before there were more here. There must be more there then* (Z).—(The situation was again reversed.)—*No, here!* (with an air of satisfaction at finding the original situation again).—How do you know?—*I'd have to count.*—All right then, count. But wait a minute. Where were these flowers (X) before?—*In the vases.*—And those (Z)?—*In the vases as well.*—And was there exactly the right number?—*Yes. Oh! they're both the same!*'

'Look at them now (arranging flowers X in a row at right angles to the vases).—*I can count them:* (doing so) *10 flowers and 10 vases.*—And now watch (putting flowers Z back into the vases Y, and then taking them out and placing them in a row parallel to X, row Z being slightly shorter so as to avoid visual correspondence).—*There's one missing!* I haven't taken any away.—*No* (puzzled). *I'll count.* (He did so.) *They're the same. I thought there was one missing.*—Why are they the same?—*They were in the vases and the vases are the same as the flowers. But I'd like to count all the same* (he counted X, Y, Z). *It's 10 and 10 and 10. Yes, all three are the same.*'

The next day, with the eggs: '*They're the same* (X and Z).—Why?— *I saw yesterday that they were the same.*—Yes, but how can we be sure?— *By counting.*—And without counting?— . . . —Where were the eggs before?—*Oh, of course! We measured with the cups* (Y) *and yesterday with the vases.*'

All these children are clearly at the second stage, i.e. they can make a one-one correspondence, but do not believe in the lasting equivalence of the corresponding sets. When it is a question of composing the equivalences, therefore, they can only do so on condition that the sets remain opposite one another and have the same perceptual character. They cannot as yet compose operationally and merely judge intuitively.

But although this is the common starting point of all these reactions, each of these children gradually succeeds, with the aid of the suggestions contained in our questions, in discovering the lasting equivalence between X and Y, then between Y and Z, and at the same time in composing the relations and finding that X is equivalent to Z. We shall now proceed to analyse the mechanism of this discovery.

Rys cannot equate X and Z as long as the two bunches are not of equal size. He passively accepts all the various perceptual changes and is incapable of any composition. This is the lowest level. Rol, who is slightly more advanced, explicitly asserts that although X = Y and Y = Z, X > Z. He even begins his reasoning by putting forward the correspondence between flowers X and the vases, then between Z and the vases, adds that 'they were put in twice' (i.e. Z as well as X), and yet concludes that X > Z because Z are closer together. Although Rol is in advance of Rys, since he discovers in the course of the experiment the lasting equivalences X = Y and Y = Z, the visual intuition which enables him to do so is inadequate to enable him to conclude that X = Z. The case of Bal shows further progress. Thinking that X > Z because of the difference in density, he decides to change what actually happened, and says 'we put them into less egg-cups'. The advantage of this bold suggestion is that as soon as the relationships are better understood, through the use of a smaller number of elements, he is able to generalize X = Z to the wider set. It is clear, however, that his discovery that X = Z was made with the aid of intuition, and not through pure logic. Uld's reaction shows that at first intuition prevails, but his spontaneous counting raises him to a higher plane and leads to more formal generalizations. The case of Hoeg, which we have purposely given in full, provides an excellent example of the conflict between intuition and logic, with the final triumph of the latter. He begins by clearly recognizing the contradiction into which intuition leads him: 'but before there were more here'. He then postulates a semi-permanence, which finally leads him to operational composition, and he rightly regards this as being due to the use of a common measure, 'we measured with the vases'. It is significant that before reaching his final conclusion he continually feels the need for empirical verification.

These then are the principal levels of development at the second stage, and their interpretation is easy. At this stage, the child relies only on his perceptual intuition, and begins by directly comparing X and Z without thinking of composing them by means of Y. Thus, according to the densities he perceives, he judges either that $X < Z$ or $X > Z$. But intuition leads to contradictory results, and when the fluctuations become impossible of acceptance, the child postulates a certain constancy. It is then that invariance of the wholes and composition of the relations of equivalence appear simultaneously as two aspects of the same reality. This change in perspective, which in certain cases is almost immediate, like the 'Aha-Erlebnis' of Bühler and the 'Einsicht' of the Gestaltists, is however quite the opposite of the crystallization during which a perceptual Gestalt is structured. It is a sudden thaw rather than a crystallization, a collapse of the perceptual structures, by the sudden melting of which, mobility and reversible composition become possible.

Finally, we come to some examples of the third stage:

Cide (5;3): ' *They're exactly the same, because I saw they were in the vases, I keep on thinking all the time that we're putting them back in the vases.*—But look at this bunch of big flowers (X) and the bunch of little flowers (Z), are they the same?—*Yes, they're the same. I think of those* (X) *and those* (Z) *and I count with the vases.*'

Frim (5;5): 'Are there as many flowers here as there?—*Oh yes! there are* . . . (reflecting). *Yes, there are a lot.*—A lot of what?—*Vases.*—But are there more flowers here than there, or less?—*There are a lot of vases, and a lot of flowers here* (X). *They were in there* (Y). *And there are a lot here* (Z), *and they were in there too. They're the same.*'

Gros (5;10). With X spaced out and Z close together: ' *They're the same.*—Why?—*There were 10 flowers and 10 vases, so there are 10 pink ones.*'

Bora (6;0): ' *They're the same because there are the vases.*'

Mar (5;8): ' *They're both the same, because there was the same length of flowers in the vases.*' And with the eggs: ' *They're the same because we measured with the egg-cups.*'

Lis (6;0). With X close together and Z spaced out: *There are more there* (X) *and less there* (Z). *No, there aren't less, because they were in the vases as well. So they're the same.'* And with the eggs: *'They're the same number, because there was the same number of cups.'*

These are striking examples of the transition from intuition to operation. When Lis, for example, corrects his perceptual impression that $X > Z$ by the equality $Z = Y$, he is compelled, as it were in spite of himself, to conclude that $Z = X$ since $X = Y$. And when Cide, struggling against his intuition, says 'I keep on thinking all the time that we are putting them back in the vases', he provides an excellent illustration of the fact that composition is an effort at reversibility which runs counter to the actual perception. When he says 'I count with the vases', he is becoming aware of the multiplicative character of this co-ordination, and this we shall examine in the next section.

§3. *Multiple correspondence and numerical multiplication*

We now have to see how composition of equivalences can be generalized in the form of one-one correspondence between *n* sets—which we shall call 'multiple correspondence', a rather unsatisfactoiy term, but which we shall only use in this connection—and numerical multiplication.

During the first stage, we find the following reactions:

Dal (5;1) did not think set X (10 flowers) and set Z (10 flowers) were equivalent, although he himself had put first one and then the other into the same 10 vases Y. 'Now we're going to put all the flowers into these little tubes (the opening of which was only large enough to contain one flower). Take enough tubes for all the flowers: you can see that we can only put one flower in each tube.—(He made a row of 10 tubes opposite the 10 vases.)—Have you got enough for all the flowers? —(He added 4.)—Is it right now?— . . . —Try them.—(He put one flower in each tube, and when he came to the twelfth he added two more, but did not grasp that he needed two tubes for each vase.) He was then told to put all the flowers into the 10 vases: 'How many will there be in each vase?—(He tried them one by one.)'

In the case of the egg-cups, he put in 10 eggs, one by one, and they were then taken out and put close together in a pan. He did the same with 10 other eggs, which were then spaced out in a second pan. 'Are they the same?—*No, there are more there* (Z).—Well now, if we give all the eggs to these children (the 10 dolls in front of which the 10 egg-cups were standing), how many can we give to each of them?—*One.*— Are you sure?—(He began putting one egg in each egg-cup, then after 3 or 4 he exclaimed): *No, a lot, 6. The children will have a lot to eat.'*

Com (4;11), after first flowers X and then flowers Z had been taken out of the same 10 vases Y, did not think X was equivalent to Z. 'If we want to put all the flowers (pointing to X and Z) in these vases, how many can we put in each vase?—(He put one in each vase, then began putting two, and then, looking at those still to come, three, after which, by successive trial and error, he finally put two in each vase. *That makes 2 for each vase.*'

Immediately afterwards: 'All right then. Now we're going to put them in these little tubes, one flower in each tube.—*Yes.*—(He put 10 tubes opposite the vases.)—Have you got enough for all these flowers?—*Yes.*—And will they all go in?—*Yes.*—Try them.—(He began, and then said): *There'll be more tubes than vases. There'll be a long line* (adding 5 or 6).'

Blu (5;6) had constructed sets X and Z corresponding to 10 vases. 'And now, if I want to put all the flowers back in these vases, how many shall I have to put in each one?—*You'll have to put one.*—Do you think they'll all go in?—(He tried it, but having reached the 5th or 6th he exclaimed): *Oh! we'll have to put more.*—(He put 2 and obtained the correct result, and then asked spontaneously): *Why did we have to put 2?* —What had we done before?—*Oh yes! 1, 1, 1* (set X), *then we took them out, and then again 1, 1, 1* (set Z).—That's right.'

Now look. We're going to take some little tubes, and we shall only put in one flower because there's only a very small hole. Take enough tubes for all the flowers.—(He put one tube in front of each vase.)— How many flowers were there in each vase?—*6, no 2.*—And how many are we going to put in each tube?—*1.*—Do you think you've got enough tubes?—*Yes, it's the same number as the vases.*—Try them then.— (He put one flower in each tube, but when he was about half-way through the series he exclaimed): *Oh! there aren't enough.*—(He added 4 and said): *I think that'll be enough* (and went on putting in the flowers). *No, there are some flowers left* (adding 3 tubes to the other end and putting 3 flowers in them.) *No, there are still 3 flowers left* (adding 3 more tubes). *They're right now, but why are they more than the vases?*—Look, in one vase there were two flowers. How many tubes did you take for two flowers? (He indicated one.)—Yes, for one flower, but what about the other?— *Oh yes!* (putting 2 tubes opposite each vase), *that's exactly right!*'

The reactions of this first stage are extremely interesting. These children, who, at least at the beginning of the test, cannot make a one-one correspondence between two sets of objects (except when the elements of one set are actually placed inside the elements of the other), are obviously equally incapable of deducing that because $X = Y$ and $Y = Z$, then $X = Z$. Thus, when they are required to make the two sets $X + Z$ correspond simultaneously with the vases Y, i.e. two flowers to each vase, or to find as many tubes as there are elements in $X + Z$, i.e. two tubes to each vase, their behaviour shows that they are quite incapable of multiplicative composition.

The most primitive reaction consists in merely identifying the new correspondence required with one of the earlier correspondences, without understanding the necessity for a correspondence of two to one, or duplication. Thus, in the test with tubes and vases, all the children began by putting out ten tubes because there were ten vases, for, as Blu said, 'it's the same number as the vases'. And yet every child clearly understood that only one flower was to be put in each tube, as they showed when they tried to verify the correspondence empirically. In the case of the other questions, each child also began by giving only one egg to each doll, and by putting only one flower in each vase.

When however the child finds that in fact there are too many flowers for the vases, and too many eggs for the egg-cups, he quickly ceases to assimilate the new situation to the former one. But he does not succeed in making the hypothesis of a definite relationship between $X + Z$ and Y, i.e. he does not understand that if X and Z correspond simultaneously to Y, it means that there are two elements, and not one, corresponding to each element Y. It does not therefore occur to children at this stage to double the number; they merely recognize the necessity for a global increase, and choose any number at random. This constitutes the characteristic feature of this level, at which there is absence of exact correspondence and also of composition of the relations of equivalence. Dal, for instance, merely adds four tubes to his original series of ten, Com adds five or six, Blu four, then three, and then three more, without understanding why: 'But why are they more than the vases?' There is the same lack of understanding in the problem of the eggs, and the number of flowers to be put in each vase.

In a word, these children merely make an arbitrary estimate of the increase and are unaware of the duplication. Although they understand that n blue flowers correspond to n vases, and that n pink flowers also correspond to the same vases, they do not understand that the n vases correspond to n pairs. And although they understand that all the flowers together correspond to the tubes, they do not understand that therefore each vase corresponds to two tubes. It should be noted that Blu, after his failures, becomes aware of this relationship, and is thus on the threshold of the second stage.

We now come to some examples of this second stage, the first of which shows the transition from the first stage to the second:

Rys (4;9) did not think flowers X and Z were equivalent (cf. §2). 'I wonder how many we'd have to put in each vase so that they'd all go in?—*I don't know* (he put them in one by one, then towards the end two by two and said): 2.'

'Now we're going to take the tubes. How many flowers did we put in one vase?—*2.*—And how many are we going to put in the tubes?— *1.*—Well then, get the tubes ready.—(He put one tube opposite each vase, put one flower into each tube, then looked at the remaining

P

flowers, without counting them, and put another row of 10 tubes opposite the vases. He then put in the flowers and said): *That's exactly right.*'

A few days later, he put 10 eggs into the egg-cups, then 10 more. 'How many eggs will each child eat?—*2.*—Why?—*One before and one after.*—And if we give them these as well (a new set of 10 that were put into the egg-cups and then placed by the other sets of 10), how many will that make for each one?—*2.*—Try it. (He put 2 in front of each, and left the last 10 on one side.)—And what about these?—*They'll be for tomorrow* (obviously brushing the question aside).'

Rol (5;4) knew that X and Z were equal to Y, but not that X and Z were equal. 'Now, if I want to put all the flowers in the vases, how many shall I have to put in each one?—*1* (he began doing so, then exclaimed): *Oh! it'll be 2 then.*'

With the eggs: 'How many eggs will that make for each child?—*2.* —And if we add these (10 more)?—*2.*—Why?—(He counted) *3.*'

Uld (5;8): 'If I put all these flowers (X + Z) in the vases (Y), how many will that make in each vase?—*2, 3 or more.*—Try it.—(He tried putting 2 and went on to the end of the row.) *That's just right.*'

'Now take just enough tubes for us to be able to put one flower in each.—(He put 1 tube in front of the 1st vase, 2 in front of the 2nd, 3rd and 4th, 1 in front of the 5th, 2 in front of the 6th and the 7th, 3 in front of the 8th and 9th, and 2 in front of the 10th. He then equalized them.)'

With 10 eggs X and 10 eggs Z: 'How many eggs will each child be able to eat?—*That one* (the 1st) *will have 2* (he went on putting 2 eggs in front of each egg-cup). *I don't think there'll be enough* (he went on). *Yes, that's right.*—And suppose we gave them these as well (10 eggs that were also put in correspondence with the egg-cups), how many would that make for each one?—*4, no 5.*—Why?—*Because they've got more.*'

Hoeg (5;11), after his replies of §2: 'And now, if we wanted to put all the flowers (X + Z) back in the vases (Y), how many would there be in each vase?—*3, 4.*—Why?—*Because we can put a lot in.*—Yes, but there must be the same number in each vase, and we must use them all.— *Yes. Then I'll put that number* (6).—Try it.—(After 3 vases he stopped.) *Well then, I'll have to put 3.*—Why?—*Because it's less* (he tried it, but stopped at about the middle of the series). *It's not right yet then. I must only put 2* (doing so). *That's right.*—Why only 2?—*Because.*—How many heaps did we have?—*Oh! 2, and they were both the same, and the vases too, so that makes 2 for each vase.*—That's right.'

'You see these little tubes? We're going to put just one flower in each tube. Take enough of them for all the flowers.—(He put one opposite each vase.)—Will all the flowers go in?—*Yes.*—Why?— *Because there are ... I'll count them* (he counted) *10, like the vases, because the flowers went into the vases. Oh! I know, I'll have to put some more everywhere, like this* (putting a second tube opposite each vase).—Try it.—(He put in the flowers.) *It's exactly right!* (surprised at the exactness of the result).'

The next day, after being questioned about the eggs (cf. §2): 'Now how many eggs will each child have eaten?—*2*.—Why?—*Because we measured 2 twice* (i.e. we twice put into the egg-cups a set of corresponding eggs).—That's right. And suppose we gave them these as well (10 more eggs)?—*That would make 3*.—And if they had these as well (10 more eggs)?—*That would make 4*.'

The difference between these reactions and those of the earlier stage is obvious. When these children make a one-one correspondence between tubes and vases, and then find that the tubes will not correspond to all the flowers, they pass straight from the system 'one to one' to the system 'two to one'. This marks an important progress towards multiplication.

Let us compare, for example, the case of Rys with that of Blu. The latter, although he finally discovers the two-one correspondence, is still at the first stage because he proceeds by arbitrary additions. Rys, on the other hand, begins by putting ten tubes for ten vases, and when he finds that there are some flowers left, does not, like Blu, attempt to estimate the number, but at once adds ten tubes, puts in the flowers without any hesitation, and says 'that's exactly right'. Similarly, Rol adds a row of ten to his original row, and Hoeg says 'Oh! I know, I'll have to put some more everywhere, like this.'

In the case of the problem of discovering how many flowers will go into each vase if X + Z is to correspond to Y, Rys, who is still at the first stage as far as this problem is concerned, begins by putting one flower in each vase, and goes on to two after the first few. Rol also begins by putting one and goes on to the end of the row, then, seeing that there are some flowers left, reacts as in the case of the tubes, and without counting says 'Oh! it'll be two then.' Uld and Hoeg, who are typical of the majority of children at this level, at once state that there will be 'two, three or more', i.e. they think in terms of n to one correspondence, and then reduce n to two.

As regards the problem with the eggs, Uld is still at the first stage and tries two eggs for each egg-cup, but without being certain, whereas the other children are certain from the start. Obviously some 'training' takes place between the first test and the present one, which may also be easier in itself. Nevertheless, it is interesting that the reasons given by Rol ('I must give two eggs each time') and Hoeg ('we measured twice') belong to the third stage, since they express awareness of the existence of two one-one correspondences that have to be multiplied.

Each of these children understands, then, that if two sets containing an equal number of elements correspond respectively to a third set 'one to one', then the first two combined will correspond to the third in the relationship 'two to one'. But is it true to say

that these children can already grasp the relationship $n + n$ as a
true multiplication, i.e. as the transition from $1 \times n$ to $2 \times n$?
To our mind there are three reasons for not accepting this view.
The first is that, as we saw in §2, these children have not yet
mastered composition of the relations of equivalence, and it
would be difficult to accept that there is understanding of arithmetical multiplication without mastery of the logical relationships
involved in the composition of these equivalences.

The second reason is that these children do not immediately
succeed with the multiple correspondence. It is only when they
discover that there is a remainder, after attempting the one-one
correspondence that they go from n to $n + n$. It is certainly a great
advance on the arbitrary procedure of the first stage, but there is
still some hesitation, and not yet immediate understanding such
as we find at the third stage.

The third and most important reason is that if the child at once
interpreted multiple correspondence as a multiplicative relationship, he would certainly be able to generalize it from $2n$ to 3,
4 or $5n$, since 3, 4, and 5 are as familiar to him as 2, as we shall
see at the third stage. Here, however, the multiple correspondence
is not generalizable. Rys, for instance, thinks that if three sets of
eggs correspond one to one with the same ten egg-cups, each child
will have two eggs, and when on making the distribution he finds
that he has ten eggs left, he puts off the solution to the next day.
In the same situation, Uld is inclined to think that each child
will have four or five eggs, finally deciding on five because 'they've
got more'. Only Hoeg is able to generalize the multiplication to
3 and 4 without hesitation, and in so doing he shows that he has
reached the third stage.

We come now to some examples of the third stage:

Gros (5;10) was convinced that $X = Z$ if $X = Y$ and $Z = Y$. 'If I put
all the flowers $(X + Z)$ in these vases (Y), how many will there be in
each?—*1 blue and 1 pink.*—How many is that?—*2.*—And if I added
these (a new set of 10), how many would there be in each vase?—*3.*—
Why?—*I'd put one, one, one.*—And now suppose we wanted to put them
in these tubes that will only hold one flower?—(He took $10 + 10 + 10$
tubes.)'

Thi (6;10): '*We'll have to put 2 flowers in each vase.*' He afterwards took
$10 + 10$ tubes. In the case of the eggs, he at once saw that when there
were $10 + 10$, each of the dolls would have 2 eggs, and that when there
were $10 + 10 + 10$ they would have 3, etc.

Bora (6;0) also understood at once that there would be 2 flowers in
each vase '*because there are 2 things* (i.e. 2 sets of 10)'. He also took 2 or
3 tubes for each vase according as there were 2 or 3 equivalent sets of
flowers.

Same reaction in the case of 2 and 3 sets of eggs. 'And if I have these

$(10 + 10 + 10 + 10)$?—*4 for each doll.*—And if I add these (10)?—*9, oh no! 5.*'

It is clear that these children, all of whom are capable of composing the equivalences (§2), are equally able to understand, by combining the relations and no longer by intuitive trial and error, the relationships of multiple correspondence involved in the problems put to them: two flowers to one vase, two eggs to one doll, and a double series of tubes for the row of vases. Moreover, and this is the interesting feature of this stage, as soon as the 'two to one' relationship is grasped, it becomes generalizable to three, four and five. From this fact, two conclusions can be drawn. Firstly, the transition from the intuitive to the operational method of procedure entails the possibility of generalization, of which we have just seen some almost instantaneous examples in the case of the small numbers familiar to the child. Secondly, the operation of correspondence is revealed in its true light, as being a multiplicative composition. In the various correspondences, one to one, two to one, three to one, etc., the value of each new set is no longer regarded only as an addition, but as a multiplication, '$1 \times n$', '$2 \times n$', '$3 \times n$', etc.

§4. *Conclusion: Multiplication of classes and numbers*

Our examination, in Chapters III and IV, of the various types of one-one correspondence showed that the equivalence reached through one-one correspondence is multiplicative in character.

It is essential, both psychologically and logically, to distinguish the various forms of equivalence. Additive and multiplicative equivalences differ by the fact that in the first, the equivalence is in respect to one attribute (e.g., blue and pink flowers are equivalent in being flowers), while in the second, two attributes are involved (e.g., the fact of being flowers, and having a certain position in a series). Such multiplicative equivalences between classes occur frequently in the comparative sciences, zoology, psychology, etc., and the whole of this volume is an illustration of them, since the stages of development of one notion have been related to those of another.

Construction of equivalences through qualitative correspondence, and co-ordination of these equivalences, are already multiplicative operations, although number as such does not yet intervene. In order that multiplication of classes shall become multiplication of numbers, all that is necessary is that the classes in question shall be 'singular', as we saw in the transition from addition of classes to addition of numbers in Chapter VIII.

We need only add, therefore, that in the case of multiplicative operations, as in that of additive operations, qualitative composition of classes is not achieved on the operational plane before that of numbers, but at the same time. There is not one stage of logical multiplication and another stage of arithmetical multiplication. During the first stage of development, neither of these compositions is possible; during the second, there is a beginning of both on the intuitive plane, and during the third, both of them become operational in the true sense. Hence the child's simultaneous success in the various tests studied in this chapter, and his immediate generalization of multiplication once it has been discovered.

CHAPTER X

ADDITIVE AND MULTIPLICATIVE
COMPOSITION OF RELATIONS AND
EQUALIZATION OF DIFFERENCES

In the previous chapter, we examined the procedure used by the child, when required to make a set Y correspond successively to two others, X and Z, in discovering that if X = Y, and Y = Z, then X = Z. This composition of relations of equivalence leads, as we saw, to the development of numerical multiplication, in the same way as the composition of qualitative correspondence of classes leads to multiplication of classes.

It now remains to analyse additive and multiplicative compositions of asymmetrical relations in relation to number. The best field for such an investigation is the one we used at the beginning of this book: that of the relationships between continuous quantities. It is true that by adding two sets or two lengths we obtain a total set or a total length, but these evoke a different idea from that of their components, whereas when a liquid is poured from one container into another, or when two units are added in a single glass, they essentially remain identical.

In each of our examinations, we have seen that the process which leads from additive and multiplicative composition of relationships to number, and conversely, necessarily presupposes the equalization of differences. We shall find this again here in a more developed and generalized form, that of elementary numerical mensuration, and hence of common measure and constitution of units. All these problems will be met here and will be discussed in connection with the relationships dealt with in Chapter I, in order to study their possible compositions.

It is satisfying to the mind to return, in this last chapter, to our starting-point, and to utilize what we have discovered in the course of our investigation. There could be no better way of seeing the interdependence and deep-seated unity of the mechanisms that explain the psychological construction of number.

§1. *Problems and results*

In the questions put to the children during this investigation there are six distinct problems.

Problem I, that of conservation of quantities, has already been studied in Chapter I. If A =B, and B is poured into a number of containers, will the new quantities C, D, E, etc., remain identical with A? Since we have already analysed the reactions to this problem, all that concerns us here is to discover what level has been reached by each child, from the point of view of conservation, when he is required to consider composition and measurement.

Problem II is that of spontaneous numerical measurement. The child is given two or three quantities of liquid in two or three containers of different shapes, such that he cannot estimate their ratio by direct perception.[1] He is asked to say whether one of the quantities is equal to, greater than, or less than, one or both of the others, and is given some empty containers which he can use at will for the solution of the problem. Our particular concern is to discover whether the child is capable of constructing a definite unit.

Problem III is similar to Problem II, but this time a common measure is imposed by the instruction. Using E_1, a small, low, narrow glass, we pour the same quantity of liquid into three containers, the first wide and tall, the second wider but lower, and the third narrower and taller. The child is then asked whether the three quantities are the same. This experiment is useful mainly as a control test, when the child has failed with Problem II, to discover whether his failure is due to incapacity to understand measure, or merely to lack of initiative in using the empty containers.

For Problem IV, the child is given a certain quantity of liquid in container U_1 (wide and low), and is asked to put the same amount into L (tall and narrow). This co-ordination of inverse relations, already studied in Chapter I, is here considered in connection with problems II–III and V–VI.

Problem V involves co-ordination of relationships of equivalence: if L =A and A =G, will L =G?

Lastly, with Problem VI, it is a question of numerical additive or multiplicative composition resulting from these relationships. From the above equation it can easily be deduced that L +G =2A, and that if A is filled with 2L, then G =½A, etc.

The replies given to these various questions can be classified according to three stages, corresponding to those we have found throughout our investigations. At the first stage, when there is

[1] Cf. Chapter I for the shapes of containers L and C.

primacy of immediate perception, we find: no conservation (I); no notion of common measure (II); disregard of the common measure used by the experimenter, and evaluation through perception only (III), and consequently complete incapacity to compose perceived relationships (IV–VI).

During the second stage, the child discovers that there is conservation in certain cases only, and cannot generalize (I). He is partially successful in measuring, but does not always choose the right container (II). When he is given a unit of measurement (III), he continues to use perceptual criteria. Problems IV and V confront him with the same difficulty, and Problem VI proves that he is still incapable of any general composition.

At the third stage, the child has grasped the fact that there is conservation (I), he is capable of measuring, making use of a common unit (II–III), and is successful with all the elementary compositions (IV–VI).

§2. Development of the notion of measure (Problems I–III)

For the sake of clarity, we shall study separately the questions involving measure (I–III) and those involving composition (IV–VI), but remembering that theoretically the first differ from the second only by the practical character of the activity they involve.

Our procedure is as follows. We give the child two or three containers of different shapes, in which there is the same quantity of liquid. He is first asked to make an evaluation by looking at them. All children, at whatever stage, are then naturally victims of the perceptual illusions due particularly to the inequality of the levels. We then say: 'What can we do to make sure? You've got all those empty glasses; pour it out and see.' If there is no reaction from the child, we ourselves show him what we mean, by pouring out the liquid from the first two containers. There are two possible alternatives. Either the child does not yet believe in conservation, in which case measurement is impossible since he thinks that any change from one container to another involves a change in quantity, or else he has sufficient grasp of conservation for the questioning to be continued so as to see the various compositions he makes.

Here are some examples of the first stage:

Bo (6;0): Problem II. He was given G_1 (blue) $= W_1$ (pink) $= L_1$ (green). 'Are they the same?—*No, there's more here* (L_1) *than there* (W_1), *but here* (G_1) *there's a little less than there* (W_1).—How do you know?—*I can see.*—Would it help you to make sure if you used the other glasses?—

Yes, one other (taking P_1 and putting it next to W_1). *I'll pour the green into it* (L_1 into P_1).—And then what are you going to do?—Would that one (L_2) be any use?—(He did not understand.)—Suppose you poured this one (W_1) into that one (L_2).—*Yes.*—How far up would it come?—(He pointed to the same level in L_2 as in W_1.)—Why?— . . . —And suppose I poured this one into there (W_1 into A_1)?—(He still pointed to the same height.)—(W_1 was then poured into A_1 and Bo saw that the level was higher.) And suppose I poured this (W_1) into that (L_2)?— *No, it won't come up as high* (as in A_1).—(W_1 was poured into L_2.) Is there more green (L_1) or more pink (L_2)?—*The same.*—And if I pour this (L_2) back into that (W_1)?—*It'll come up higher. There's more.*—(This was then done.) Is there the same amount of pink (W_1) and green (L_1)? —*No, there's more green.*—If I drink this (W_1) and you drink that (L_1), shall we both have drunk the same amount?—*No, not the same.*—And if I pour this (W_1) into that (L_2)?—*The same.*—And into that one (W_1)? —*No.*'

'Look, I'm putting the same here (W_1) and there (W_2). Is there the same amount?—*Yes.*—And now that I've poured that one (W_2) into those (C_1 and C_2)?—*No. It's higher, and there are 2 glasses. That makes more.*'

Problem III. 'I'm putting that and that and that (3 times E_1) into each of these glasses (P, very wide and low, T, less wide and a little taller, and L, tall and narrow). Now tell me what I did.—*You poured it with that one* (E_1).—Is there the same amount in the three glasses?— *Here* (L) *it's more than there* (T), *and there* (T) *it's more than there* (P).—Can you do it again?—(Bo poured E_1 three times into each of the large glasses.)—So if we give 3 glasses to each of these little girls, they'll have the same amount, will they?—*No, that one has a lot* (L), *and that one hasn't* (T). *And that one's got less still* (P).—But what did you pour with? —*With that one* (E_1) *I poured three times in each one.*—Then aren't they the same?—*No, there's more there* (L), *then there* (T), *then there* (P).'

Jol (6;0). Problem II. He was given three equal quantities of different coloured liquids. $L_1 = W_1 = G_1$: 'Are they the same?—*Here* (G_1) *it's the least.*—And there (W_1)?—*Medium.*—And there (L_1)?—*A lot. That one* (G_1) *is the least.*—Can you do anything with these empty glasses to see if you're right?—(He took A.) *I'll have to put the green* (L_1) *into this. No, it's too big. I'll have to put it in there* (L_2) *to see if there's the same amount in it. And in there* (pouring W_1 into W_2). *It's the same, because it's the same size* (pouring back W_2 into W_1).—You remember, don't you, that you're trying to find out if there's the same amount here (L_1) and here (W_1)?—*I'll have to put this* (L_1) *into that* (L_2).—And will it help if you pour this (L_1) into that (W_2)?—*No.*—If I put this (L_1) into that (W_2), will it be the same height here (W_2) and there (W_1)?—*I think it'll be higher there* (W_2) *than there* (W_1).—(L_1 was poured into W_2.)—*Oh! They're both the same!*—(W_2 was then poured back into L_1.)—*Not the same. It isn't the same any more.*'

'Suppose I pour this (W_1) into that (L_2)?—*It'll come up to here* (pointing to the level of W_1 on L_2.)—(I poured it out.) Look.—*Oh! They're both the same* (L_1 and L_2)!—Why?—*Because you poured out the pink* (W_1)

it was too small: you poured it out of a little glass (W$_1$, lower but wider) *into a big glass* (L$_2$, tall and narrow).—And suppose I pour it back?—*It'll come up to there* (indicating the same height as before).—(I did so.) Why does it come up to there?—*Because there's more green* (L$_2$); *the pink's less* (L$_2$ poured into W$_1$).—But were they (L$_1$ and L$_2$) the same before?— *Yes, but you poured the pink* (W$_1$) *into the very big one* (L$_2$)!'

Problem III: 'And now watch (pouring E$_1$ three times into U$_1$, then into G$_1$, then into L$_1$). Is there the same amount in all three?— *No.*—What did I do?—*You took it in that* (E$_1$) *and poured it into those.*—Is there the same amount?—*No, there's a little more there* (L$_1$).—What did I pour it out with (pointing to E$_1$ and repeating the action with my finger). Did I take the same amount with that (E$_1$)?—*Yes.*—And is there the same amount in these three glasses?—*No.*'

These reactions of the first stage are extremely important for the understanding of measure. There could be no more striking evidence that measure is impossible without conservation of the quantities to be measured, for the very good reason that quantities that are not conserved cannot be composed.

These children not only provide a clear confirmation of our findings in Chapter I with regard to conservation in general, but they also indicate in the most obvious way their pre-logical attitude. For instance, Bo thinks there is more liquid in L$_1$ than in W$_1$, When W$_1$ is poured into L$_2$ (identical with L$_1$), he agrees that they are equal, and yet when L$_2$ is poured back into W$_1$ he no longer accepts the equality. Similarly, Jol thinks that the green and pink liquids are equal in W$_1$ and W$_2$, but that they are not equal when W$_2$ is poured into L$_1$, etc.

Obviously in such a situation measure has no meaning, and the child does not understand what he is supposed to do when he is asked to verify his evaluations by means of the empty glasses given to him. Thus Jol, in order to compare L$_1$ and W$_1$, wanted to pour L$_1$ into L$_2$ and W$_1$ into W$_2$, regardless of the fact that it would make no difference. Then, when it was suggested that L$_1$ should be poured into W$_2$ he completely failed to see any use in such a transfer.

The position is even clearer in the case of Problem III, which involves the simplest form of measure through additive composition, glass E being poured three times into each of the containers G, U and L, or P, T and L. The children understand the data perfectly, and Bo himself repeats the operation correctly. But at this level the child does not conclude from the fact that the distribution was equal that the resulting quantities are also equal. Jol says explicitly that the same amount was taken with E, but that there is not the same amount in G, U and L. If the terms 'pre-logical' and 'pre-numerical' have a meaning, they must surely be used to qualify a behaviour in which there is complete negation of the axioms of equivalence.

We now come to the reactions of the second stage:

Vis (6;9), Problem II. G_1 (blue) $=W_1$ (pink) $=L_1$ (green): 'Are they the same?—*No. There's more here* (L_1) *than there* (W_1) *and this one* (W_1) *is more than that* (G_1).—How do you know?—*I can see.*—Take these empty glasses and see if you're right.—(He took L_2). *It's the same size as that one* (L_1).—Well then, what must you pour into it?—*The pink* (pouring W_1 into L_2). *Oh! There's just the same amount. I thought there was more green.* —(L_2 was poured back into W_1.)—Is there the same amount of pink and green?—*No* (hesitating). *I don't know.*—If I drink this (W_1) and you drink that (L_1), shall we both have the same amount to drink?— *No, I'll have more* (L_1).—And if I pour this (W_1) back into that (L_2)?— *Both the same.*—And if I drink it out of this one (W_1)?—*No, not the same.*'

Similarly, after recognizing that '*there's just the same amount*' in A_1 (pink) and A_2 (green), when A_2 was poured into $B_1 + E_1 + E_2 + E_3 + E_4$ there was more green (while if A was poured into $B_1 + B_2$ the green remained constant.) 'And when all the green was in there (A_2)?—*It was the same* (as the pink).—And if I put all the green back into there (A_2), where will it come up to?—*The same height.*—Then are the green $(B_1 + 4 E)$ and the pink (A_1) the same?—*Yes, the same* (hesitating and pouring $B_1 + 4E$ into A_2).—Why are you pouring it out?—*To see if they're the same. No. it'll come up higher. . . . No, it'll be the same. Yes, it is.*

Ree (6;0): $L_1 = W_1 = G_1$. Ree thought $L_1 > W_1 > G_1$ and to find out if he was right took L_2. 'Show me how far up it will come.—(He pointed on L_2 to the level of W_1 and poured.) *Why, it goes up to the top!*—Why? —*They're both the same.*—(L_2 was poured back into W_1.)—*It's getting very low* (laughing).—Shall we have drunk the same amount?—*Yes, when you pour it into there* (L_2), *it's the same height because it's bigger.*—And what about those $(W_1$ and $G_1)$?—*This one* (G_1) *is much bigger.*—Which glass will you take to find out?—(He poured G_1 into W_2.) *It's the same.*— (W_2 was then poured back into G_1.)—*It's the same.*—And what about those $(G_1$ and $L_1)$?—*I don't know. We'll have to find out. There's more there* (L_1).—And if we pour this (G_1) into that (L_2)?—*It might come up to the top. I can't tell.*'

Ree was then given G and P containing the same quantity of liquid, but without duplicates for comparison. He had however W_1 and W_2 which were empty. 'What can you do to measure?—*I don't know.* (He poured P into W_1.)—Are this (W_1) and that (G) the same?—*No.*— What can we do then?—*I don't know.*—Can we pour it out?— . . .—(G was then poured into W_2.)—*Oh!*'

Pro (7;0) also was half-way towards the notion of conservation and measure in problems I and II. Problem III: He was given the containers D_1, O_1, and L_1, and the same quantity, 3 E_1 was poured into each. 'Is there the same amount in all three?—*No. There's more here* (L_1), *less here* (D_1) *and very little here* (O_1).—Do you remember how I poured it out?—*Yes, three times that* (E_1) *here, then here, then here.*—Then are they the same?—*No. Here* (O_1) *you've only put half.*—(All the liquid was emptied out.) Now you pour it out as I did before.—(He poured

3 E_1 into each one.)—Are they the same?—*No. This glass* (L_1) *is bigger.*
—How did you pour it out?—*I put one there, and one there, and one there.*—
Then is there the same?—*Yes, there's the same. That one* (O_1) *is wider, and this one* (L_1) *is narrower.*—How do you know now that they're the same?
—*There was the same amount in that* (E_1).'

Pos (6;11) was almost at the third stage as far as problems I and II were concerned. For problem III he was given 4 containers, G, L, W and B, into each of which we poured 2 E: "What did I do?—*You poured with that* (E).—Is there the same amount in all three?—*No. There's more here* (L).'

Cot (7;6). Problem III: He was given P, L and A empty, and 3 E was poured into each: 'Is there the same amount in each of them?—*There's less yellow* (P).—(We began again.) And now?—*Less yellow.*—Tell me what I did.—(He reproduced the process exactly and said): *No, they're the same. You filled that* (E). *You had the same every time in the little one* (E).

As far as conservation is concerned, these reactions fully confirm our findings in Chapter I. There is conservation when the changes are only slight and not too easily perceptible, non-conservation when the changes are more obvious, then gradual belief in constancy as a result of successive verifications. Vis, for instance, does not at first think that $L_1 = W_1$, although he agrees that $L_1 = L_2$ when W_1 is poured into L_2. He sees that $A_1 = B_1 + B_2$ if A_2 is poured into $B_1 + B_2$, but refuses at first to recognize that $A_1 = B_1 + 4E$ when B_2 is poured into $4E$; etc.

In such circumstances, measurement begins to be possible, but without as yet any systematization. Unlike the children of the first stage, these children spontaneously make use of the empty glasses as instruments for measurement, and even (towards the end of the stage) as common measures. Thus Vis, when told to see whether the quantity in L_1 was equal to that in W_1, poured W_1 into L_2, and Ree used W_2 to compare W_1 and G_1, and so on.

In spite of the fact that these children spontaneously discover the notion of measure, which makes its appearance at the same time as the notion of conservation, it is essential to notice the limitations of their metrical capacity. In the first place, as the construction of conservation is not yet completed, their estimate of the measurement depends on the elements taken into account (as for instance, when Vis judges the quantity in W_1 by comparing its level with that in L_2). In the second place, as there is no rigorous composition, there cannot be co-ordination of successive measurements. Thus Ree, after using L_2 to measure W_1 and seeing that L_1 and W_1 are equal, also measures W_1 and G_1 but is incapable of deducing that $L_1 = G_1$. It is obvious that this incapacity to combine equivalent relationships (cf. Chapter IX) affects measurement. W_1 ought to be the common measure between L_1 and G_1, and since composition is lacking, there can be no general unit. In comparing W_1 and L_1 by means of L_2 these children were not measuring in the true sense, because L_2 was not a mean term distinct from L_1, but a duplicate identical with it. When the mean term is different in shape and dimensions, these children find great difficulties. The same Ree, for instance, when he had to compare G and P without duplicate glasses, was unable to find a common measure without assistance.

This brings us to the third limitation, which is revealed in Problem III. At the second stage, there are not yet 'units' of measurement, i.e. there is no common measure susceptible of being added or multiplied. Thus, when E is poured three times into various containers which the child has to compare, he encounters great difficulties. Even Pos and Cot, who for the other problems were on the borderline between stages two and three, declined to accept E as the unit of measurement and estimated the quantities by the level reached in the various containers. Pos, for example, knew that the same quantity had been poured out from E, but did not deduce that there was the same amount of liquid in the four containers. Cot was unaware that an equal quantity had been distributed until he was made to repeat the process in detail. As for Pro, even when he had himself poured out the liquid, using E, he refused to accept the equivalence, and was only prepared to do so after being made aware of the units by means of a story.

There is a very close relationship between all the reactions of this stage, those we have seen in this section and those in the next and in Chapter IX. They show that the child at this level is not yet capable of operational composition in any field. This accounts for his lack of understanding of the common measure, as distinct from simple measurement or comparison between two terms, and also for his lack of understanding of the unit, the unit being precisely a common measure.

We now come to the third stage, at which the child is capable of operational constructions. Here are some examples, the first being a borderline case between the second and third stages:

Ar (6;8). He was given the same quantity of liquid in L_1, W_1, G_1 and thought that $L_1 > W_1 > G_1$: 'How do you know?—*I can see.*—Wouldn't you be able to tell better if you took one of those glasses?—(He took L_2, put it by L_1, poured L_1 into it and said): *It's the same size. I'll pour out this one* (W_1).—Where will it come up to?—(He pointed to about half-way up L_1 and poured it out.) *It's the same.*—(L_1 was poured back into W_1.)—And now?—*They're both the same!* (L_2 and W_1).' Then, to see if W_1 was equal to G_1 he wanted to pour G_1 into W_2: 'Where will it come up to?—(He pointed to the same height as in W_1 and poured it out.)

They're both the same.—And is there as much here (L_1) and here (G_1)?—
No, there's more here (L_1).—And what about those (W_1 and G_1)?—
They're the same.—And these two (L_1 and G_1)?—*Oh yes! When we poured
that* (W_1) *into a glass like that* (L_1) *it was the same. So those* (L_1 and G_1)
are the same.—Have we tried it, to see?—*No.*—Then how do you know?
—*Because there's the same amount of pink* (indicating $W_1 = G_1$), *so there's
the same in all three.*'

Problem III: E was poured 3 times into B, W and P. 'Is there the
same amount to drink?—*There's the same in all of them because you put the
same amount in with that* (E).—But why is it higher and lower in those
(B, W and P)?—*This one* (P) *is smaller, that one* (W) *is medium-sized, and
that one* (B) *is bigger, but there's the same amount. You put the same amount in
although it's lower and higher.*'

San (6;3). Problem II. $L_1 = A_1 = G_1$. San thought that $L_1 > A_1 > G_1$.
'Try with these glasses.—(He poured A_1 into L_2.) *They're the same.*—
(L_2 was poured back into A_1.) And those (A_1 and L_1)?—*The same.*—
How do you know?—*I measured it with the same one.*—And those (A_1 and
G_1)?—*I think they're the same. We must measure.* (He poured G_1 into L_2
then L_2 into A_2.) *They're the same* (pouring back).—And those (G_1 and
L_1)?—*They're the same, because we've measured: we could see that those* (G_1
and A_1) *were the same.*—Yes, but what about these two (L_1 and G_1)?—
Because we measured that (A_1) *with that* (L_2).'

Problem III: E was poured twice into G, P and L: 'Is there the same
amount in all three?—*Yes, you put 2 in each time.*'

Jan (6;6). Problem III: E was poured twice into G, P and D. 'Is
there the same amount?—*No.*—Why?—*There's less here* (G) *because you
put in 2 of that one* (E), *and there and there* (P and D) *you put in 3.*—(The
process was repeated.)—*Oh! It was 2 in each one and they're the same. I
thought there were 3.*'

Problem II. When Jan was asked to compare G_1 and P_1 without
using the duplicates G_2, P_2, he poured G_1 into D_1, marked the level
with his finger, poured out P_1 and compared the two levels!

Van (7;0), Problem II. O_1 (blue) = H_1 (pink) = L_1 (green). The
child thought that $H_1 > L_1 > O_1$. 'What can we do to make sure?
You've got the glasses, you can do anything you like.—*Yes, what can we
do? Pour it into a glass, but which one?* (He poured O_1 into A_1 and compared A_1 with H_1 which was more or less the same shape, then took
L_1 and said): *There's more green.* (He poured a little from L_1 into L_2 and
D_1, leaving some in L_1, then poured $L_1 + L_2 + D_1$ into A_2 and compared it with A_1.) *No, there isn't more. It's the same. I thought there was more
green.*—And what about the pink (H_1) and the blue (D_1 poured into
A_1)?—*They're the same.*—And the pink (H_1) and the green (A_2)?—
They're the same: I poured it in.'

Van was also given G and P without duplicates. He poured G into
W_1 and P into W_2. When he had to estimate the quantity in A_1 (partly
filled) without using A_2, he poured A_1 into $L_1 + L_2 + L_3$ (full) and W_2
into $L_4 + L_4 + L_4$.

In the case of problem III he at once said: '*They're the same because
each time you put a little one* (E) *in each one.*'

230 ADDITIVE & MULTIPLICATIVE COMPOSITIONS

The difference between these reactions and those of the second stage is obvious. There is no need to point out that all these children assume that there is conservation, but in addition to this, they can measure of their own accord, Ar with some hesitation, but the others systematically. The most interesting case is that of Van, who spontaneously discovers a common measure A_1 for D_1 and A_2 and for $L_1 + L_2 + D_1$. Even when there are no duplicates of G and P Van and Jan find a solution to their problem, Van by a common measure, and Jan by calculation. Moreover, the co-ordination of the measurements is spontaneous, as is shown by the case of San, who at once assumes that $L_1 = G_1$ if $L_1 = A_1$ and $A_1 = G_1$, without being asked about them. What is still more important is that Problem III is solved without hesitation, which means that the child at once discovers the relation 'in each con-tainer, so many units'. In a word, what is new at this stage is the discovery of the common measure and the unit, and these define operational composition as distinct from mere intuitive co-ordination.

§3. *Composition of relations and of numerical units*

From what has been said above it is clear that there is a logic of measurement: in measuring, we compose units that are con-served, and introduce a system of equivalences between these compositions. We shall therefore now analyse the logical and numerical compositions that intervene, not only in the preceding questions, but also in Problems IV, V and VI, each of which has a specific lesson to teach in this respect. It will be remembered that Problem IV has already been considered briefly in Chapter I, and that Problem V is an application of the findings of the previous chapter to continuous quantities, but in order to under-stand the answers given to Problem VI, which particularly concerns us here, it is important to know each child's reactions to questions IV and V.

Here are some examples of the first stage:

Fum (5;0). Problem IV: 'Take this glass (U_1, $\frac{1}{6}$ full of pink liquid). It's for you. Now put the same amount for Remi into that one (L_1).— (He poured blue liquid into L_1 to the same height as in U_1.) *It's the same amount.*—(U_1 was poured into L_2, which was then full.) Who has got more?—*I have.*—(L_2 was poured back into U_1.) Now make them the same.—(Fum put in a little more than before, about $\frac{2}{6}$ of L_1.) *Remi has more.*—Are you sure? (U_1 was poured into L_2.)—*Oh no! I've got more.*— Why?—*Remi has drunk some.*'

Problem VI (simplified): 'Look, this is for me (A_1) and that (A_2) is for you. Is there the same in both?—*Yes.*—(A_1 was poured into B_1 and B_2.) Have we both got the same amount?—*No, there's more for you*

because there's just a little more in there.—Where has it come from?—
There's more because you poured it into there, it's different, it's more.—And if I
pour those $(B_1 + B_2)$ back into that (A_1) where will it come up to?—
(He indicated that the glass would be full, then almost full.) *Before, it
was the same as mine* (A_2). *Now it'll come up to there.*—Why?—*It was in two
glasses.*—(It was poured back.)—*Oh! It's the same.*' Similarly Fum, in
order to have more liquid than I had, poured A_2 into $E_1 + E_2 + E_3 + E_4$
and expected that when they were poured back into A_2 the level
would be higher than before.

In answer to the question 'What must you do so that yours will be
higher than mine?' Fum, whose liquid was in 4 E while mine was in
A_1, picked up L_1 (rightly so, because it was narrower than A_1), but
went no further, and said: '*It won't be higher because you've got a bigger
glass.*' He then tried to find a glass bigger than A_1 and took P (wide and
low) and poured 3 of his 4 E into it. Then he tried pouring it into H
(taller than A_1 but almost as wide), into S (big and wide) and finally,
disappointed, said: '*It's still you.*' He was thus expecting that the level
would increase as the size of the glass increased, and he only used 3 of
his 4 glasses, as though the whole was not the sum of the parts.

Mol (6;0). Problem IV (U_1 was $\frac{1}{2}$ full): Mol filled L_1 to the same
level. U_1 was then tilted, and Mol looked at the slanting surface of the
liquid: '*There's more here* (U_1). *No, there's more here* (L_1), *because it's
higher.*'

Problem V (simplified): 'Take that one (W_1) and pour it into there
(G_1) and then into there (A_1).—(He did so.)—Tell me what you did.
—*I poured with that* (W_1) *into that one and that one.*—Then is there the
same amount to drink in both?—*No. There's more here* (A_1) *than there*
(G_1) *because it's higher.*—But how much was there in that one (W_1)?—
It was quite full, but it doesn't make the same amount.'

Problem VI (simplified): 'Is there the same amount here (L_1) and
there (L_2)?—*Yes.*—Watch (pouring L_2 into $E_1 = E_2$).—*It's the same,
because that one* (E) *is half those* (pointing to 2 E).—And if I do this (L_1
poured into P)?—*Oh no! I've got more* (2 E).—But where did I get this
(P) from?—*From there* (L_1), *but it's not the same any more.*'

Sot (5;6) reacted in the same way as the others in the case of conservation and measurement. In spite of this he was tried with problem
VI, without simplification, after he had compared P_1 and L_1 and said
'*They're the same.*—Well now, watch what I'm doing (pouring 2 L_1
into A_1). Is there the same amount for me ($A_1 = 2 L_1$) and for you
$(L_1 + P_1)$?—*No. I've got more. Oh no! It's the same if I do that* (pouring L_1
into A_2). . . . *No, I've got more.*—Why?— . . . —What did I do?—*You
poured two of those* (L_1) *into that* (A_1).—Well then?—*I've got more.*—Are
these the same (L_1 and P_1)?—*Yes.*—Well then?—*But that one* (P_1) *is
round, it makes more.*—But isn't this (L_1) the same as that (P_1)?—*Yes, if
you pour it out.*—Then are they the same?—*No, here it's like that* $(L_1 + P_1)$
and there there's that (A_1).—If we pour this (P_1) into that (A_2) where
will it come up to?—*The same height* (as $A_1 = 2 L_1 = 2$ P).—And that
one (L_1)?—*Lower* (pointing to $\frac{1}{3}$).'

Her (7;0) had just poured E into P: 'Watch (pouring 2 E into B).

Those are for you (E + P) and this is for me (B). What is there here (B)?
—*Twice that one* (E).—Have we got the same amount then?—*Yes, I've
got more. No, you've got more, because it's bigger* (B).—If I pour this (P) into
that (B) where will it come up to?—(He pointed to $\frac{1}{3}$).—And that one
(E)?—(He pointed higher, almost to the level of B.)—And are they the
same, that and that (E and P)?—*Yes.*'

Further examples are unnecessary to show that children at this
level are incapable of any composition, either logical or numerical.
As we found in Chapter I, §2, they are not capable of multiplying
the two inverse relations of height and cross-section of the
columns of liquid.

As for Problem V, it is obvious that this incapacity to multiply
relations, combined with the absence of any notion of conservation
and of measurement, precludes even an intuitive understanding
of composition of equivalences. In Problem V, it is no longer
merely a matter of equating three classes, as in the case of the
composition studied in Chapter IX, but of the equalization of
three pairs of relations, each of which is a multiplication of height
by cross-section. As we saw in §2 of this chapter, Bo and Jol were
incapable of understanding that two of the three quantities L_1,
W_1 and G_1 were equal. There was therefore no question of asking
them to compose them, and we simplified the problem by letting
the children themselves pour the contents of one glass into the
two others in turn. Mol, for example, poured W_1 first into G_1 and
then into A_1, and yet he did not conclude that $A_1 = G_1$. Although
as he said, W_1 was 'quite full', it did not 'make the same amount'.

As for Problem VI, it was reduced to its simplest form, the
questions asked being of the following type: if $A_1 = B_1 + B_2$, will
$B_1 + B_2 = A_1$? If $L_2 = E_1 + E_2$, and if $L_2 = P$, shall we have $E_1 + E_2$
$= P$? Fum thought that $B_1 + B_2$ would not reach the initial level
in A_1, and Mol, who agreed that $L_2 = E_1 + E_2$, did not deduce that
$E_1 + E_2 = P$. P came 'from there' (L_1), but was 'not the same any
more'. When, as in the case of Sot and Her, Problem VI is presented in its entirety, two interesting reactions can be observed.
Firstly, the equation $a + a = 2a$, presented in the form $P_1 + L_1 = A_1$,
or $P_1 + E_1 = B_1$ is not understood because the child judges from
his perception and not from the composition. Sot, for instance
concluded that $P_1 + L_1$ was more than A_1, although he knew
that $A_1 = 2L_1$ and that $P_1 = L_1$, the reason he gave being that
there was more because P was round. Her decided that B was
more than $P + E$, although $B = 2E$ and $P = E$. The second reaction
is even stranger, Although he remembered that $P_1 = L_1$ and
$A_1 = 2L_1$, Sot thought that when P_1 was poured into A_1 it would
reach the present level in A_1, while L_1 would reach only to one-
third, and Her, while agreeing that $P = E$, thought that P would

come up to one-third of the level of B, while E would reach almost the same level as B! Children at this stage have therefore not yet divided the liquid into fractions, because there is no notion of conservation, and therefore no possibility of additive composition.

This absence of composition is so amazing that one constantly wonders whether there is not some misunderstanding on the part of the child, i.e. whether when he says 'there's more' or 'less' he is not merely thinking of the level, instead of the total quantity. This interpretation must, however, be excluded, for we have always taken the greatest care to see that the instructions were understood, and specified 'more (or less) to drink' in order to ensure that there was no ambiguity. Moreover, when the child thinks of the level, it is precisely because he is unable, for want of adequate logical tools, to picture the total quantity otherwise than by means of one of its aspects, without co-ordinating this particular relationship with the others. He frequently attempts to take the cross-section into consideration (Fum, etc.), but he then forgets the level. Generally speaking, there can be no doubt that the child understands what is required of him, since he spontaneously transfers the liquids from one container to another in his attempts to measure and verify his results.

We now come to the reactions of the second stage:

Vis (6;6). Problem IV: P_1 was $\frac{1}{6}$ full and L_1 empty. To find the same quantity, Vis filled L_1 to the same level as P_1. 'Is there the same amount?—*No, I've got more* (L_1). (He poured some back from L leaving about $\frac{2}{3}$).—*Oh no! Now you've got more* (He made them equal again, then made L $\frac{1}{4}$ full.) *No, I've got more*, etc.'

Problem V. L_1 (blue) $= W_1$ (pink) $= G_1$ (green). The equality was shown by simply pouring the blue into W_1 then into L_1, and then pouring the same amount of pink into W_1. 'Is the blue the same amount as the pink?—*Yes.*—Is there the same amount of pink and green?—*Yes.*—And is the blue the same as the green?—*Yes* (hesitating).—Are you sure?—*No.*—Why?—*This one* (L_1) *is narrow and that one* (G_1) *is bigger.* (He took W_2 and W_3, poured L_1 into W_2 and G_1 into W_3 and only then seemed to be sure): *They're the same.*'

Ree (6;6). Problem IV. P_1 was $\frac{1}{6}$ full and L_1 empty. 'Put the same amount in here (L_1) as there is there (P_1).—*I don't know how far up it will come* (filling L_1 $\frac{1}{2}$ full. *That's right. No, this one's wider* (P_1). *I'll have to see* (pouring P_1 into L_2). *Oh! It comes higher.*—(L_2 was filled, using $\frac{1}{6}$ of P_2, and P_1 was $\frac{1}{6}$ full). Is there the same amount to drink?—*Yes, but I'd like to try again with a glass like that one* (P_2).—(He poured L_2 into P_2). *They're the same* (He poured back P_2 into L_2 and P_1 into L_1). *They're just the same height.*'

Problem V. We saw in §2 that, after seeing that L_1 and W_1 were equal, then W_1 and G_1, Ree thought that if G_1 was poured into L_1 'it might come up to the top. I can't tell'.

Problem VI. E_2 was poured twice into A_1. The child himself poured E_1 once into U_1. He was then given U_1 and E_1: 'Tell me what I did.— *You poured twice* (into A_1).—You're going to drink those $(E_1 + U_1)$ and I'm going to drink this (A_1). Shall we both drink the same amount?— *No, I don't think so. I want to try who'll have the most. This one* (U_1) *is a little glass with only a little in it.*—But are this (U_1) and that (E_1) the same?— *Yes.*—And how many of those (E_1) are there in this (A_1)?—*Two.*— Well then?—*Then both of us will have the same amount. These two* $(E_1$ and $E_2)$ *were put in. They're the same height. We'll have to try.*—Are you sure?— *We'd better try.'*

He was then asked: 'If I pour this (U_2) into that (A_2) how far up will it come?—(He pointed to half the level in A_2, which was correct.)— Why?—*Because it's the middle. This one* (U_2) *is the same as that* (E_1).— Why will it come to the middle?—*I don't know if it will be exactly the middle* (pouring U_2 into A_2). *Yes, look, it's the middle.'* A_2 was then poured back into U_2 for the next test.

He was given $E_1 + U_2 + A_1$ (with $A_1 = 2$ E) full of pink liquid: 'How many of this (E) must I pour into that (A_2) so as to have the same amount as all those?—*Two.*—Try. (He touched each glass with his finger and counted.)—*No, 4, that'll come to the same height.*—E (blue) was poured 4 times into A_2.)—*Yes.'* Then Ree, who was never convinced at once, took B_1 and said: '*I'd like to see the pink* (beginning to pour out $E_1 + U_2 + A_1$).—How far up will that come?—(He pointed to the height in A_2, although B_1 was narrower.) *Here, I think. I don't know* (going on pouring). *It's higher. I don't understand now.*—(B_1 was then poured into U_1 and A_2 into U_2.) *Oh! They're the same height!'*

Bor (7;0). Problem V. He had difficulty in establishing the fact that $L_1 = W_1$, and that $W_1 = G_1$. When he was asked if $L_1 = G_1$ he pointed to the set of glasses and said: '*There was always the same amount.'*

Problem VI. 'Watch what I'm doing (pouring 2 E_2 into A_1).— *You've poured that glass* (E_2) *in twice.*—And now watch this (pouring E_1 into P_1). Are these $(E_1 + P_1)$ the same amount as that (A_1)?—*No. There* (A_1) *it's twice, and here* $(E_1 + P_1)$ *it's four times.*—Are this (E_1) and that (P_1) the same?—*Yes.*—And if I pour that (E_2) into this (E_1)?—*It'll come to the top. It's exactly the same amount.*—And what did I pour into there (A_1)?—*Twice that glass* (E_2).—And if I drink this (A_1) and you drink those $(E_1 + P_1)$?—*I'll drink more. These are four times, and that* (A_1) *is two.* —Why four?—*Because that's bigger* (P_1). *I've got two glasses and that as well. That's a big glass* (P_1) *and this is a little one* (E_1) *so that make four times.'* He was therefore counting E_1 and P_1 as 2, then arbitrarily adding 2 more because P_1 was large.

If I pour that (E_1) into this (A_2), how far up will it come?—(He indicated half the contents of A_1.).—And if I pour that (P_1)?—(He again pointed to half the contents of A_1, which was correct.)—And if I pour these two $(E_1 + P_1)$?—(He pointed to a considerably higher level than that of the liquid in $A1$.) *That'll make four times.*—Explain how.— *There* (E_1) *and there* (P_1) *it's the same. If we measured that* (P_1) *it would get higher. . . .* (He seemed puzzled, took P_1 in one hand, E_1 in the other, and looked both at them and at E_2). *That's two glasses. . . . Oh no! It'll come to the same height!*—How did you find out?—*I saw that that* ($P_1 + E_1$) *is the same amount, and this* (E_2) *the same glass.*'

Gis (7;0). Problem V: After measuring the equality of G_1 and W_1 and then of W_1 and L_1, he thought that $L_1 = G_1$, but instead of deducing it he simply inferred it: '*It'll be the same, because there* (G_1) *it's more stretched out* (looking at it carefully), *bigger and thinner. You think it's more because* . . . (pointing to the level) *but it must be the same.*'

Problem VI: Gis poured P_1 into E_1 and I poured 2 E_1 into B_1. 'I'm going to drink this (B_1) and you'll drink that ($P_1 + E_1$). Shall we drink the same amount?—*Yes, I'll have the same as you. Yours is bigger. If we put those* ($P_1 + E_1$) *into there* (B_2) *it would make the same amount.*—How do you know?— . . . —(B_1 was then reduced by half.) Are they still the same? —*No, I've got more.*—Then how do you know?— . . . —What did I do when I poured it in?—(He pointed to E_1.) *You did it with that. Once that* (E_1) *and the half* (of B_1).—Are this (P_1) and that (E_1) the same?—*Yes.* —And that one (B_1, into which the other half had been poured back), is it the same as that ($P_1 + E_1$)?—*Yes.*'

'If I pour this (P_1) into that (E_1) how far up will it come?—(He pointed to the same level as P_1.)—And if I pour that (B_1) into those (E_1 and E_2)?—*That will make one and the half.*—(E_1 and P_1 were poured into B_2.) Are they the same?—*Yes.*—(They were poured back.)—If I pour this (E_1) into that (B_2) how far up will it come?—(He pointed to the same level as E_1.) *The same height.*—Is it the same amount (P_1 and E_1)?—*Yes.*—If I pour this ($E_1 + P_1$) into that (B_2) how far up will it come?—*It'll be quite full* (pointing to a higher level than B_1.)—If I drink this (B_1) and you that?—*Mine will be more.*—($E_1 + P_1$ were poured into B_2.)—*They're the same!*'

'Then that and that (E_1 and P_1) are the same?—*Yes.*—And if I pour all that ($E_1 + P_1$) into there (B_2)?—*It'll come to the same height* (as B_1).— Yes, that's right. And if I only pour in this one (E_1)?—(He pointed to $\frac{5}{8}$ of the liquid.)—And if I only pour in that one (P_1)?—*The same amount* ($\frac{5}{8}$ of the liquid).—And if I pour them both in?—*The same height* (as B_1).—And if I only pour in this one (E_1)?—*A little less* ($\frac{5}{8}$).—And that one (P_1)?.—*A little less* ($\frac{5}{8}$).'

Lois (7;0). Problem V: He measured the equality of G_1 and W_1, then of W_1 and L_1. 'And will there be the same amount to drink in these two (G_1 and L_1)?—*I think so.*—Why?—*Because here* (G_1) *it's more spread out. That's why it's low down.*'

Problem VI: 'Look, those ($E_1 + P_1$) are for you. This one (A_1 into which 2 E_2 was poured) is for me. Tell me what I did when I poured it out.—*You poured twice with that one* (E_2).—And is there the same amount in this (P_1) and that (E_1)?—*Yes.*—And in that (E_2)?—*The same.*—Then have we both got the same amount to drink, if this (A_1) is mine and those ($P_1 + E_1$) are yours?—*I've got more because I'll drink two glasses and you only that* (A_1).—But is that (P_1) the same amount as that (E_1)?—*Yes.*—And what about these two (E_1 and E_2)?—*Oh yes! It's the same. These two* ($E_1 + P_1$) *are the same, and you poured out that* (E_1) *twice, so that makes the same amount.*'

'And if I pour that (P_1) into there (A_1), how far up will it come?—

(He pointed to $\frac{3}{4}$.)—And that one (E_1)?—*The same height* ($\frac{3}{4}$).—And both of them?—*The same height as that* (level in A_1).'

These reactions show, as usual, that at the second stage there is a beginning of co-ordination, but that it is merely intuitive, without operational composition.

This can be clearly seen in the solutions given to Problem IV. These children, in contrast to those at the first stage, consider simultaneously height and cross-section, and expect the level in the narrow container to be higher than in the wide one. Instead, however, of finding a principle of composition and measurement, they confine themselves to empirical evaluations.

The results obtained in the case of Problem V are exactly parallel. At the earlier stage, the children were not capable of deducing the equality $G_1 = L_1$ from the equalities $G_1 = W_1$ and $W_1 = L_1$, since any notion of conservation or measurement was absent. At the present stage, on the contrary, the child succeeds in discovering the equalities $G_1 = W_1$, and $W_1 = L_1$, gradually comes to recognize their constancy, and finally concludes that $G_1 = L_1$. Nevertheless, in spite of appearances, it would be wrong to assume that the child reaches this conclusion as a result of true deduction, which would consist in composing the general equalities $L_1 = W_1$; $W_1 = G_1$; therefore $L_1 = G_1$. He discovers the correct result merely by virtue of an inductive analogy. In establishing the equalities $L_1 = W_1$ and $W_1 = G_1$ he has to establish at least four equivalences, and when he is further questioned as to whether $L_1 = G_1$ he is inclined to think that probably the equivalence will continue, but for him it is a matter of probability and not of logical necessity. Ree, for example, thinks that 'perhaps' L_1 will equal G_1, but is not prepared to make a categorical statement about it until he has verified it empirically. Bor also accepts the equivalence, but merely because 'there was always the same amount' on other occasions, and Vis, Gis and Lois use the same type of reasoning.

A comparison of the reactions to Problems V and VI shows that in both cases there is composition of the relations of height and cross-section, and also of equivalences. In Problem IV, however, the equivalence is given and the multiplicative relation has to be constructed, while in Problem V the situation is the opposite. It is therefore of interest to find that at this level the same method of intuitive co-ordination, and not deduction, is used in both cases.

The key to these reactions is to be found in the answers given to Problem VI, for here the correct solution requires an arithmetization of the additive and multiplicative compositions of the relations in question. None of the children quoted had any difficulty in understanding that $E_1 = U_1$, all of them remembered that $2E_1$ had been poured into A_1, and yet none of them arrived at a complete deductive solution.

As for the equality $E_1 + U_1 = A_1$, Ree, for example, is torn between the idea of equivalence and that of non-equivalence, because U_1 'is a little glass with only a little in it'. The struggle between reasoning, which strongly suggests that $E + E = 2E$, and perception, which suggests that there is inequality, finally leads Ree to the conclusion that 'we must try it'. Later, he understands almost at once that to obtain a quantity equal to $E_1 + U_1 + A_1$ it will be necessary to pour $4E_1$ into A_2, but is still anxious to verify it, and when he has poured $E_1 + U_1 + A_1$ into B_2 he fails to see why the level in the narrower container B_2 differs from that in A_2. Bor also is torn between reasoning which tells him that $E_1 + P_1 = A_1$ since $P_1 = E_1$ and $A_1 = 2E_1$, and perception which suggests that P_1 is larger: hence his conclusion that $P_1 + E_1$ 'makes four times' and A_1 only 'twice'. The term 'four times' must here be merely the expression of a perceptual evaluation, since Bor himself says that only one E_1 was poured into P_1. Gis has from the start the impression that $P_2 + E_1 = B_1$, but it is only by analogy with the previous equivalences he has met. He is incapable of giving an explanation for his belief, and when asked to be more precise about his original intuition he goes so far as to say that $E_1 + P_1$ will give a higher level than that in B_1, and that 'there's more'. Lois, although he clearly understands the data, begins by saying that there is more in $P_1 + E_1$ than in A_1, 'because I'll drink two glasses', but he afterwards recognizes the equivalence.

These children, then, are not yet capable of composing three of four elements into two equivalent totalities. Or rather, while they find no difficulty in so doing when there is no opposition between the relations and perception (e.g. when $E_1 + E_2 = E_3 + E_4$) they have not yet reached the point at which rational composition triumphs over perception.

The position is even clearer in the second part of the problem which involves decomposition. All these children are aware that $A_1 = 2E_1$, and that $E_1 = P_1$, and yet when asked about the level of the liquid in E_1 if it is poured into A_2 (which is placed next to A_1), none of them are certain that it will be half the level in A_1, that the same will be true of the contents of P_1, and that $E_1 + P_1$ will give the same level as in A_1. Ree alone says 'half-way because it's the same amount as there' (E_1), but he at once adds 'I don't know if it's exactly half-way', as if to make quite clear that it is not a matter of deduction but of intuitive probability. Bor also begins by attributing half the height of A_1 to E_1, and also to P_1, but for $E_1 + P_1$ he indicates a level much higher than that in A_1

(more than three times the unit E_1), because 'if we measured that
(P_1) it would get higher'. Thus for Bor $1 + 1$ does not give 2 if the
two units differ too much in appearance. Gis thinks that when he
has $P_1 + E_1 = B_1$, if $E_1 = P_1$, the contents of E_1 will reach the same
level in B_2 as in E_1, while $P_1 + E_1$ will reach a higher level than
in B_1. Then, when he grasps that $P_1 + E_1$ poured into B_2 will
reach the present level in B_1, he thinks that E_1 alone represents
five-sixths of the amount, and that the same is true of P_1 alone.
Thus for Gis, each of the two halves of a whole, when taken
separately, is equivalent to five-sixths of the whole. Similarly,
for Lois, $E_1 + P_1$ represents the same level as that in A_1, but E_1
alone is equivalent to three-quarters of the total.

The contradiction in these compositions is a further and even
more striking proof of the conflict between perception and reasoning at this stage. It shows more particularly that the construction
of the unit, necessary for measurement, involves equalization of
differences, and this we now see to be the essential condition for
the transition from compositions of purely qualitative relations to
truly numerical compositions.

We now come to the reactions of the third stage:

Fol (7;0). Problem IV: ' *This* (L) *is long and that* (P) *is wide. For that*
($P\frac{1}{6}$) *you have to fill this* (L) *quite full. If we measured they'd be the same.*'
Problem V: O_1 (pink) $= A_1$ (yellow) $= P_1$ (blue).—Is there the same
amount of pink and blue?—*Yes.*—Are you sure, or do you only think
so?—*There was the same amount of pink and yellow, then the same of yellow
and blue, so there's the same of pink and blue* (pointing to the glasses as he
spoke).'
Problem VI. 2 E_1 was poured into A_1, then E_1 into U_1: 'Are these
($U_1 + E_1$) and that (A_1) the same?—*Yes, because you put the two into there*
(A_1).—(U_1 was poured into L_1.)—Is there still the same here ($L_1 + E_1$)
and there (A_1)?—*Yes.*—(L_1 was poured into B_1.)—And what about
these ($B_1 + E_1$) and that (A_1)?—*Yes, they're the same. That one* (E_1) *is the
same amount as that* (B_1), *and for this one* (A_1) *you took the little glass* (E_1).'
$U_1 = U_2$. U_1 was poured into L_1, and L_1 into $E_1 + E_2$; then E_1 was
poured into M_1: 'Are these ($E_2 + M_1$) and that (U_2) the same?—*Yes.*—
And is this (B_1) the same as that (E_1)?—*Yes.*—And the same as that
(M_1)?—*Yes.*—($\frac{1}{2}U_2$ was poured into M_2.)—Are those ($U_2 + M_2$) the
same as those ($M_1 + E_1$)?—*Yes. There are the two little ones, and you
poured it out before with the same little one* (E). M_2 was then replaced by E_2,
etc., and in every case his answer was correct.

Nao (6;10). Problem VI. 2 L_1 was poured into A_1 and the child was
given $P_1 + L_1$ (which he had just recognized as equal): 'Which has
more, these ($P_1 + L_1$) or that (A_1)?—*They're both the same, because those*
(L_1 and P_1) *are the same and you've put 2 like that* (L_1) *into there* (A_1).—
And if we pour those ($L_1 + P_1$) into that (A_2) how far up will it come?—
The same height.—And this one (P_1) by itself?—*Half-way up, because it's
half.*—And this one (L_1) by itself?—*That'll come half-way as well.*—(A

third L was added to A_1.)—*You've got more than me: you've put three.*—If I put this (L_1) into that (A_2) how far up will it come?—(He pointed to $\frac{1}{3}$ of the existing level.)—Why?—*Because you had put in 2 like that one* (L_1) *and it was up to there* (the original level).—And suppose we poured this (A_1) into 3 glasses like that (L_1)?—*It would make 3 full ones* (correct).'

Schen (6;11). Problems IV and V quite correct. Problem VI: $A_1 = 2$ E_1 and $E_1 = P_1$: '*There's more here* (A_1) *than there* (P_1).—And are these $(P_1 + E_1)$ less than that (A_1)?—*The same. You put 2 into that* (A_1).— And if I pour this (P_1) into that (A_2), how far up will it come?—(He indicated half-way.) *Lower; half.*—And what about this one (E_1)?— *That'll be half too.*—And those $(P_1 + E_1)$?—*As much as that* (A_1).'

San (7;0). Problem VI: $A_1 = 2$ L_1 and $L_1 = P_1$. '*They're the same because you put 2 like that* (L_1) *and these* $(L_1 + P_1)$ *make twice as well.*—If we poured this (P_1) into that (A_2), how far up would it come?—*Half.*— Well now, you've got all those $(P_1 + L_1 + A_1)$. How many of this one (L_1) must we pour into there (A_2) so as to have the same?—*3, no 4, because there* (A_1) *there are 2.*'

Chou (7;0). Problem V. L_1 (blue) $= W_1$ (pink) and $W_1 = G_1$ (green). '*There* (G_1), *there's as much as there* (L_1). *They're both the same.*—Why?—*I looked at all three of them.*—But did you look at these two together (blue and green)?—*No, but I saw by the pink.*'

Problem VI. $P_1 = E_1$ and $A_2 = 2$ E_1: 'You'll have all those $(P_1 + E_1 + A_1)$. How many little ones (E_2) must I take so as to have the same amount here (A_2)?—*6.*—Why?—(He pointed to the 3 glasses one after the other.) *2, 4, 6 . . . Oh no! I thought there were two everywhere* (his reasoning was therefore correct).'

If we compare these reactions with those of the previous stage the contrast between operation and intuition is clearly to be seen. At this stage, Problem IV no longer presents any difficulty (cf. Chapter I) and there is extreme precision in the solution of Problem V. Chou, for instance, is well aware that he used glass W_1 as a common measure in comparing L_1 and G_1 as his words indicate: 'I looked at all three of them . . . I saw by the pink.'

A comparison of Problem VI with the two earlier ones clearly proves that when the child becomes capable of rigorous composition of elementary operations of logic or relations, he also becomes capable of numerical composition involving the same relations.

From the point of view of logic of relations, Problem VI is indeed only the synthesis of Problems IV and V, since in order to establish that $E_1 + U_1 = A_1$, where $A_1 = 2E_1$ and $U_1 = E_1$, it must be understood: (1) that the increase in height of the liquid in a narrow container is compensated by the decrease in cross-section, and conversely (Problem IV), and (2) that if $U_1 = E_1$ and $E_1 = \frac{1}{2}A_1$, then $U_1 = \frac{1}{2}A_1$ (Problem V). Something more, however, is involved in Problem VI, since it also presupposes the constitution of units susceptible of addition and multiplication.

It is in fact, when Problems IV and V are solved operationally that Problem VI also is solved. Fol's certainty of the equivalence of the units or of their sums is proof against a whole series of successive transformations. In the case of Nao, Schen, San and Chou, composition of the type E + E + E . . . acquires a character that is both multiplicative and additive, as Chou, for example, shows when he thinks that the sum is equal to six because two units were poured into each glass. Conversely, we find that these same children indicate half, and even a third, of a given column of liquid as corresponding to the units. To sum up, in contrast to those of the earlier stages, these children can combine one with another the units of measure obtained by a rigorous equalization of differences.

§4. Conclusions

We must emphasize, if the relation between numerical operations and qualitative logical relations is to be understood, that the compositions dealt with in this chapter are already implicit in the elaboration of conservation itself (cf. Chapter I). In the case of the problem of conservation, however, the child is unaware of their existence, whereas in the present case he has to discover and 'think' them.

The problem we put to the children in Chapter I, using exactly the same material as in this chapter, was that of deciding whether a quantity A_1, equivalent to A_2, remains equivalent when subdivided or poured into a different container. Obviously the solution of such problems requires on the part of the child the capacity to unite parts into a whole, to divide a whole into parts, to co-ordinate equivalences and to multiply relationships. In other words, it involves all the additive and multiplicative compositions studied in this chapter. It is therefore in no way surprising that the stages of the construction of conservation are exactly synchronic with those of the development of these compositions. It may even have seemed to the reader that we were merely repeating, with only slight changes in the language used, the tests of Chapter I. But it is one thing to postulate the equivalence of A_1 and A_2 from the point of view of perception and to discover whether the equivalence is conserved in spite of successive transformations, and it is quite another thing to construct the equivalence by measurement (Problems II and III of this chapter) or by various deductions (Problems IV–VI). In the first case, the child has to justify a given solution, while in the second he has to find the solution. The same compositions are thus the result, in the first situation, of an analysis which may involve varying degrees of awareness, and in the second, of a synthesis which demands clear and precise thinking. This fact explains why for the child the problems of operational composition appear to be new, while for the adult they are immanent in every problem of quantification.

What we have just said is equally applicable to each of the investigations in Chapters VII to IX concerning additive and multiplicative compositions. Addition and multiplication of classes, relations and numbers are implicit in the construction of every class, every relation and every number. But it is not at all the same thing to construct such elements without any knowledge of the operations involved, as it is to link the elements, once they have been constructed, by means of the same operations explicitly and consciously performed. In both cases the same 'groupings' or the same 'groups' are in question, but in the first case the mind is proceeding from the result to the analysis of its composition, while in the second it proceeds from the synthetic composition to its results.

The reason why the stages of composition are the same as those of conservation is now clear, since the latter is at the same time the result of composition and the invariant that makes composition possible.

At the first stage, the child is unaware of both conservation and composition. Perceived relationships, which change with each change of container, are not co-ordinated operationally, or even intuitively, with the result that the child's evaluation is based entirely on the qualities and their immediate relationships (gross quantity), awareness of one relationship preventing awareness of others, co-ordination thus being impossible.

With the progress of intuition, the perceptual relationships gradually begin to be co-ordinated, provided that the transformations are not too great, and this beginning of intuitive co-ordination characterizes the second stage. Until co-ordination of relationships becomes generalized, however, there can be no rigorous system of compositions, and as at the second stage the relationships resulting from extensive transformations are not co-ordinated, the child relying on his actual perception rather than on any rule of composition, this stage remains intuitive, intuition being merely representation constructed by means of interiorized, fixed perceptions. How then are we to explain the transition from this intermediary stage to the rigorous composition to be found in all the various fields we have examined?

It seems that the third stage only becomes possible with the constitution of two interdependent systems, the 'grouping' of multiplications of relations, and the 'group' of numerical multiplications, both of which co-ordinate into a closed and reversible whole the operations involved, the one on the qualitative and the other on the numerical plane.

What is lacking in the multiplications of asymmetrical relations characteristic of the second stage is the possibility of their grouping. At the third stage, on the contrary, grouping is achieved. Let us take as a typical example the case of Fel, who is capable of co-ordinating a sequence of equivalences which it is difficult for the reader to follow without putting them on paper: $U_1 = U_2$; then $U_2 = L_1$; $L_1 = E_1 + E_2$; then $E_1 = M_1$; therefore $E_2 + M_1 = U_2$; then $\frac{1}{2}U_2 = M_2$; therefore $\frac{1}{2}U_2 + M_2 = M_1 + E_1$; and if $E_2 = M_2$, then $\frac{1}{2}U_2 + E_2 = M_1 + E_1$, etc. It is clear that, in addition to the equating of differences and the constitution of mathematical operations, this sequence involves as a minimum the following logical operations:

(1) Composition of multiplications of relationships.

(2) A sequence of equivalences such that two successive transformations are reducible to a single one.

(3) Generalization, which consists in passing from an intuitive relationship between two objects to an operational relationship between three objects, then four, and so on. These complete the grouping of multiplications of asymmetrical relations.

The progress of the third stage does not, however, consist merely in the completion of the qualitative co-ordinations (in this particular case, grouping of the multiplications of relationships), but also in the synchronic constitution of the group of arithmetical multiplications through the process of equalization of differences.

This process can clearly be seen in the correct solutions to Problem II. When, in comparing L_1 and G_1, the child spontaneously pours G_1 into L_2, or, in comparing G and P, pours G into W_1 and P into W_2, he is not merely seriating the differences between G_1 and L_1 or between G and P, but is trying to reduce the relations of difference to equalities, and this is characteristic of measurement. The simplest form of this equalization consists in pouring G into L_2 in order to compare it with L_1, thus showing that the decrease in cross-section from G to L is compensated by the increase in level. In this case, the equating of differences consists merely in the reduction of G to L, L serving as the measure for G. When, however, G is poured into W_1 and P into W_2, the differences between G and P are cancelled out through the use of a common measure W, which thus constitutes an elementary unit, distinct from the terms to be compared, but not yet composed with itself through additions or multiplications.

With the correct solutions to Problem III, equalization of differences is completed by the constitution of units that can be additively and multiplicatively composed, i.e. of a common measure in the ordinary sense.

At the third stage, when the child is capable of solving Problem VI in its form P (=E) +E =A (if A =2E), he also understands that the successive levels in A are susceptible of graduation into a system of units and fractions according to the number of E poured into A.

Thus by children at this level, questions III, V and VI are regarded as multiplicative problems. When, for instance, in the case of Problem VI, San says that for P +L +A, glass L must be poured in 'four times . . . because there (A) there are two', we have a particularly explicit example of the process that takes place in all measurement, the very notion of a common measure depending on that of multiplicative equivalence.

We thus find, as at the conclusion of Chapter IX, that while multiplication of classes and multiplication of relations are two distinct operations, the one bringing into correspondence terms that are qualitatively equivalent, and the other asymmetrical relations between non-equivalent terms, all that is necessary in order to make the terms of these relations equivalent and thus to fuse multiplication of relations and that of classes into a single operational whole, is that the differences shall be equalized. We then have multiplication of numbers. Once again, therefore, number is seen to be the synthesis of class and asymmetrical relation. This general conclusion is supported by the whole of our analysis of number in the preceding pages.

GLOSSARY

a priori analytic deduction—deduction which is not based on any experiment (*a priori*) and which does not say anything about its object that is not contained in its premises (analytic).

extensive quantity—the name given to any magnitude that is susceptible of actual addition, as for example mass or capacity—the mass of a body formed of two bodies is the sum of the masses of the original bodies.

intensive quantity—the name given to any magnitude which is not susceptible of actual addition, as for example temperature. Two quantities of water at 15° and 25° respectively do not produce a mixture at 40°.

logical groupings—by this expression the author understands a type of organization of propositions such that the four following conditions are satisfied: (i) there exisits a law of composition; (ii) this law is associative; (iii) there exists an inverse for each operation; (iv) there exists an identical operation.

logical multiplication—expresses the fact that two or more attributes are considered simultaneously. Thus, to consider red round beads as opposed to red square beads or black round beads, is to make use of the logical multiplication of two attributes; red, round; red, square; black, round.

INDEX

Words marked with an asterisk occur so frequently throughout the book that page references have not been given.

International Library of Psychology, Philosophy & Scientific Method

Editor: C K Ogden

(Demy 8vo)

Philosophy

Anton, John Peter, **Aristotle's Theory of Contrariety** *276 pp. 1957.*
Black, Max, **The Nature of Mathematics** *242 pp. 1933.*
Bluck, R.S., **Plato's Phaedo** *226 pp. 1955.*
Broad, C. D., **Five Types of Ethical Theory** *322 pp. 1930.*
    The Mind and Its Place in Nature *694 pp. 1925.*
Burtt, E. A., **The Metaphysical Foundations of Modern Physical Science**
    A Historical and Critical Essay *364 pp. 2nd (revised) edition 1932.*
Carnap, Rudolf, **The Logical Syntax of Language** *376 pp. 1937.*
Cornford, F. M., **Plato's Theory of Knowledge** *358 pp. 1935.*
    Plato's Cosmology, The Timaeus of Plato *402 pp. Frontispiece. 1937.*
    Plato and Parmenides *280 pp. 1939.*
Crawshay-Williams, Rupert, **Methods and Criteria of Reasoning**
    312 pp. 1957.
Hulme, T. E., **Speculations** *296 pp. 2nd edition 1936.*
Lazerowitz, Morris, **The Structure of Metaphysics** *262 pp. 1955.*
Mannheim, Karl, **Ideology and Utopia** *360 pp. 1954.*
Moore, G. E., **Philosophical Studies** *360 pp. 1922. See also* Ramsey, F.P.
Ogden, C. K. and Richards, I. A., **The Meaning of Meaning**
    With supplementary essays by B. Malinowski and F. G. Crookshank
    394 pp. 10th Edition 1949. (6th Impression 1967.)
Ramsey, Frank Plumpton, **The Foundations of Mathematics and other**
    Logical Essays *318 pp. 1931.*
Richards, I. A., **Principles of Literary Criticism** *312 pp. 2nd edition, 1926.*
    Mencius on the Mind. Experiments in Multiple Definition
    190 pp. 1932.
Smart, Ninian, **Reasons and Faiths** *230 pp. 1958.*
Vaihinger, H., **The Philosophy of As If**
    428 pp. 2nd edition 1935.
Wittgenstein, Ludwig, **Tractatus Logico-Philosophicus** *216 pp. 1922.*
Wright, Georg Henrik von, **Logical Studies** *214 pp. 1957.*
Zeller, Eduard, **Outlines of the History of Greek Philosopohy**
    248 pp. 13th (revised) edition 1931.

Psychology

Adler, Alfred, **The Practice and Theory of Individual Psychology**
    368 pp. 2nd (revised) edition 1929.
Eng, Helga, **The Psychology of Children's Drawings**
    240 pp. 8 colour plates. 139 figures. 2nd edition 1954.
Koffka, Kurt, **The Growth of the Mind** *456 pp. 16 figures. 2nd edition*
    (revised) 1928.